FANTASTIC FOUR

Mr. and Mrs. Grimm

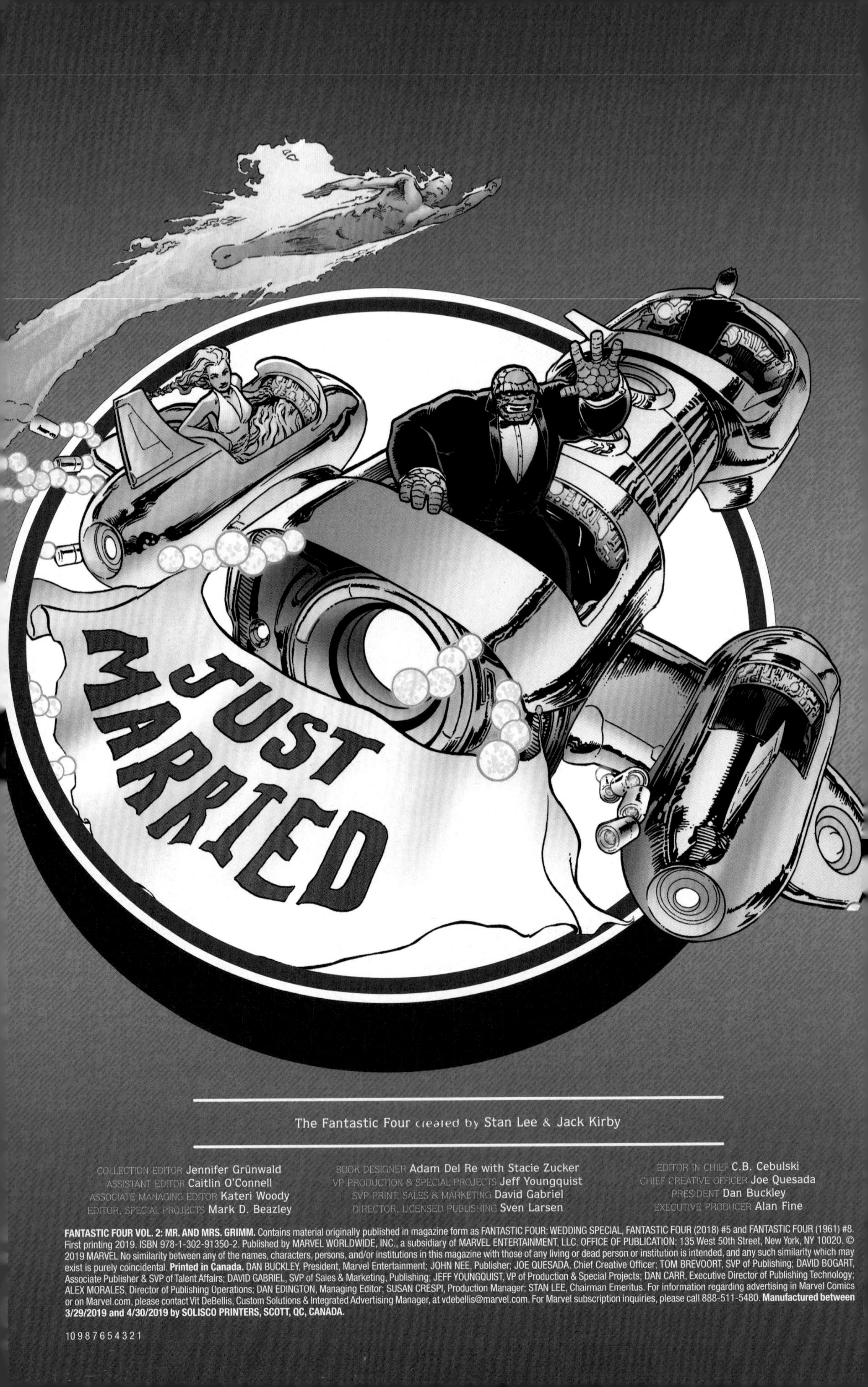
JUST MARRIED

The Fantastic Four created by Stan Lee & Jack Kirby

COLLECTION EDITOR Jennifer Grünwald
ASSISTANT EDITOR Caitlin O'Connell
ASSOCIATE MANAGING EDITOR Kateri Woody
EDITOR, SPECIAL PROJECTS Mark D. Beazley

BOOK DESIGNER Adam Del Re with Stacie Zucker
VP PRODUCTION & SPECIAL PROJECTS Jeff Youngquist
SVP PRINT, SALES & MARKETING David Gabriel
DIRECTOR, LICENSED PUBLISHING Sven Larsen

EDITOR IN CHIEF C.B. Cebulski
CHIEF CREATIVE OFFICER Joe Quesada
PRESIDENT Dan Buckley
EXECUTIVE PRODUCER Alan Fine

FANTASTIC FOUR VOL. 2: MR. AND MRS. GRIMM. Contains material originally published in magazine form as FANTASTIC FOUR: WEDDING SPECIAL, FANTASTIC FOUR (2018) #5 and FANTASTIC FOUR (1961) #8. First printing 2019. ISBN 978-1-302-91350-2. Published by MARVEL WORLDWIDE, INC., a subsidiary of MARVEL ENTERTAINMENT, LLC. OFFICE OF PUBLICATION: 135 West 50th Street, New York, NY 10020. **Printed in Canada.** DAN BUCKLEY, President, Marvel Entertainment; JOHN NEE, Publisher; JOE QUESADA, Chief Creative Officer; TOM BREVOORT, SVP of Publishing; DAVID BOGART, Associate Publisher & SVP of Talent Affairs; DAVID GABRIEL, SVP of Sales & Marketing, Publishing; JEFF YOUNGQUIST, VP of Production & Special Projects; DAN CARR, Executive Director of Publishing Technology; ALEX MORALES, Director of Publishing Operations; DAN EDINGTON, Managing Editor; SUSAN CRESPI, Production Manager; STAN LEE, Chairman Emeritus. For information regarding advertising in Marvel Comics or on Marvel.com, please contact Vit DeBellis, Custom Solutions & Integrated Advertising Manager, at vdebellis@marvel.com. For Marvel subscription inquiries, please call 888-511-5480. **Manufactured between 3/29/2019 and 4/30/2019 by SOLISCO PRINTERS, SCOTT, QC, CANADA.**

10 9 8 7 6 5 4 3 2 1

FANTASTIC FOUR

With the Baxter Building occupied, the FF have taken up residence in Ben's apartment building at 4 Yancy Street. But they won't have much time to settle in, because Ben and Alicia's wedding is just around the corner! Can Marvel's First Family make it through the ceremony without any super-powered shenanigans this time? Read on and find out, True Believers!

Mr. and Mrs. Grimm

FANTASTIC FOUR: WEDDING SPECIAL #1

Gail Simone, Dan Slott & Fred Hembeck
WRITERS

Laura Braga, Mark Buckingham, Mark Farmer & Fred Hembeck
ARTISTS

Jesus Aburtov, Matt Yackey & Megan Wilson
COLOR ARTISTS

VC's Joe Caramagna & Fred Hembeck
LETTERERS

Carlos Pacheco & Romulo Fajardo Jr.
COVER ART

FANTASTIC FOUR #5

Dan Slott
Writer

"4-MINUTE WARNING"

Aaron Kuder
ARTIST

Marte Gracia & Erick Arciniega
COLOR ARTISTS

"CHANGE PARTNERS"

Michael Allred
ARTIST

Laura Allred
COLOR ARTIST

"GUYS' NIGHT OUT"

Adam Hughes
ARTIST

VC's Joe Caramagna
LETTERER

Esad Ribić
COVER ART

Alanna Smith
ASSOCIATE EDITOR

Tom Brevoort
EDITOR

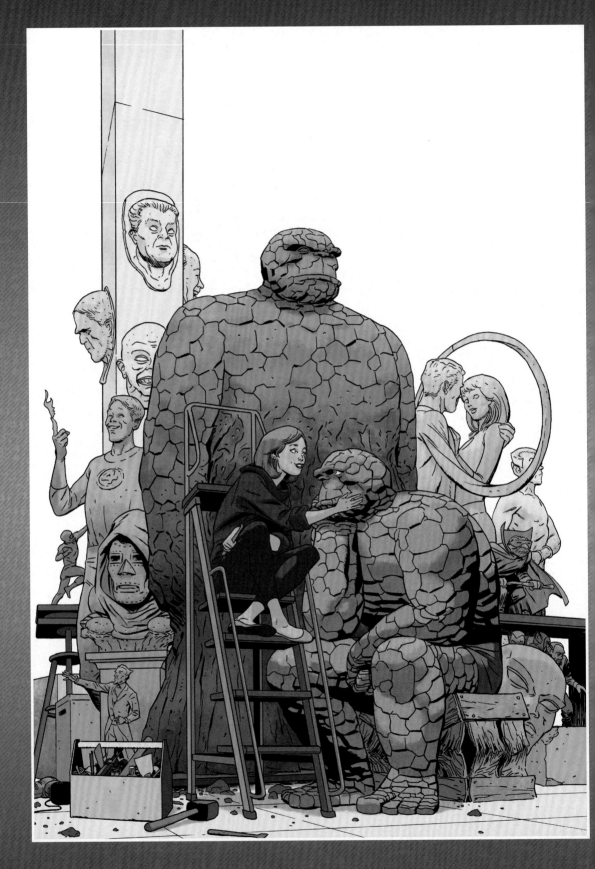

Wedding Special #1 variant by **Marcos Martin**

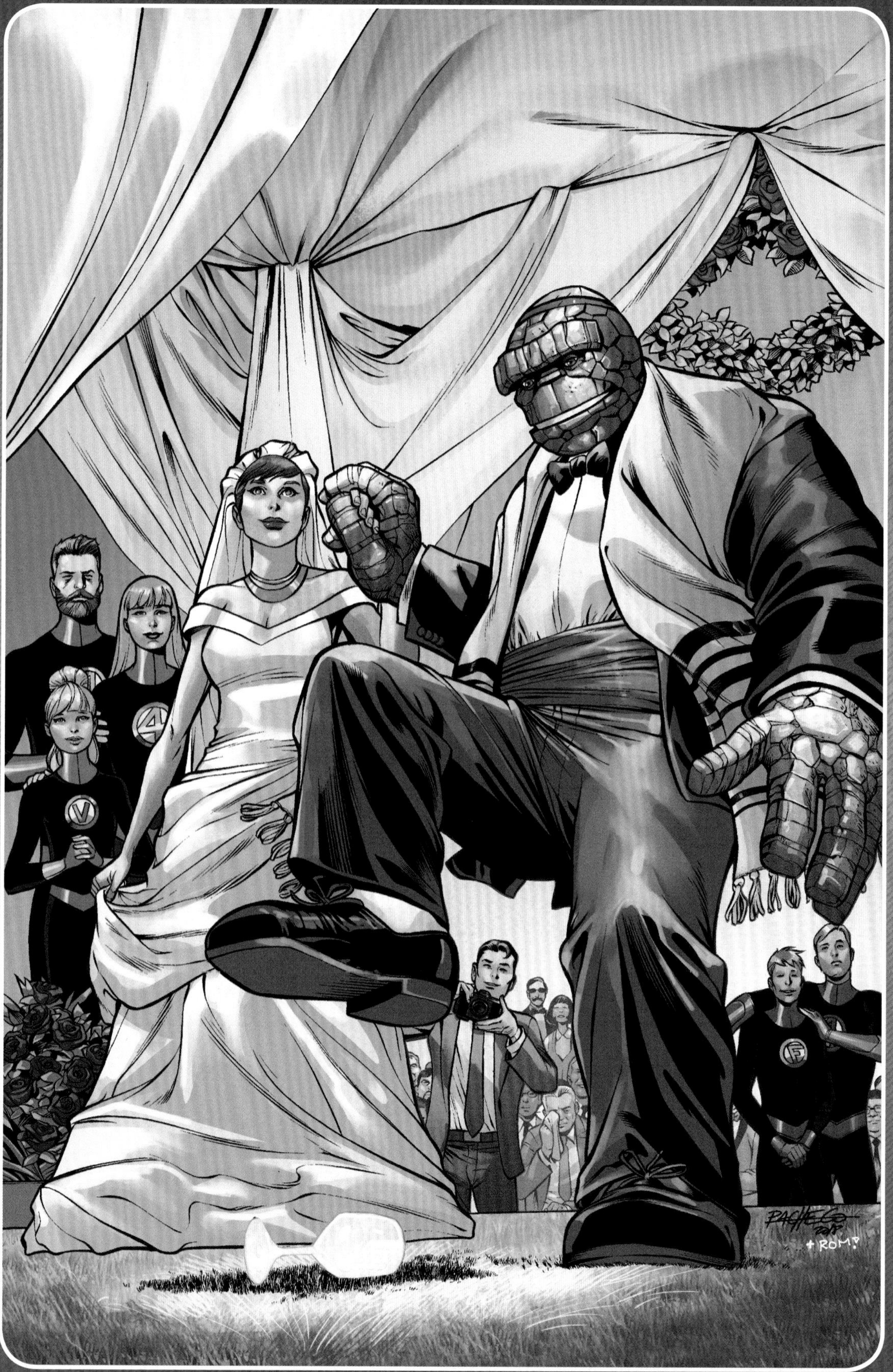

WEDDING SPECIAL 1

WE CORDIALLY INVITE YOU TO
THE WEDDING OF

Alicia Reiss Masters

AND

Benjamin Jacob Grimm

"(INVISIBLE) GIRLS GONE WILD"

Writer: **Gail Simone**
Artist: **Laura Braga**
Color Artist: **Jesus Aburtov**
Letterer: **VC's Joe Caramagna**

"FATHER FIGURE"

Writer: **Dan Slott**
Penciler: **Mark Buckingham**
Inker: **Mark Farmer**
Color Artist: **Matt Yackey**
Letterer: **VC's Joe Caramagna**

"THE PUPPET MASTER'S LAMENT"

By **Fred Hembeck**
Color Artist: **Megan Wilson**

Cover • **Carlos Pacheco & Romulo Fajardo Jr.**
Variant Covers • **Marcos Martin; Mike McKone &**
Matt Yackey; Artgerm; Pasqual Ferry & Chris Sotomayor
Graphic Designer • **Carlos Lao**   Associate Editor • **Alanna Smith**
Editor • **Tom Brevoort**
Editor in Chief • **C.B. Cebulski**
Chief Creative Officer • **Joe Quesada**
President • **Dan Buckley**
Executive Producer • **Alan Fine**
The Fantastic Four Created by **Stan Lee & Jack Kirby**

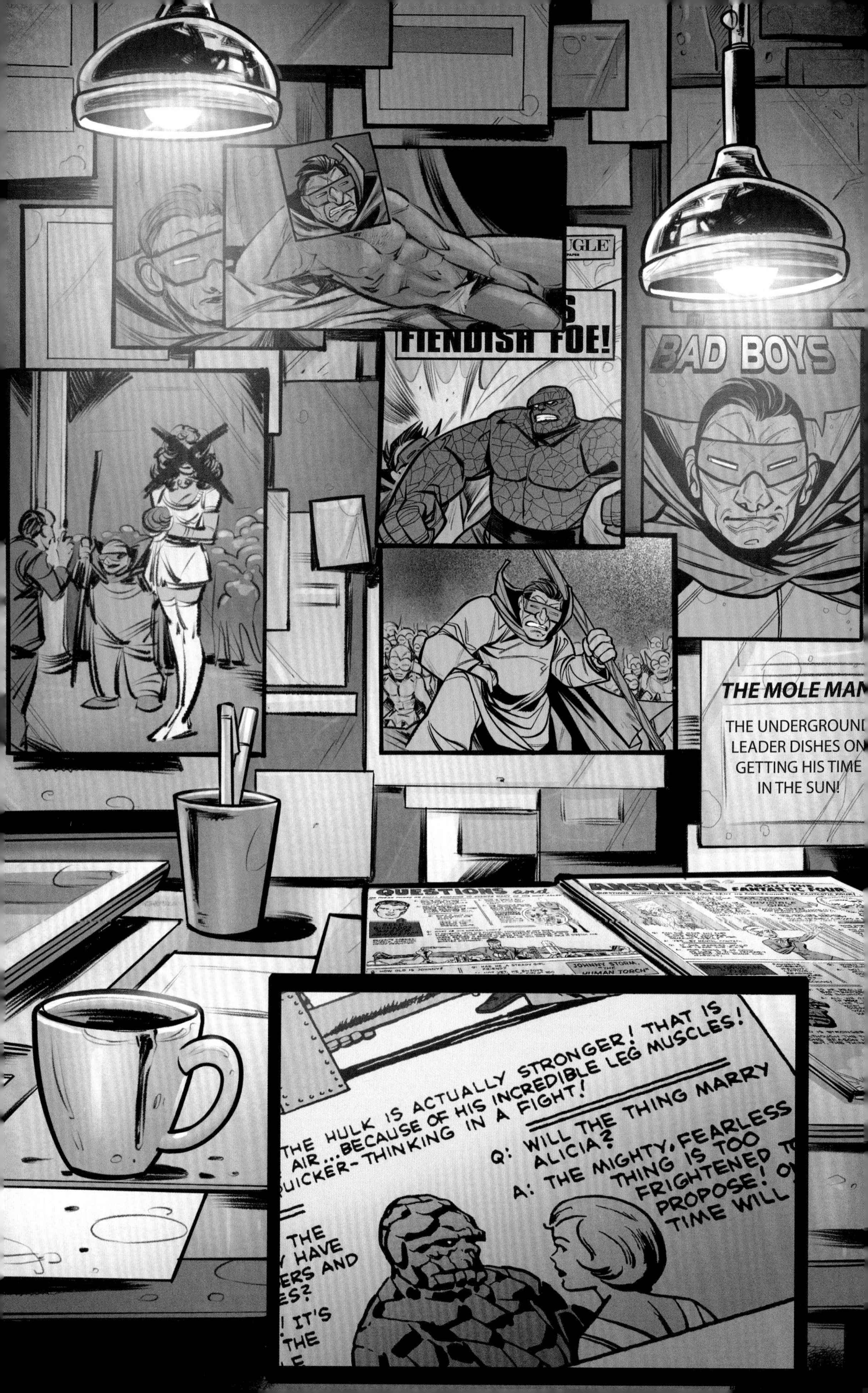

FIENDISH FOE!
BAD BOYS
THE MOLE MAN
THE UNDERGROUNI
LEADER DISHES ON
GETTING HIS TIME
IN THE SUN!
QUESTIONS and
ANSWERS
FANTASTIC FOUR
JOHNNY STORM
THE HULK IS ACTUALLY STRONGER! THAT IS
AIR... BECAUSE OF HIS INCREDIBLE LEG MUSCLES!
QUICKER-THINKING IN A FIGHT!
Q: WILL THE THING MARRY ALICIA?
A: THE MIGHTY, FEARLESS THING IS TOO FRIGHTENED T PROPOSE! O TIME WILL
THE
Y HAVE
ERS AND
ES?
! IT'S
THE

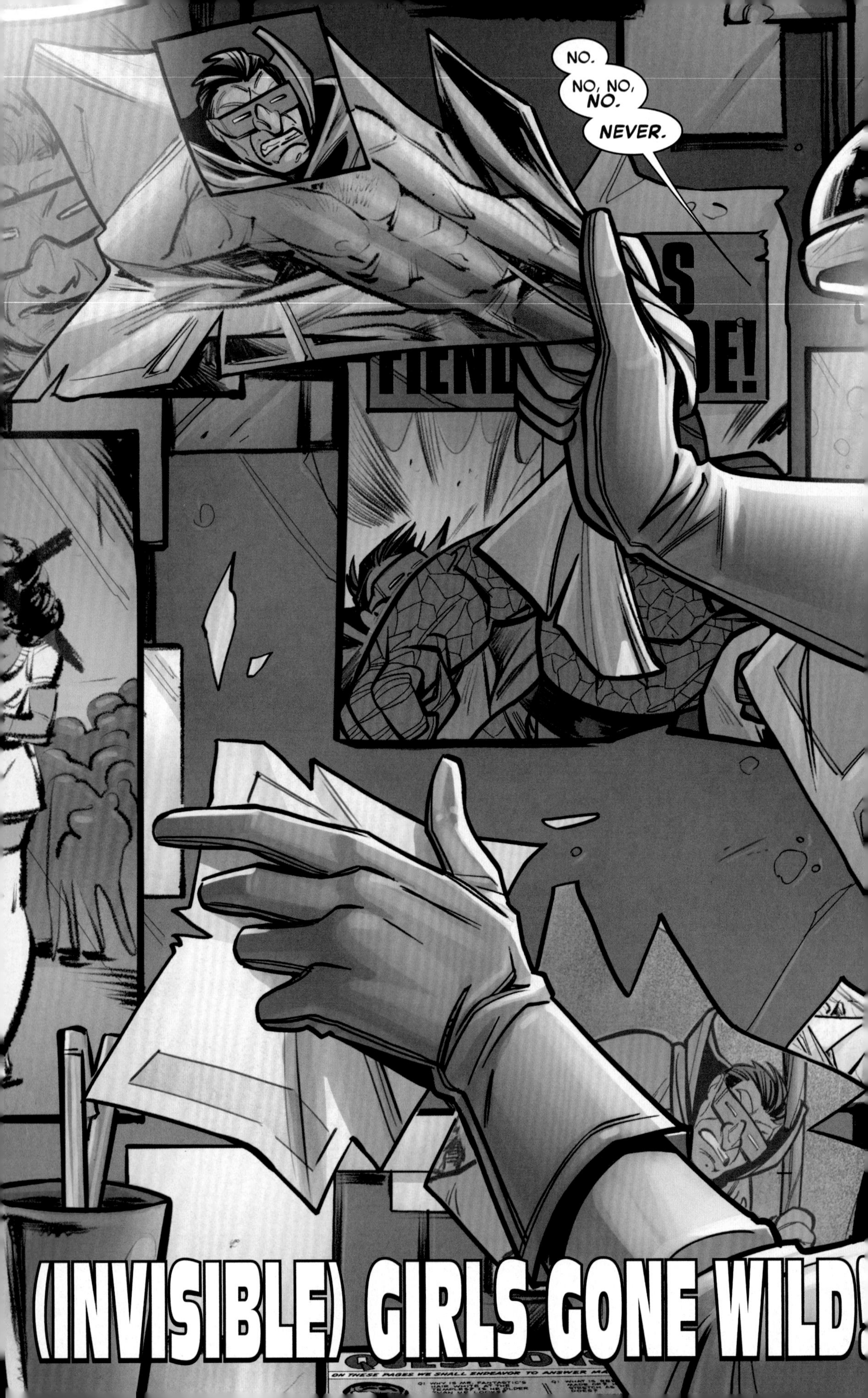
NO.
NO, NO, NO.
NEVER.
(INVISIBLE) GIRLS GONE WILD!

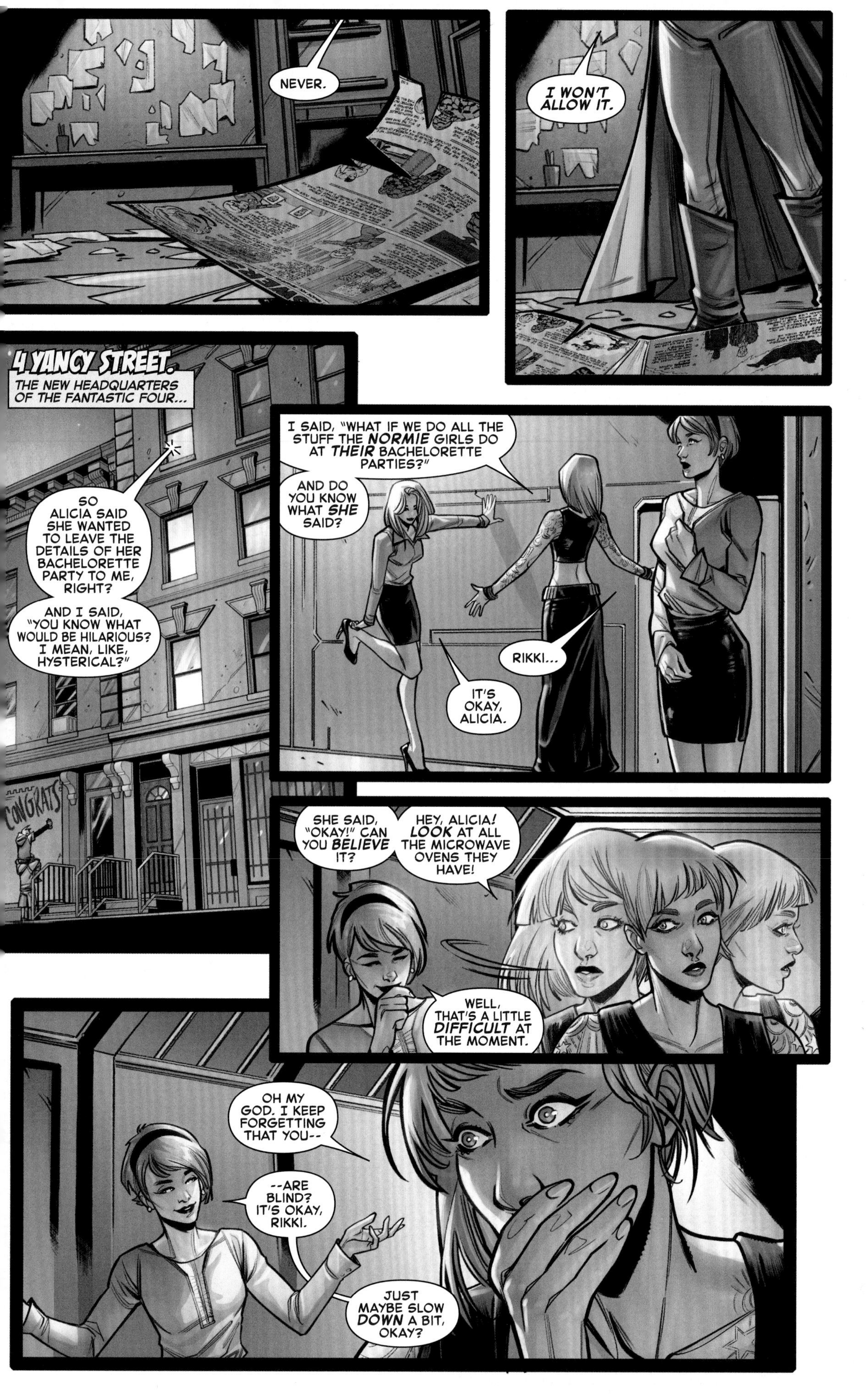
NEVER.
I WON'T ALLOW IT.
4 YANCY STREET.
THE NEW HEADQUARTERS OF THE FANTASTIC FOUR...
SO ALICIA SAID SHE WANTED TO LEAVE THE DETAILS OF HER BACHELORETTE PARTY TO ME, RIGHT?
AND I SAID, "YOU KNOW WHAT WOULD BE HILARIOUS? I MEAN, LIKE, HYSTERICAL?"
CONGRATS
I SAID, "WHAT IF WE DO ALL THE STUFF THE NORMIE GIRLS DO AT THEIR BACHELORETTE PARTIES?"
AND DO YOU KNOW WHAT SHE SAID?
RIKKI...
IT'S OKAY, ALICIA.
SHE SAID, "OKAY!" CAN YOU BELIEVE IT?
HEY, ALICIA! LOOK AT ALL THE MICROWAVE OVENS THEY HAVE!
WELL, THAT'S A LITTLE DIFFICULT AT THE MOMENT.
OH MY GOD. I KEEP FORGETTING THAT YOU--
--ARE BLIND? IT'S OKAY, RIKKI.
JUST MAYBE SLOW DOWN A BIT, OKAY?

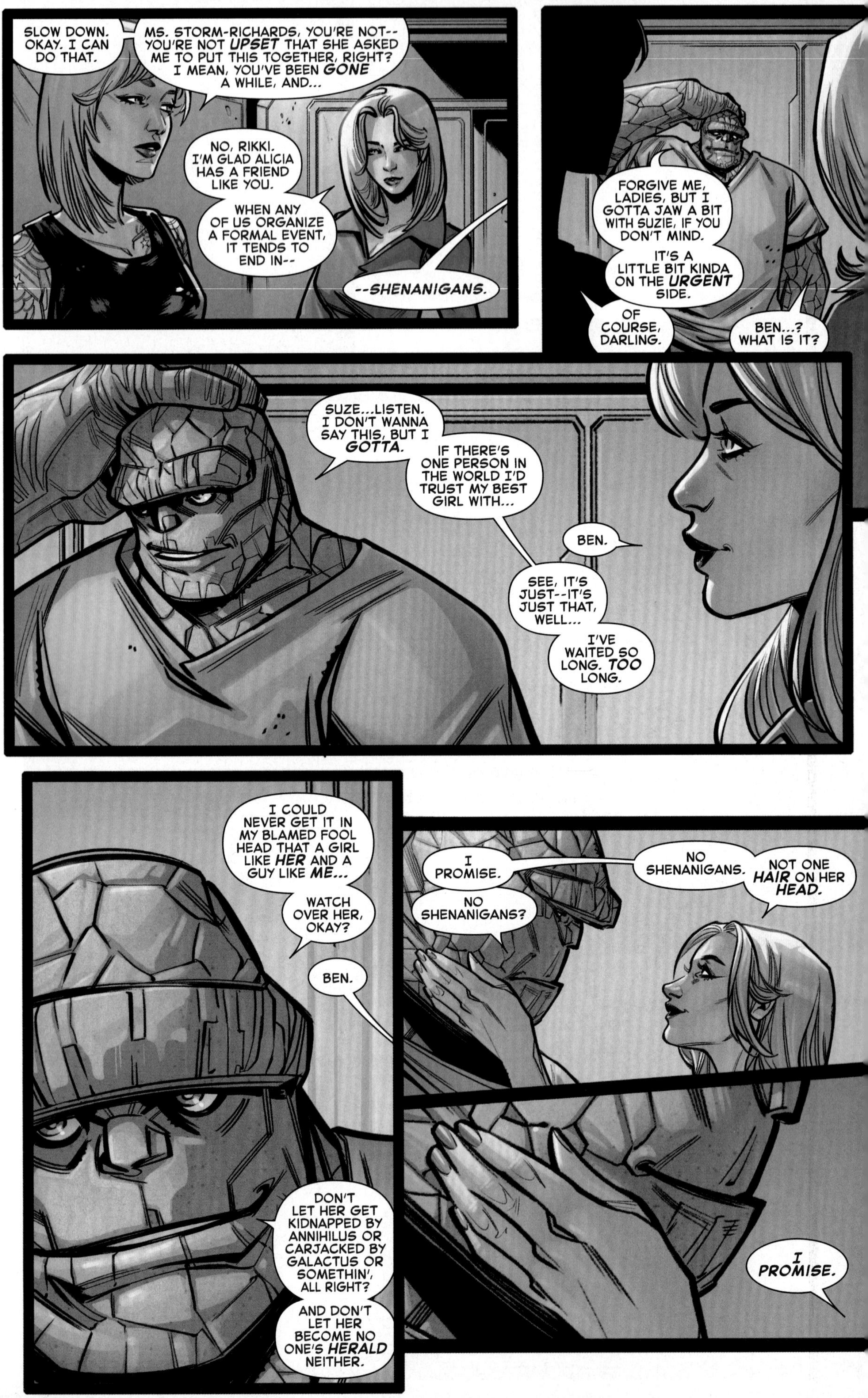
SLOW DOWN. OKAY. I CAN DO THAT.
MS. STORM-RICHARDS, YOU'RE NOT-- YOU'RE NOT UPSET THAT SHE ASKED ME TO PUT THIS TOGETHER, RIGHT? I MEAN, YOU'VE BEEN GONE A WHILE, AND...
NO, RIKKI. I'M GLAD ALICIA HAS A FRIEND LIKE YOU.
WHEN ANY OF US ORGANIZE A FORMAL EVENT, IT TENDS TO END IN--
--SHENANIGANS.
FORGIVE ME, LADIES, BUT I GOTTA JAW A BIT WITH SUZIE, IF YOU DON'T MIND.
IT'S A LITTLE BIT KINDA ON THE URGENT SIDE.
OF COURSE, DARLING.
BEN...? WHAT IS IT?
SUZE...LISTEN. I DON'T WANNA SAY THIS, BUT I GOTTA.
IF THERE'S ONE PERSON IN THE WORLD I'D TRUST MY BEST GIRL WITH...
BEN.
SEE, IT'S JUST--IT'S JUST THAT, WELL...
I'VE WAITED SO LONG. TOO LONG.
I COULD NEVER GET IT IN MY BLAMED FOOL HEAD THAT A GIRL LIKE HER AND A GUY LIKE ME...
WATCH OVER HER, OKAY?
BEN.
DON'T LET HER GET KIDNAPPED BY ANNIHILUS OR CARJACKED BY GALACTUS OR SOMETHIN', ALL RIGHT?
AND DON'T LET HER BECOME NO ONE'S HERALD NEITHER.
I PROMISE.
NO SHENANIGANS?
NO SHENANIGANS.
NOT ONE HAIR ON HER HEAD.
I PROMISE.

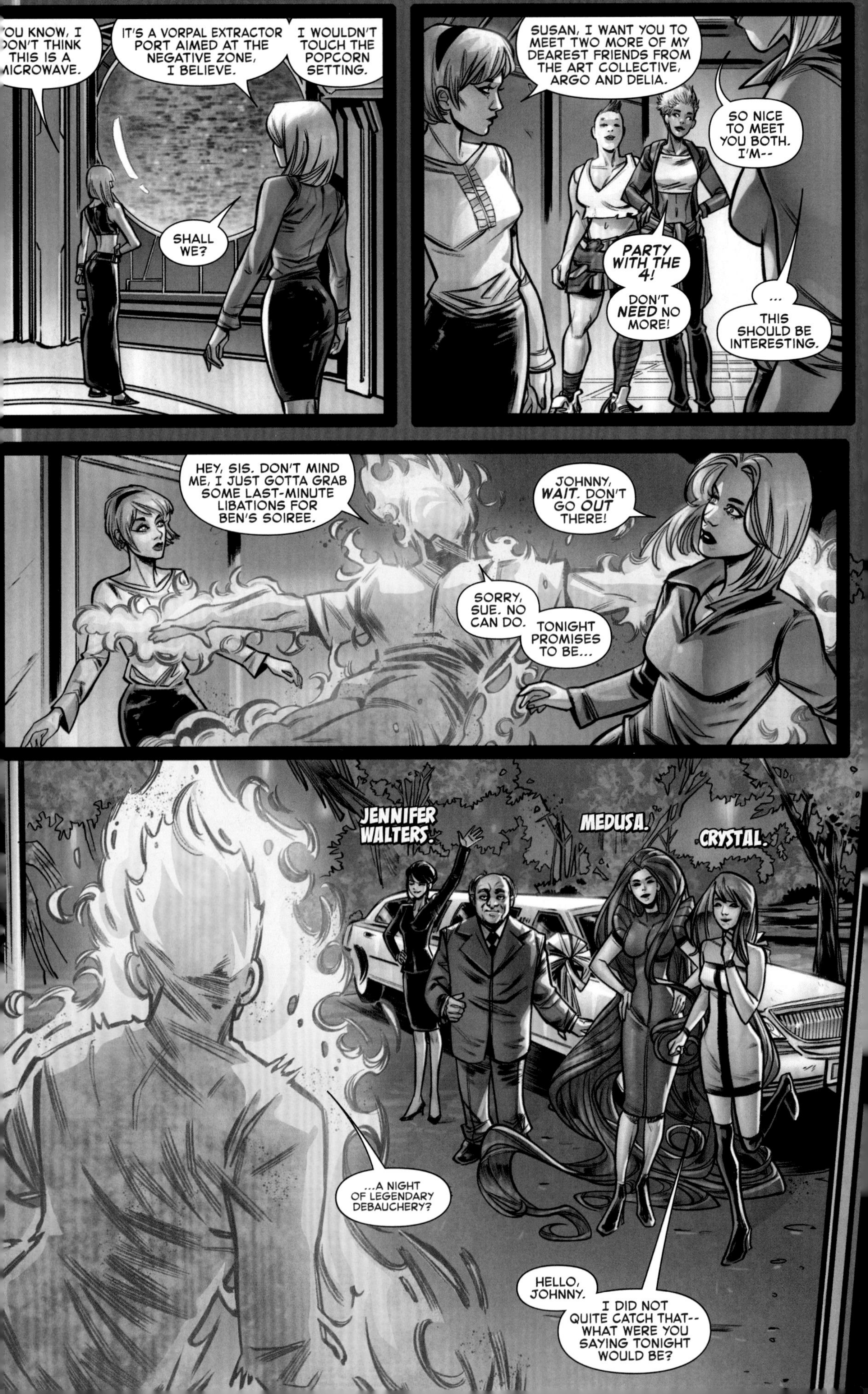

YOU KNOW, I DON'T THINK THIS IS A MICROWAVE.
IT'S A VORPAL EXTRACTOR PORT AIMED AT THE NEGATIVE ZONE, I BELIEVE.
I WOULDN'T TOUCH THE POPCORN SETTING.
SHALL WE?
SUSAN, I WANT YOU TO MEET TWO MORE OF MY DEAREST FRIENDS FROM THE ART COLLECTIVE, ARGO AND DELIA.
SO NICE TO MEET YOU BOTH. I'M--
PARTY WITH THE 4!
DON'T NEED NO MORE!
...
THIS SHOULD BE INTERESTING.
HEY, SIS. DON'T MIND ME, I JUST GOTTA GRAB SOME LAST-MINUTE LIBATIONS FOR BEN'S SOIREE.
JOHNNY, WAIT. DON'T GO OUT THERE!
SORRY, SUE. NO CAN DO.
TONIGHT PROMISES TO BE...
...A NIGHT OF LEGENDARY DEBAUCHERY?
JENNIFER WALTERS.
MEDUSA.
CRYSTAL.
HELLO, JOHNNY.
I DID NOT QUITE CATCH THAT-- WHAT WERE YOU SAYING TONIGHT WOULD BE?

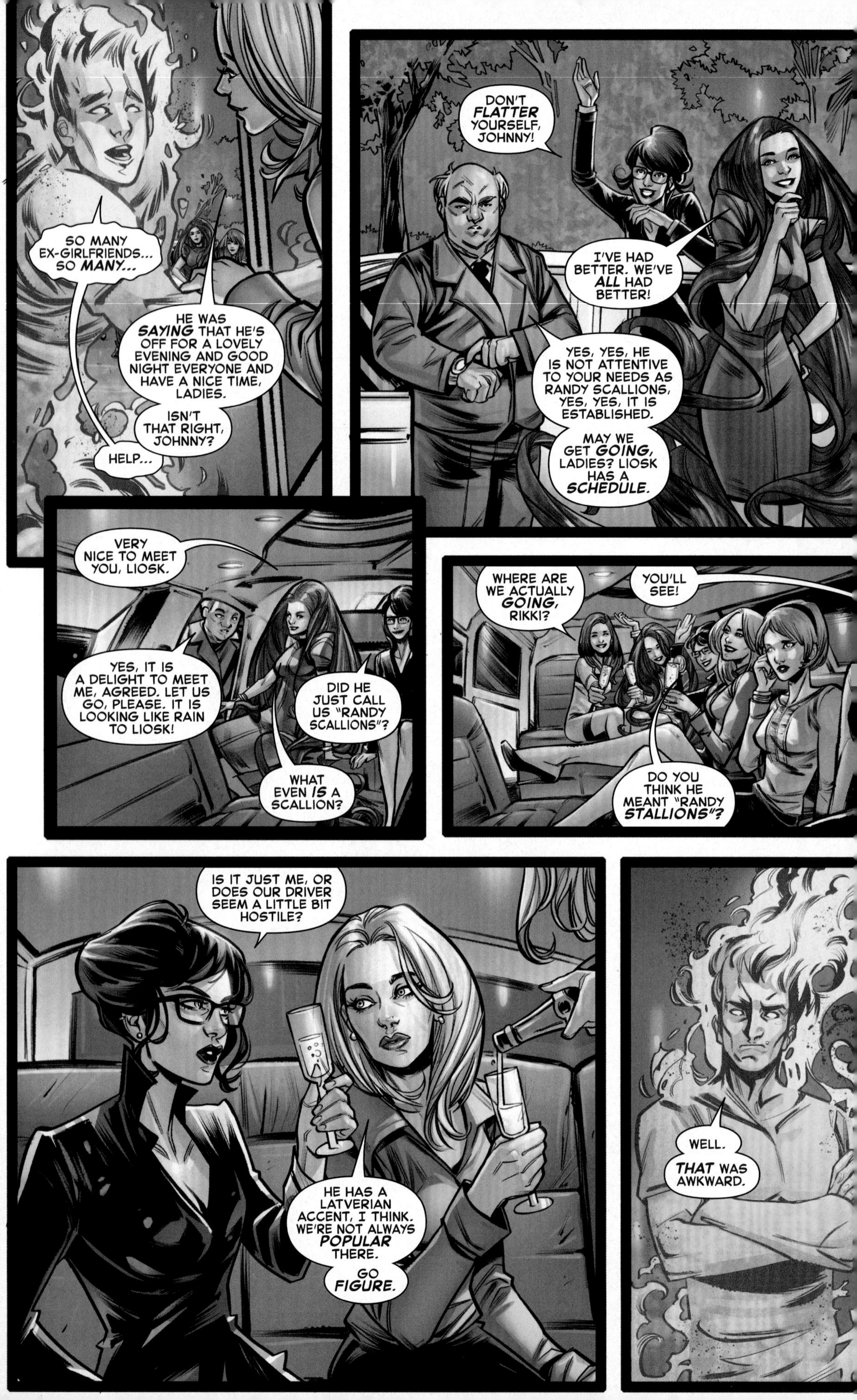
SO MANY EX-GIRLFRIENDS... SO MANY...
HE WAS SAYING THAT HE'S OFF FOR A LOVELY EVENING AND GOOD NIGHT EVERYONE AND HAVE A NICE TIME, LADIES.
ISN'T THAT RIGHT, JOHNNY?
HELP...
DON'T FLATTER YOURSELF, JOHNNY!
I'VE HAD BETTER. WE'VE ALL HAD BETTER!
YES, YES, HE IS NOT ATTENTIVE TO YOUR NEEDS AS RANDY SCALLIONS, YES, YES, IT IS ESTABLISHED.
MAY WE GET GOING, LADIES? LIOSK HAS A SCHEDULE.
VERY NICE TO MEET YOU, LIOSK.
YES, IT IS A DELIGHT TO MEET ME, AGREED. LET US GO, PLEASE. IT IS LOOKING LIKE RAIN TO LIOSK!
DID HE JUST CALL US "RANDY SCALLIONS"?
WHAT EVEN IS A SCALLION?
WHERE ARE WE ACTUALLY GOING, RIKKI?
YOU'LL SEE!
DO YOU THINK HE MEANT "RANDY STALLIONS"?
IS IT JUST ME, OR DOES OUR DRIVER SEEM A LITTLE BIT HOSTILE?
HE HAS A LATVERIAN ACCENT, I THINK. WE'RE NOT ALWAYS POPULAR THERE.
GO FIGURE.
WELL.
THAT WAS AWKWARD.

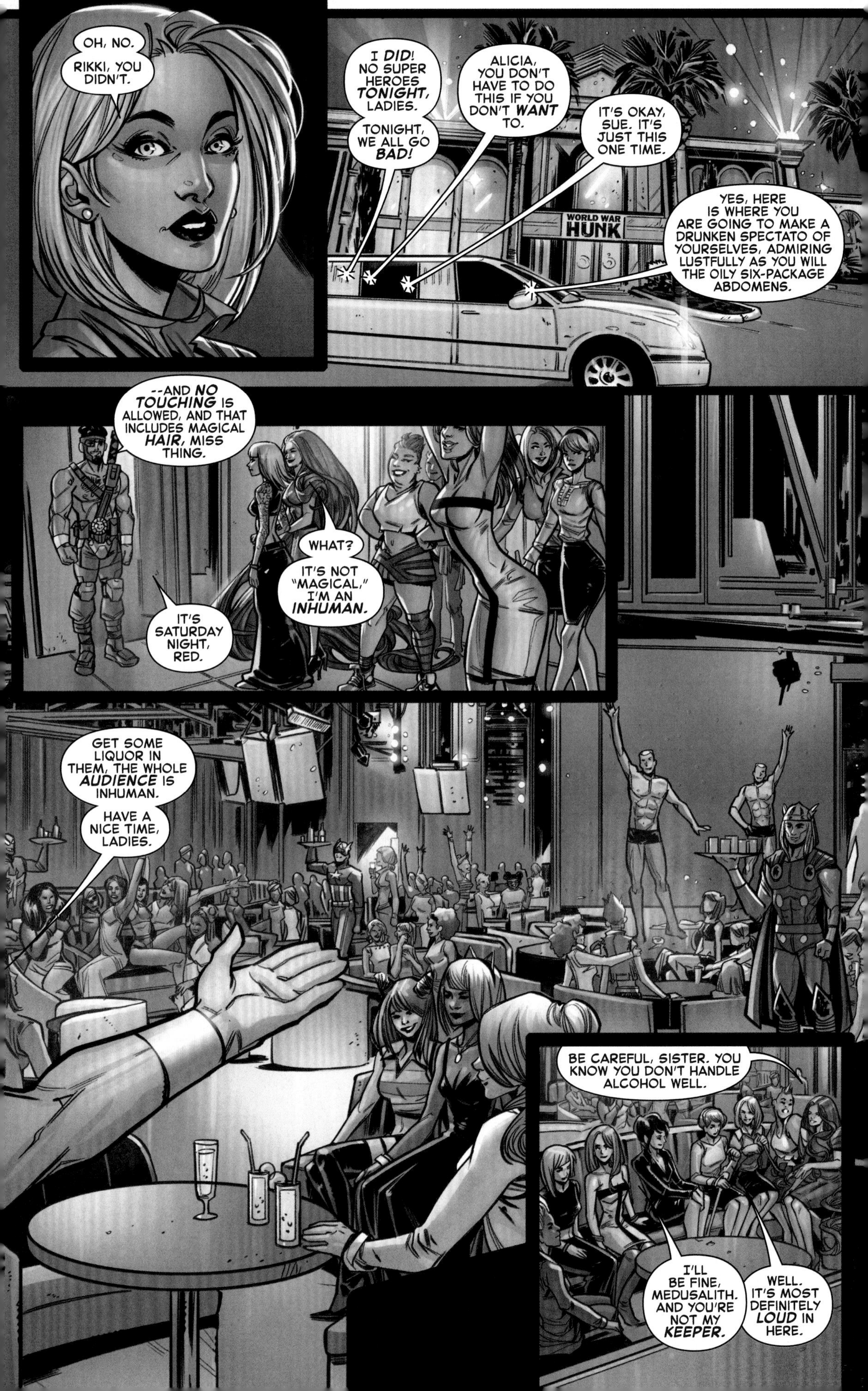
OH, NO.
RIKKI, YOU DIDN'T.
I DID! NO SUPER HEROES TONIGHT, LADIES.
TONIGHT, WE ALL GO BAD!
ALICIA, YOU DON'T HAVE TO DO THIS IF YOU DON'T WANT TO.
IT'S OKAY, SUE. IT'S JUST THIS ONE TIME.
WORLD WAR HUNK
YES, HERE IS WHERE YOU ARE GOING TO MAKE A DRUNKEN SPECTATO OF YOURSELVES, ADMIRING LUSTFULLY AS YOU WILL THE OILY SIX-PACKAGE ABDOMENS.
--AND NO TOUCHING IS ALLOWED, AND THAT INCLUDES MAGICAL HAIR, MISS THING.
WHAT?
IT'S NOT "MAGICAL," I'M AN INHUMAN.
IT'S SATURDAY NIGHT, RED.
GET SOME LIQUOR IN THEM, THE WHOLE AUDIENCE IS INHUMAN.
HAVE A NICE TIME, LADIES.
BE CAREFUL, SISTER. YOU KNOW YOU DON'T HANDLE ALCOHOL WELL.
I'LL BE FINE, MEDUSALITH. AND YOU'RE NOT MY KEEPER.
WELL. IT'S MOST DEFINITELY LOUD IN HERE.

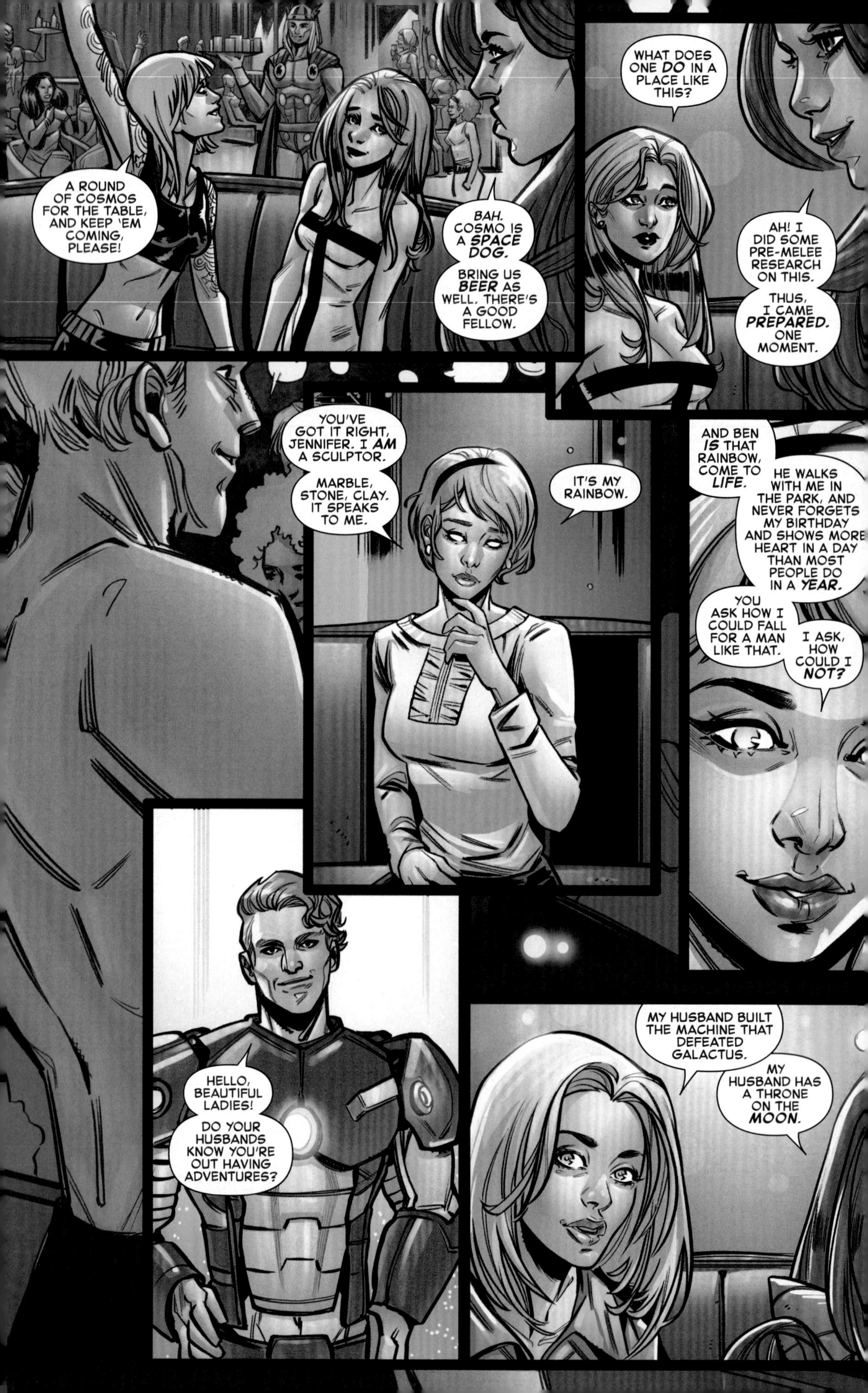
A ROUND OF COSMOS FOR THE TABLE, AND KEEP 'EM COMING, PLEASE!
BAH. COSMO IS A SPACE DOG.
BRING US BEER AS WELL. THERE'S A GOOD FELLOW.
WHAT DOES ONE DO IN A PLACE LIKE THIS?
AH! I DID SOME PRE-MELEE RESEARCH ON THIS.
THUS, I CAME PREPARED. ONE MOMENT.
YOU'VE GOT IT RIGHT, JENNIFER. I AM A SCULPTOR.
MARBLE, STONE, CLAY. IT SPEAKS TO ME.
IT'S MY RAINBOW.
AND BEN IS THAT RAINBOW, COME TO LIFE.
HE WALKS WITH ME IN THE PARK, AND NEVER FORGETS MY BIRTHDAY AND SHOWS MORE HEART IN A DAY THAN MOST PEOPLE DO IN A YEAR.
YOU ASK HOW I COULD FALL FOR A MAN LIKE THAT.
I ASK, HOW COULD I NOT?
HELLO, BEAUTIFUL LADIES!
DO YOUR HUSBANDS KNOW YOU'RE OUT HAVING ADVENTURES?
MY HUSBAND BUILT THE MACHINE THAT DEFEATED GALACTUS.
MY HUSBAND HAS A THRONE ON THE MOON.

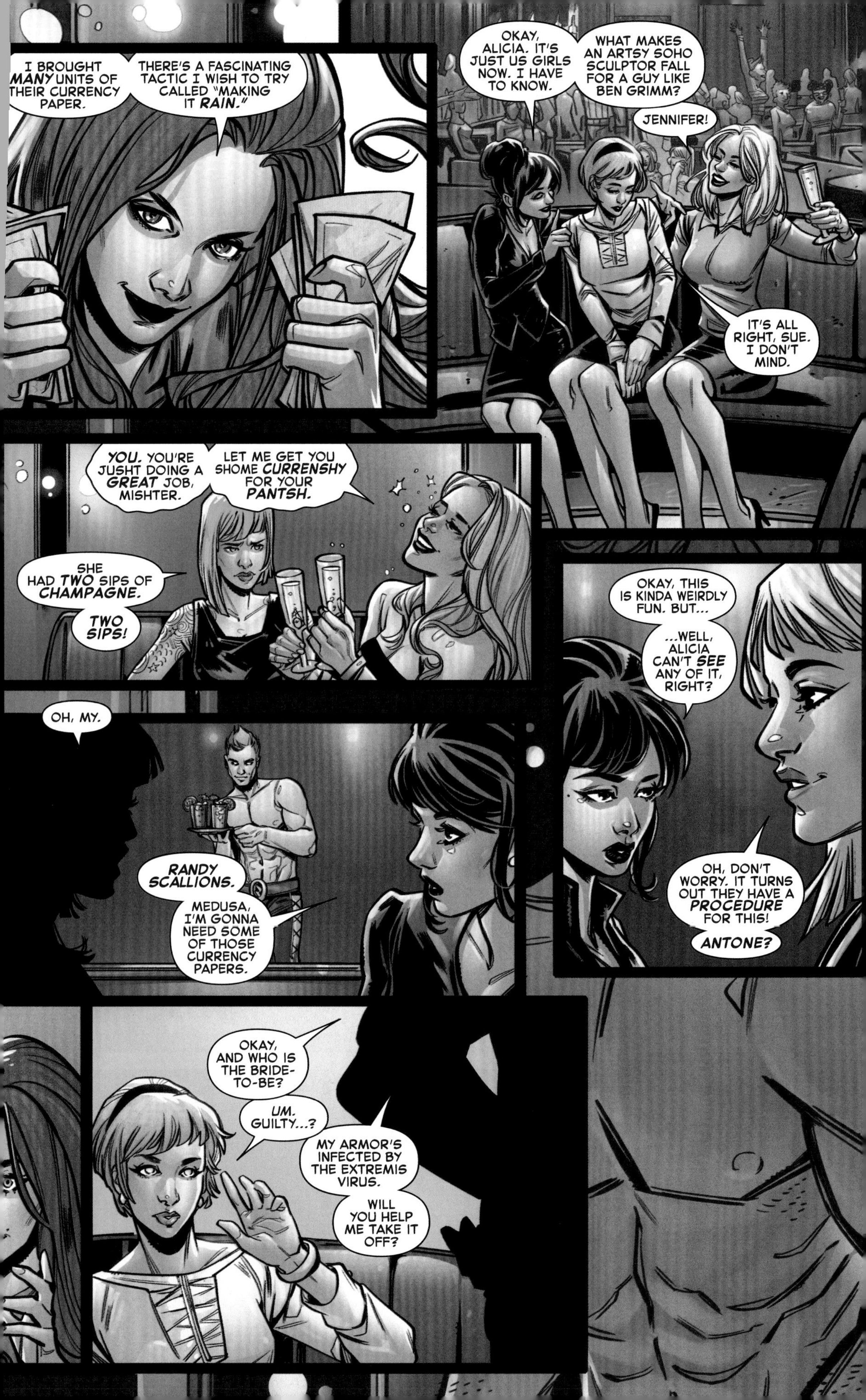
I BROUGHT MANY UNITS OF THEIR CURRENCY PAPER.
THERE'S A FASCINATING TACTIC I WISH TO TRY CALLED "MAKING IT RAIN."
OKAY, ALICIA. IT'S JUST US GIRLS NOW. I HAVE TO KNOW.
WHAT MAKES AN ARTSY SOHO SCULPTOR FALL FOR A GUY LIKE BEN GRIMM?
JENNIFER!
IT'S ALL RIGHT, SUE. I DON'T MIND.
YOU. YOU'RE JUSHT DOING A GREAT JOB, MISHTER.
LET ME GET YOU SHOME CURRENSHY FOR YOUR PANTSH.
SHE HAD TWO SIPS OF CHAMPAGNE.
TWO SIPS!
OKAY, THIS IS KINDA WEIRDLY FUN. BUT...
...WELL, ALICIA CAN'T SEE ANY OF IT, RIGHT?
OH, DON'T WORRY. IT TURNS OUT THEY HAVE A PROCEDURE FOR THIS!
ANTONE?
OH, MY.
RANDY SCALLIONS.
MEDUSA, I'M GONNA NEED SOME OF THOSE CURRENCY PAPERS.
OKAY, AND WHO IS THE BRIDE-TO-BE?
UM. GUILTY...?
MY ARMOR'S INFECTED BY THE EXTREMIS VIRUS.
WILL YOU HELP ME TAKE IT OFF?

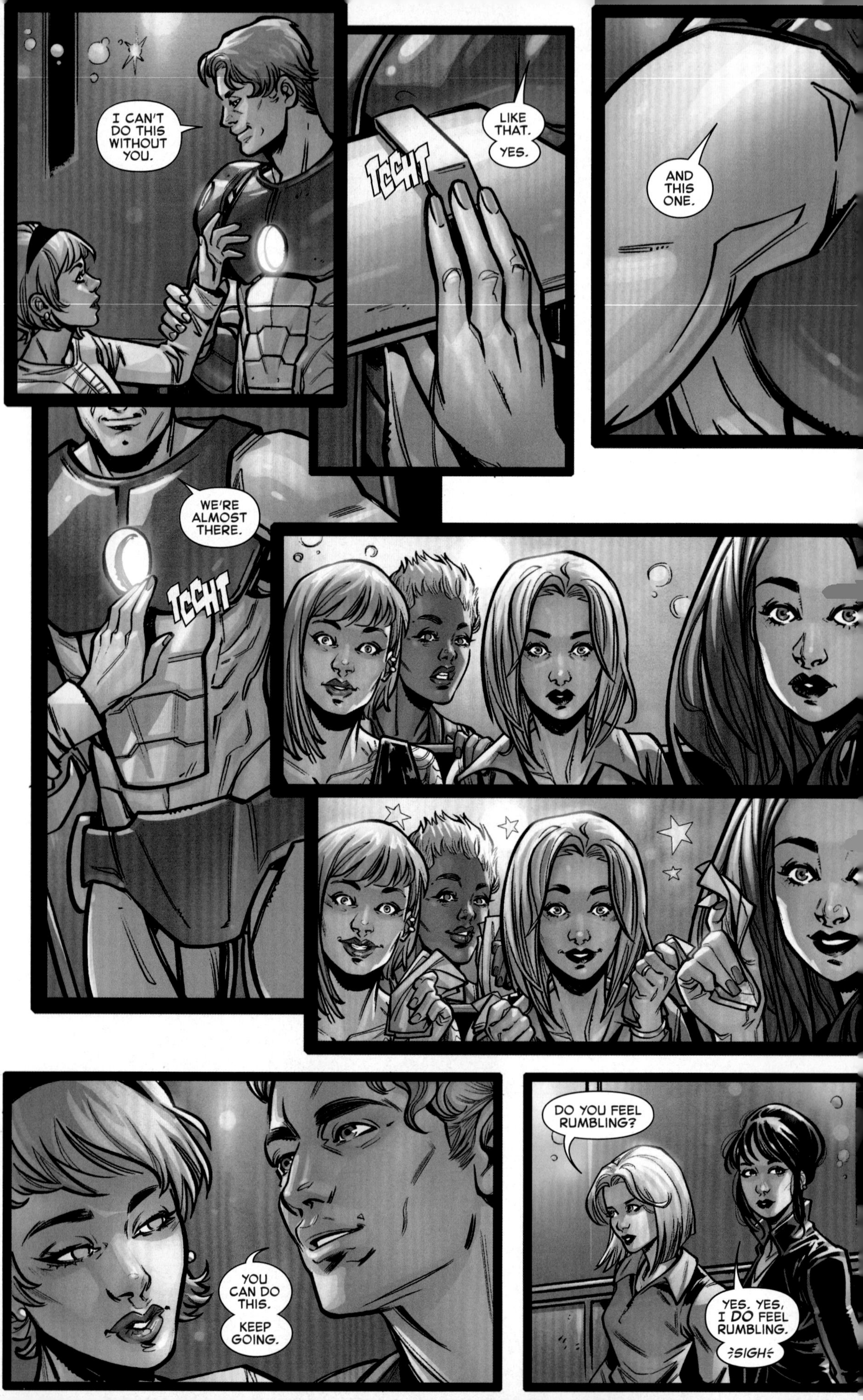
I CAN'T DO THIS WITHOUT YOU.
TCCHT
LIKE THAT.
YES.
AND THIS ONE.
WE'RE ALMOST THERE.
TCCHT
YOU CAN DO THIS.
KEEP GOING.
DO YOU FEEL RUMBLING?
YES. YES, I DO FEEL RUMBLING.
SIGH

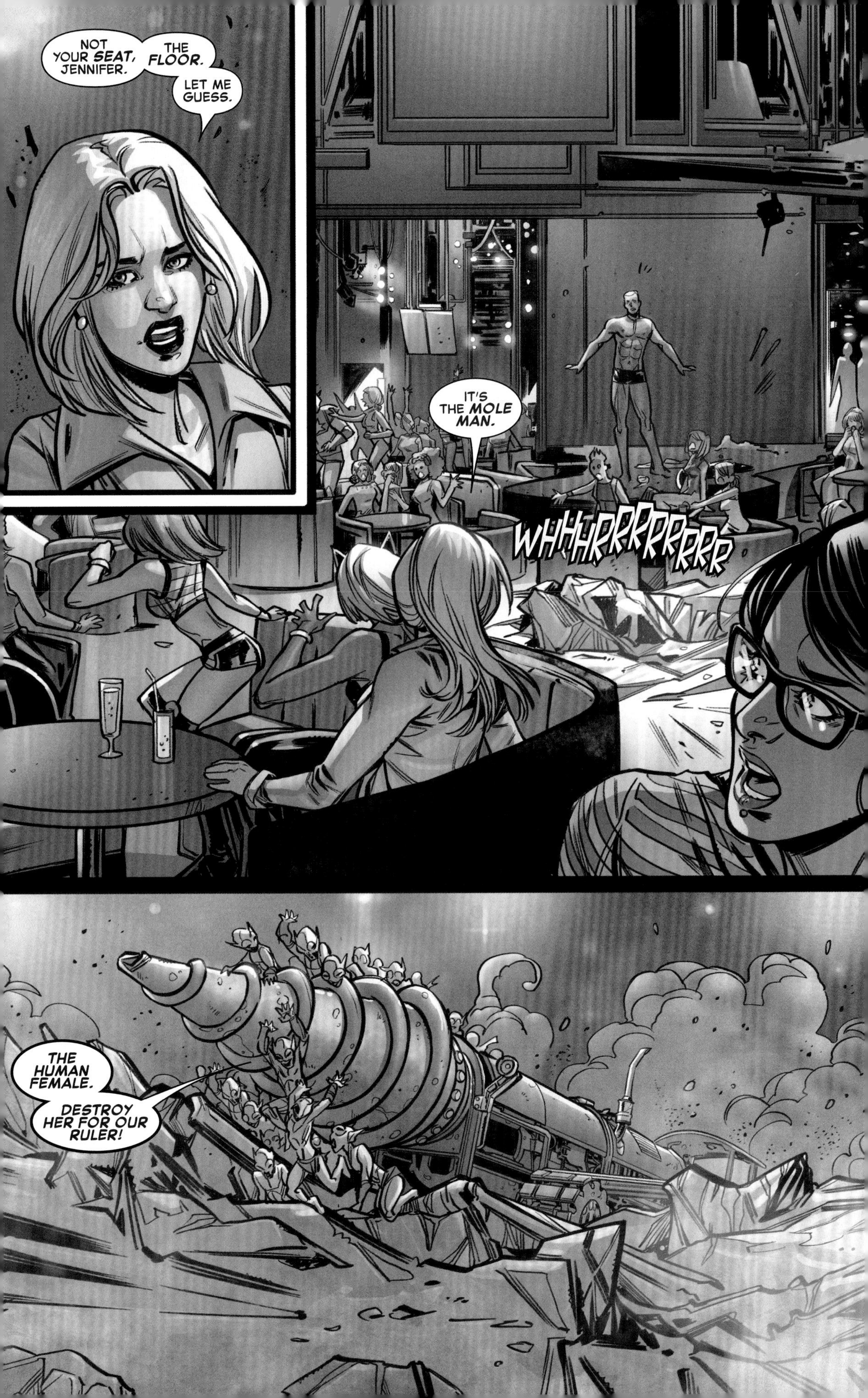
NOT YOUR SEAT, JENNIFER.
THE FLOOR.
LET ME GUESS.
IT'S THE MOLE MAN.
WHHHRRRRRRRRR
THE HUMAN FEMALE.
DESTROY HER FOR OUR RULER!

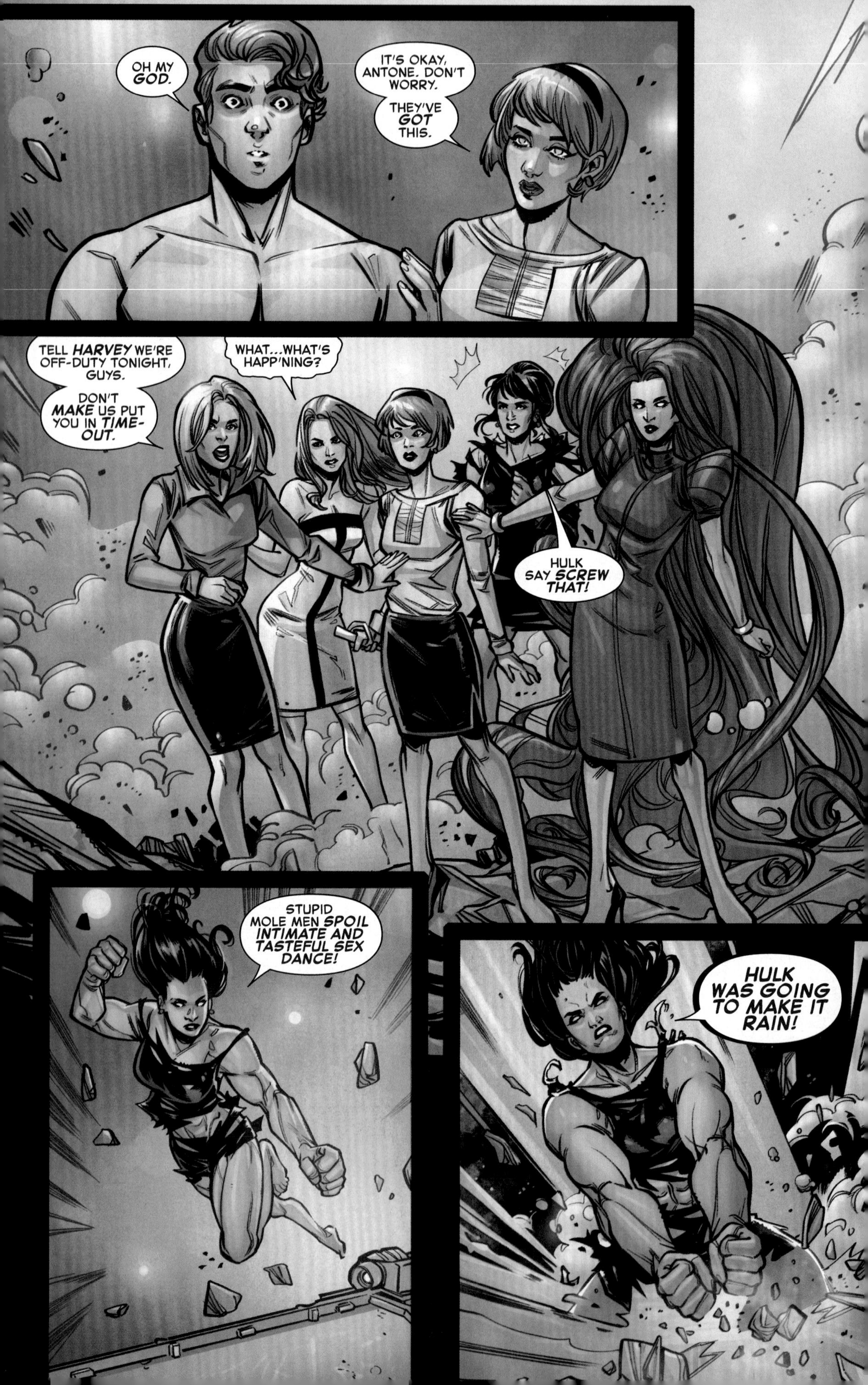
OH MY GOD.
IT'S OKAY, ANTONE. DON'T WORRY.
THEY'VE GOT THIS.
TELL HARVEY WE'RE OFF-DUTY TONIGHT, GUYS.
DON'T MAKE US PUT YOU IN TIME-OUT.
WHAT...WHAT'S HAPP'NING?
HULK SAY SCREW THAT!
STUPID MOLE MEN SPOIL INTIMATE AND TASTEFUL SEX DANCE!
HULK WAS GOING TO MAKE IT RAIN!

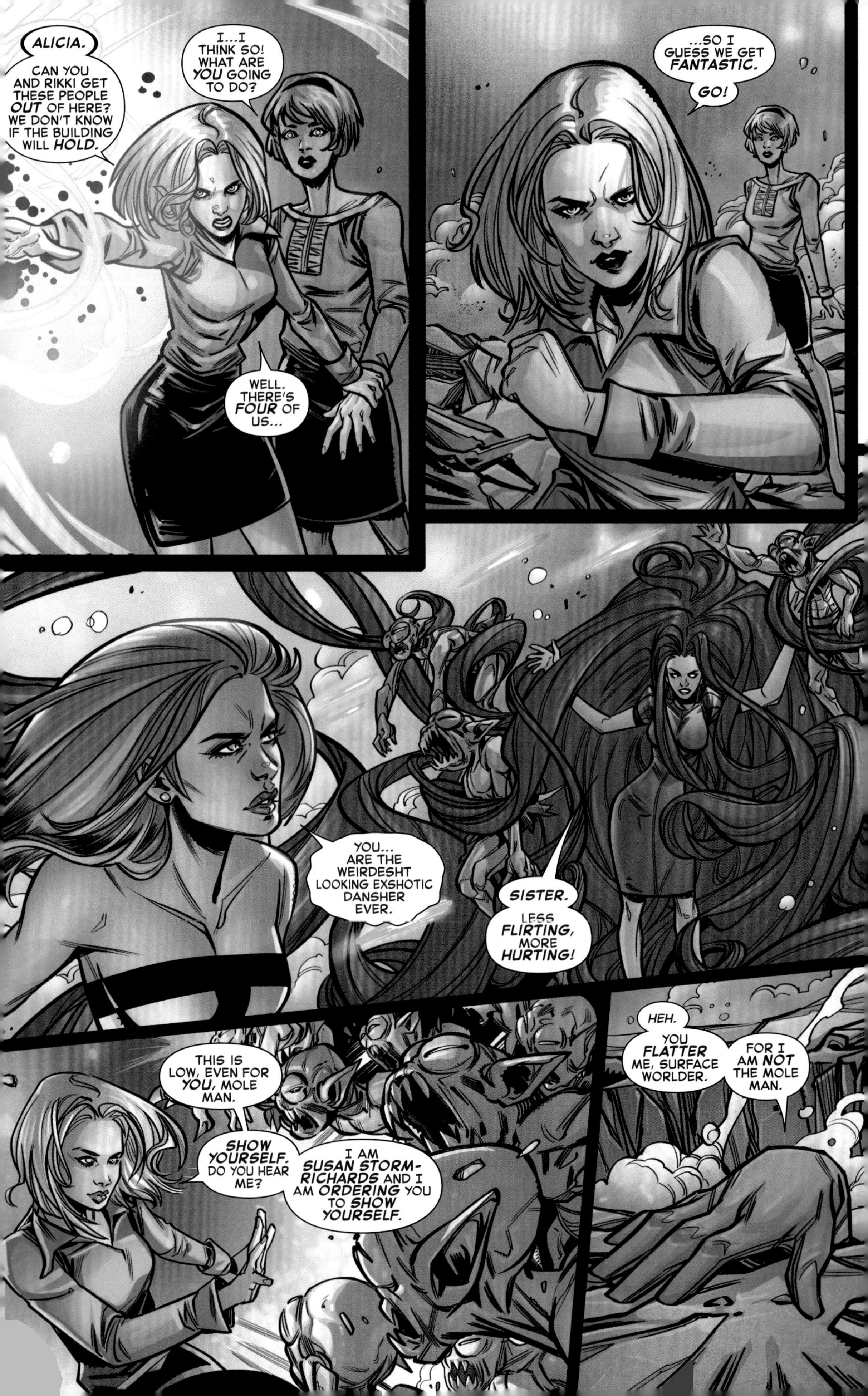
ALICIA.
CAN YOU AND RIKKI GET THESE PEOPLE OUT OF HERE? WE DON'T KNOW IF THE BUILDING WILL HOLD.
I...I THINK SO! WHAT ARE YOU GOING TO DO?
WELL. THERE'S FOUR OF US...
...SO I GUESS WE GET FANTASTIC.
GO!
YOU... ARE THE WEIRDESHT LOOKING EXSHOTIC DANSHER EVER.
SISTER.
LESS FLIRTING, MORE HURTING!
THIS IS LOW, EVEN FOR YOU, MOLE MAN.
SHOW YOURSELF. DO YOU HEAR ME?
I AM SUSAN STORM-RICHARDS AND I AM ORDERING YOU TO SHOW YOURSELF.
HEH.
YOU FLATTER ME, SURFACE WORLDER.
FOR I AM NOT THE MOLE MAN.

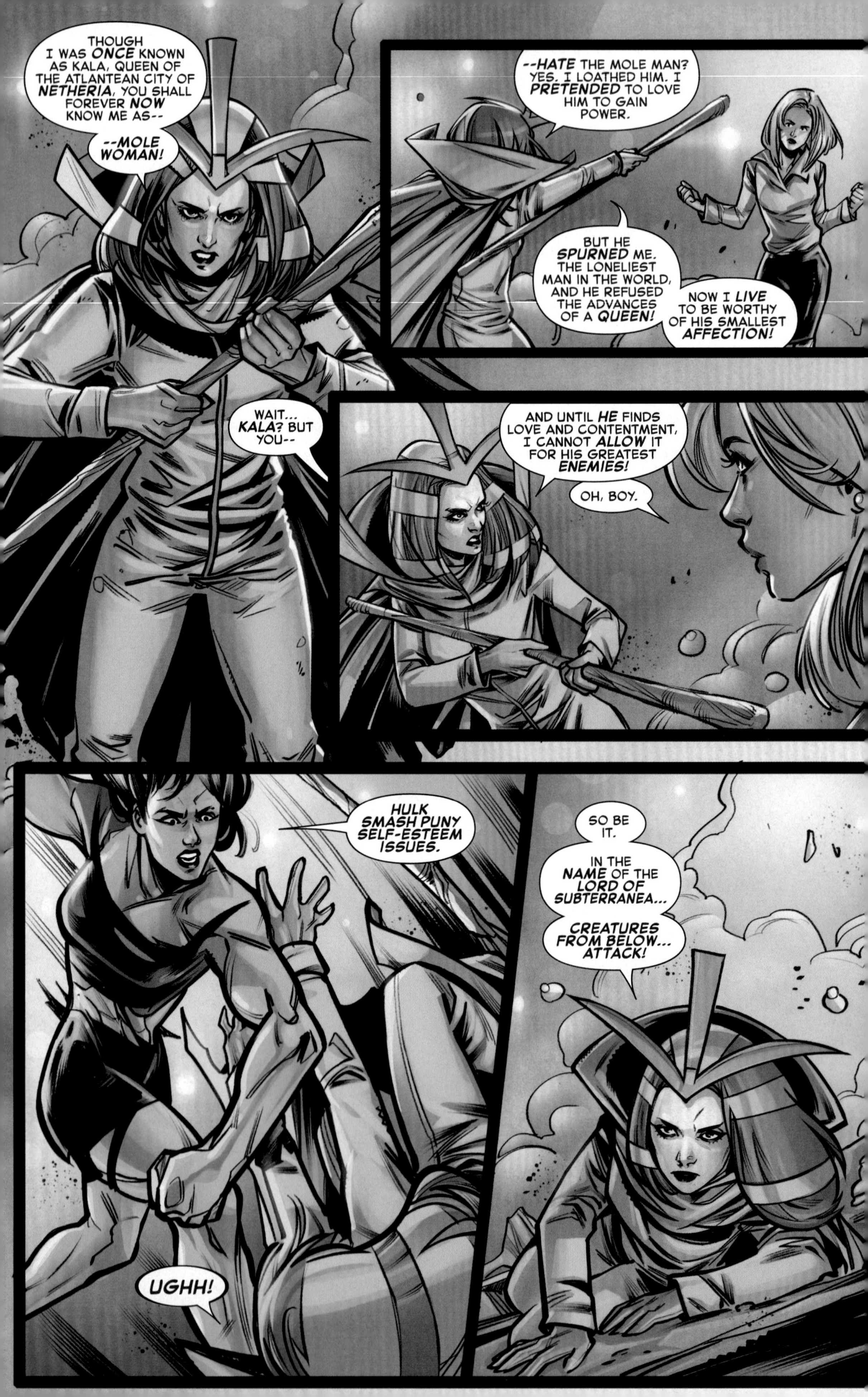
THOUGH I WAS ONCE KNOWN AS KALA, QUEEN OF THE ATLANTEAN CITY OF NETHERIA, YOU SHALL FOREVER NOW KNOW ME AS--
--MOLE WOMAN!
WAIT... KALA? BUT YOU--
--HATE THE MOLE MAN? YES. I LOATHED HIM. I PRETENDED TO LOVE HIM TO GAIN POWER.
BUT HE SPURNED ME. THE LONELIEST MAN IN THE WORLD, AND HE REFUSED THE ADVANCES OF A QUEEN!
NOW I LIVE TO BE WORTHY OF HIS SMALLEST AFFECTION!
AND UNTIL HE FINDS LOVE AND CONTENTMENT, I CANNOT ALLOW IT FOR HIS GREATEST ENEMIES!
OH, BOY.
HULK SMASH PUNY SELF-ESTEEM ISSUES.
UGHH!
SO BE IT.
IN THE NAME OF THE LORD OF SUBTERRANEA...
CREATURES FROM BELOW... ATTACK!

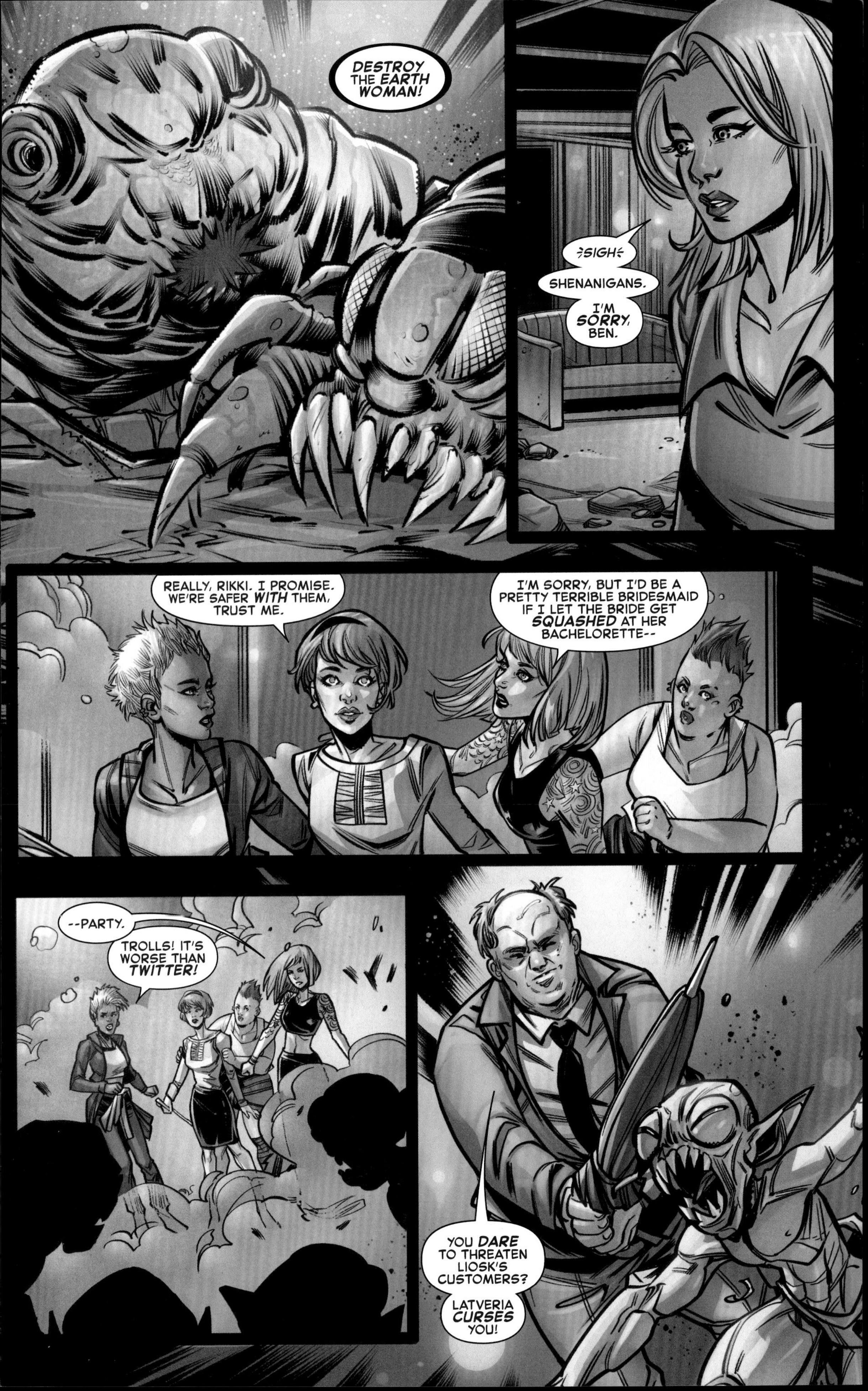
DESTROY THE EARTH WOMAN!
SIGH
SHENANIGANS.
I'M SORRY, BEN.
REALLY, RIKKI. I PROMISE. WE'RE SAFER WITH THEM, TRUST ME.
I'M SORRY, BUT I'D BE A PRETTY TERRIBLE BRIDESMAID IF I LET THE BRIDE GET SQUASHED AT HER BACHELORETTE--
--PARTY.
TROLLS! IT'S WORSE THAN TWITTER!
YOU DARE TO THREATEN LIOSK'S CUSTOMERS?
LATVERIA CURSES YOU!

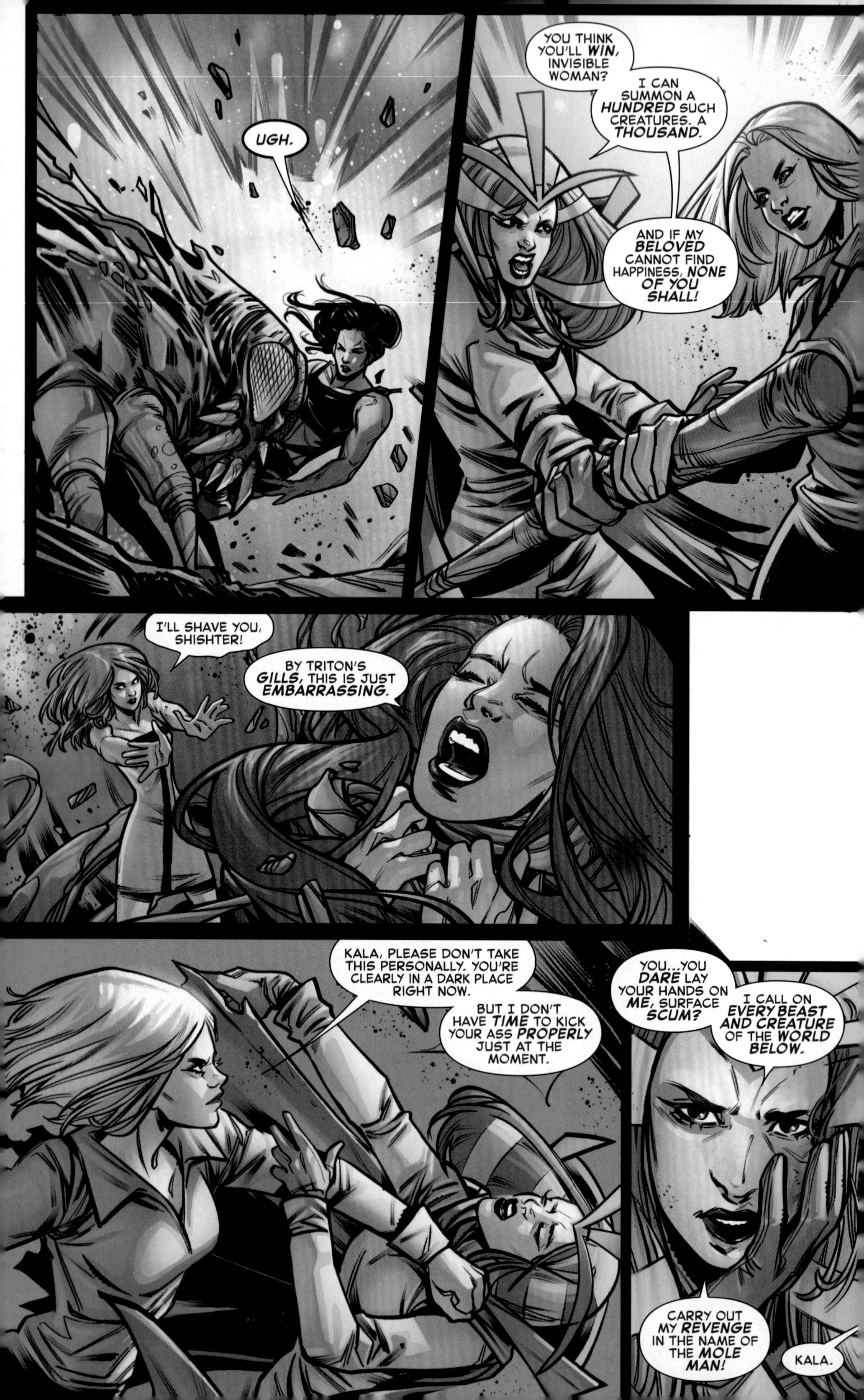
UGH.
YOU THINK YOU'LL WIN, INVISIBLE WOMAN?
I CAN SUMMON A HUNDRED SUCH CREATURES. A THOUSAND.
AND IF MY BELOVED CANNOT FIND HAPPINESS, NONE OF YOU SHALL!
I'LL SHAVE YOU, SHISHTER!
BY TRITON'S GILLS, THIS IS JUST EMBARRASSING.
KALA, PLEASE DON'T TAKE THIS PERSONALLY. YOU'RE CLEARLY IN A DARK PLACE RIGHT NOW.
BUT I DON'T HAVE TIME TO KICK YOUR ASS PROPERLY JUST AT THE MOMENT.
YOU...YOU DARE LAY YOUR HANDS ON ME, SURFACE SCUM?
I CALL ON EVERY BEAST AND CREATURE OF THE WORLD BELOW.
CARRY OUT MY REVENGE IN THE NAME OF THE MOLE MAN!
KALA.

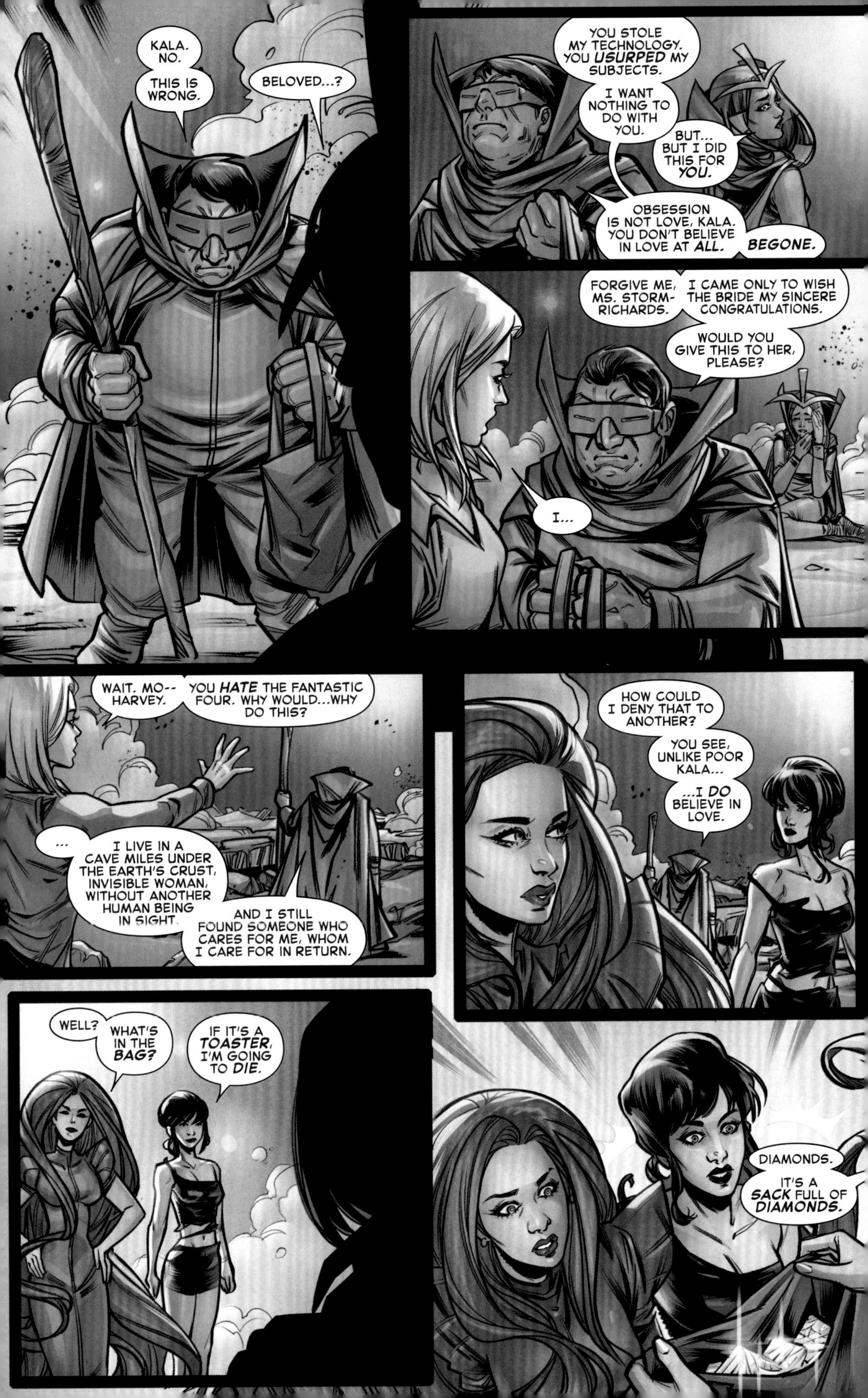
KALA. NO.
THIS IS WRONG.
BELOVED...?
YOU STOLE MY TECHNOLOGY. YOU USURPED MY SUBJECTS.
I WANT NOTHING TO DO WITH YOU.
BUT... BUT I DID THIS FOR YOU.
OBSESSION IS NOT LOVE, KALA. YOU DON'T BELIEVE IN LOVE AT ALL.
BEGONE.
FORGIVE ME, MS. STORM-RICHARDS.
I CAME ONLY TO WISH THE BRIDE MY SINCERE CONGRATULATIONS.
WOULD YOU GIVE THIS TO HER, PLEASE?
I...
WAIT. MO-- HARVEY.
YOU HATE THE FANTASTIC FOUR. WHY WOULD...WHY DO THIS?
...
I LIVE IN A CAVE MILES UNDER THE EARTH'S CRUST, INVISIBLE WOMAN, WITHOUT ANOTHER HUMAN BEING IN SIGHT.
AND I STILL FOUND SOMEONE WHO CARES FOR ME, WHOM I CARE FOR IN RETURN.
HOW COULD I DENY THAT TO ANOTHER?
YOU SEE, UNLIKE POOR KALA...
...I DO BELIEVE IN LOVE.
WELL?
WHAT'S IN THE BAG?
IF IT'S A TOASTER, I'M GOING TO DIE.
DIAMONDS.
IT'S A SACK FULL OF DIAMONDS.

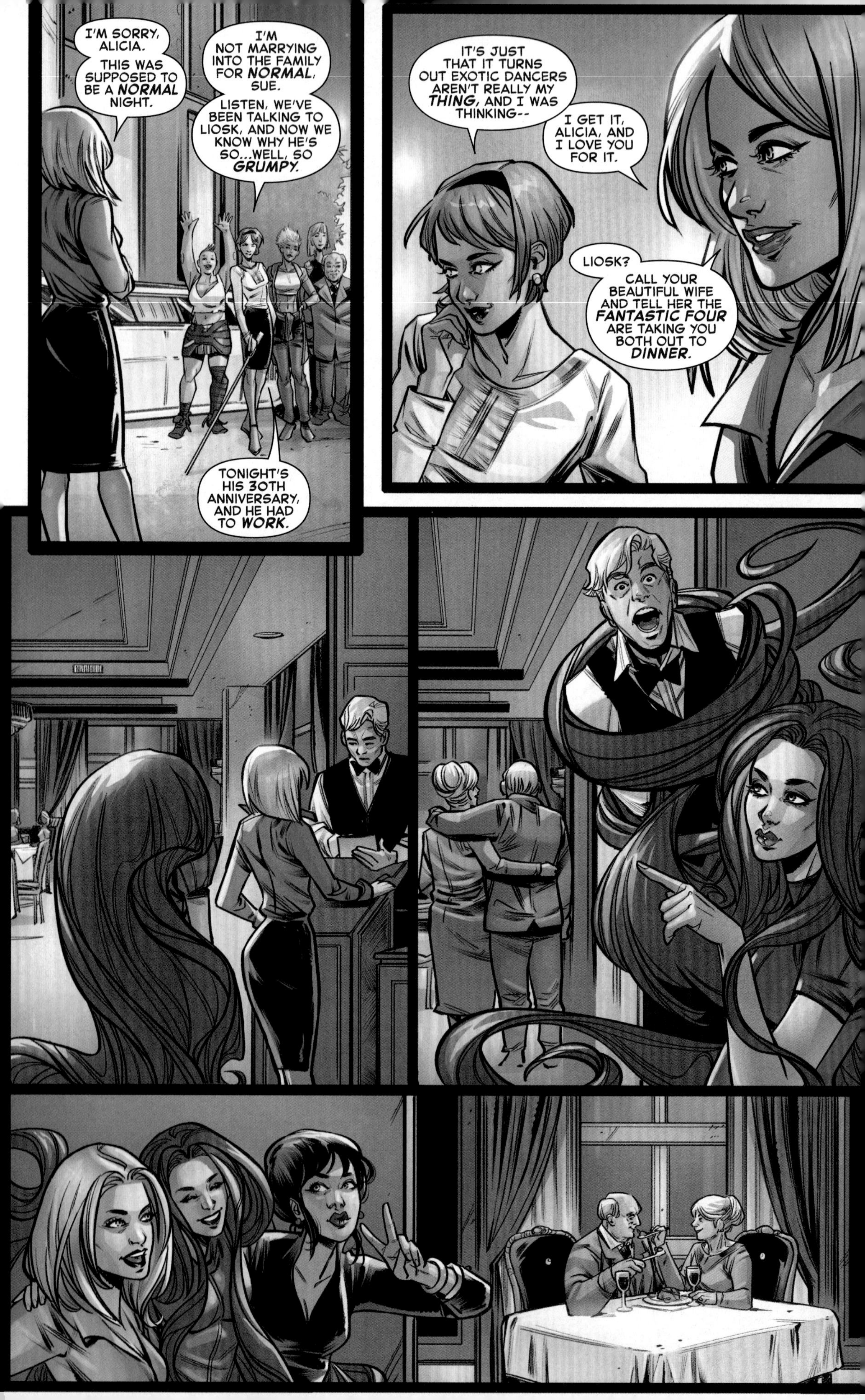
I'M SORRY, ALICIA.
THIS WAS SUPPOSED TO BE A NORMAL NIGHT.
I'M NOT MARRYING INTO THE FAMILY FOR NORMAL, SUE.
LISTEN, WE'VE BEEN TALKING TO LIOSK, AND NOW WE KNOW WHY HE'S SO...WELL, SO GRUMPY.
TONIGHT'S HIS 30TH ANNIVERSARY, AND HE HAD TO WORK.
IT'S JUST THAT IT TURNS OUT EXOTIC DANCERS AREN'T REALLY MY THING, AND I WAS THINKING--
I GET IT, ALICIA, AND I LOVE YOU FOR IT.
LIOSK?
CALL YOUR BEAUTIFUL WIFE AND TELL HER THE FANTASTIC FOUR ARE TAKING YOU BOTH OUT TO DINNER.

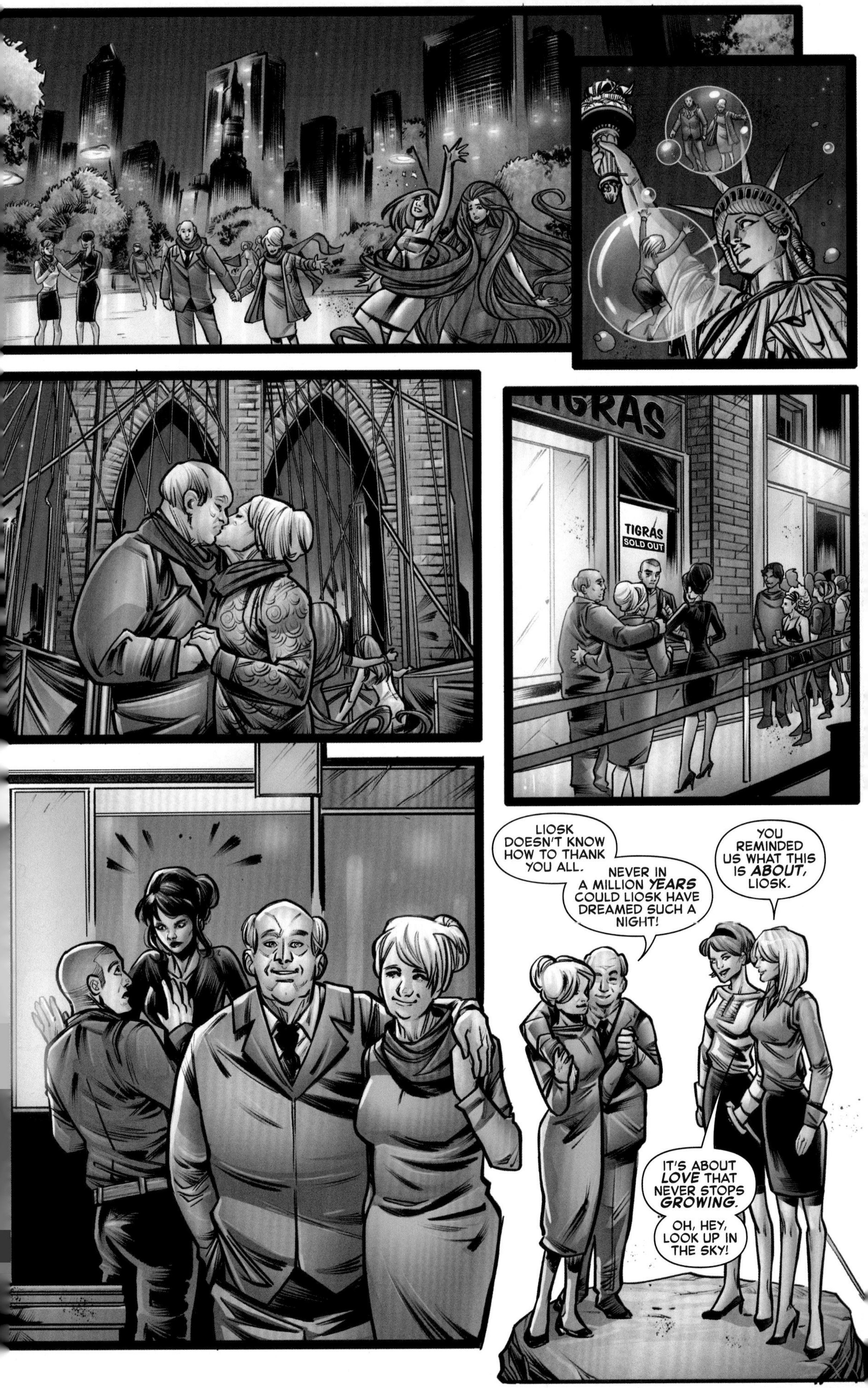

TIGRAS
TIGRAS
SOLD OUT
LIOSK DOESN'T KNOW HOW TO THANK YOU ALL.
NEVER IN A MILLION YEARS COULD LIOSK HAVE DREAMED SUCH A NIGHT!
YOU REMINDED US WHAT THIS IS ABOUT, LIOSK.
IT'S ABOUT LOVE THAT NEVER STOPS GROWING.
OH, HEY, LOOK UP IN THE SKY!

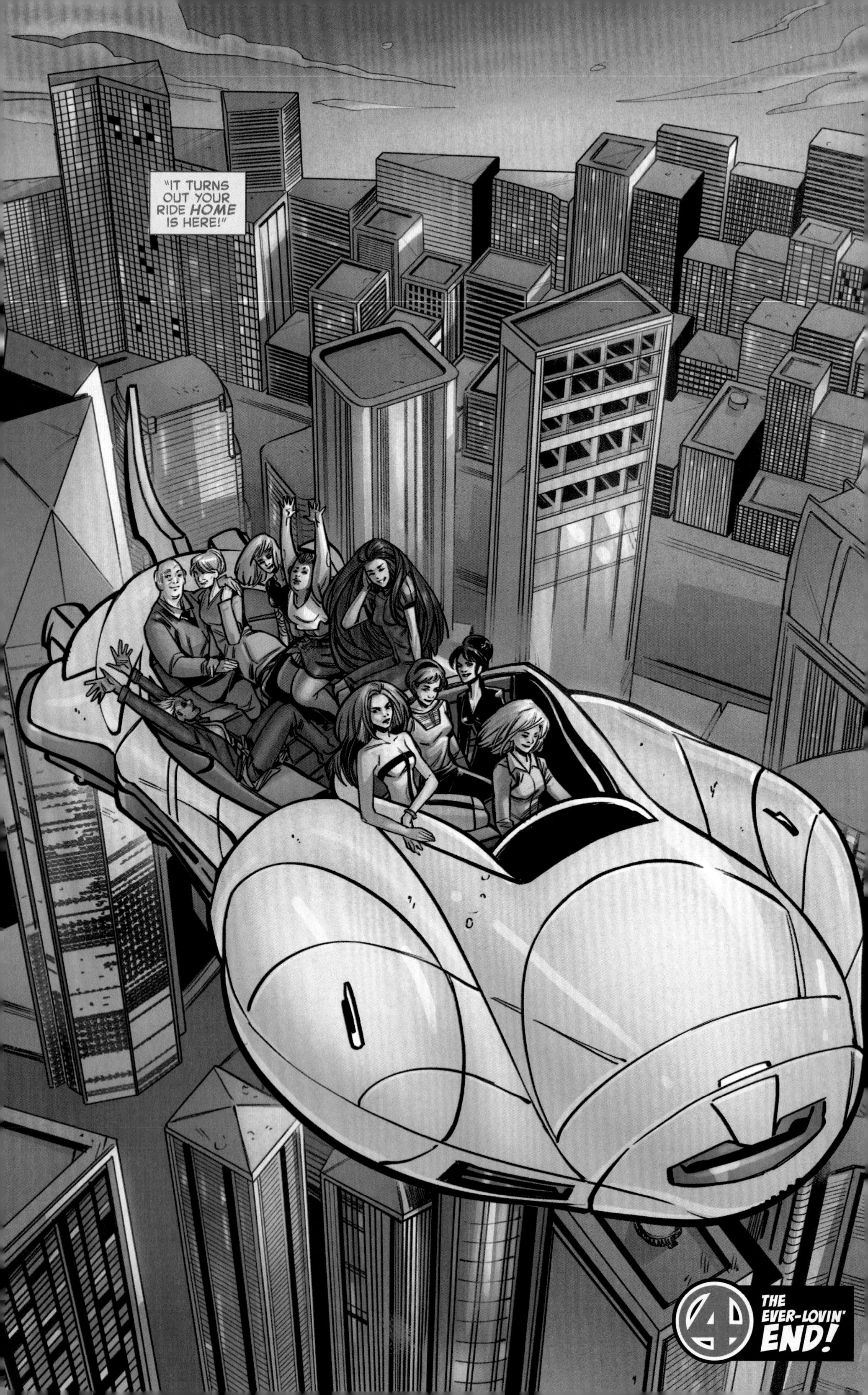
"IT TURNS OUT YOUR RIDE HOME IS HERE!"
THE EVER-LOVIN' END!

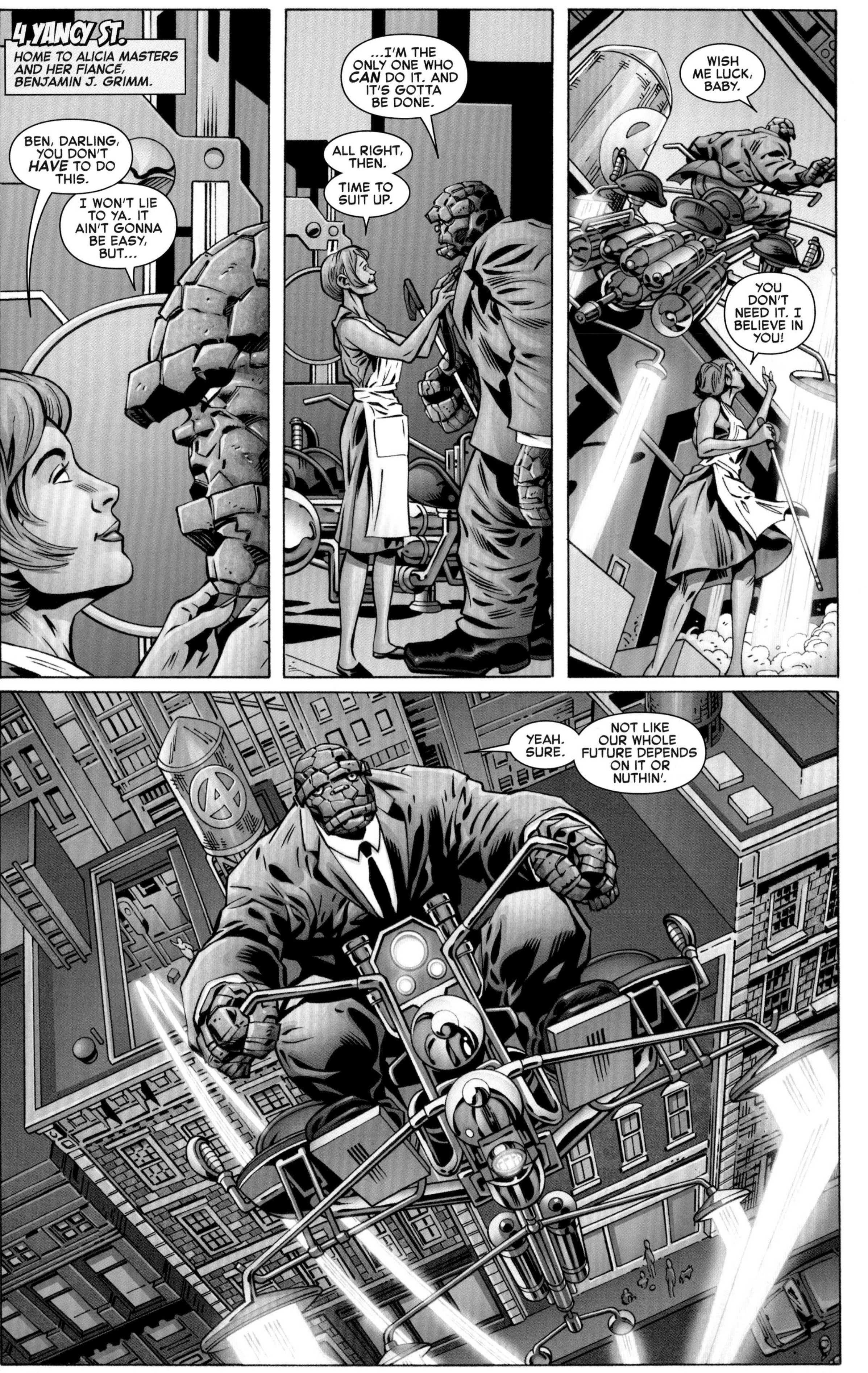
4 YANCY ST.
HOME TO ALICIA MASTERS AND HER FIANCÉ, BENJAMIN J. GRIMM.
BEN, DARLING, YOU DON'T HAVE TO DO THIS.
I WON'T LIE TO YA. IT AIN'T GONNA BE EASY, BUT...
...I'M THE ONLY ONE WHO CAN DO IT. AND IT'S GOTTA BE DONE.
ALL RIGHT, THEN.
TIME TO SUIT UP.
WISH ME LUCK, BABY.
YOU DON'T NEED IT. I BELIEVE IN YOU!
YEAH. SURE.
NOT LIKE OUR WHOLE FUTURE DEPENDS ON IT OR NUTHIN'.

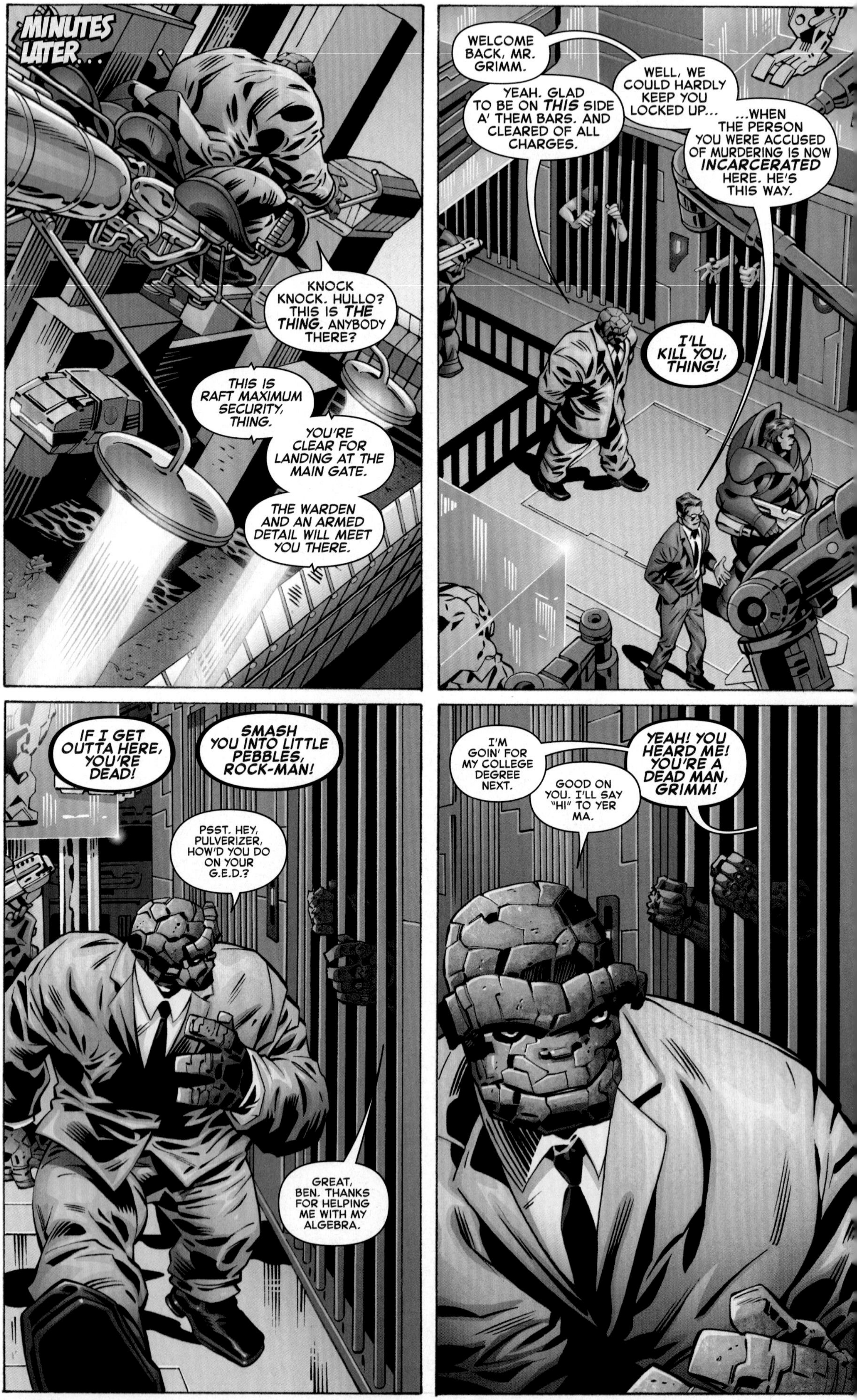
MINUTES LATER...
KNOCK KNOCK. HULLO? THIS IS THE THING. ANYBODY THERE?
THIS IS RAFT MAXIMUM SECURITY, THING.
YOU'RE CLEAR FOR LANDING AT THE MAIN GATE.
THE WARDEN AND AN ARMED DETAIL WILL MEET YOU THERE.
WELCOME BACK, MR. GRIMM.
YEAH. GLAD TO BE ON THIS SIDE A' THEM BARS. AND CLEARED OF ALL CHARGES.
WELL, WE COULD HARDLY KEEP YOU LOCKED UP...
...WHEN THE PERSON YOU WERE ACCUSED OF MURDERING IS NOW INCARCERATED HERE. HE'S THIS WAY.
I'LL KILL YOU, THING!
IF I GET OUTTA HERE, YOU'RE DEAD!
SMASH YOU INTO LITTLE PEBBLES, ROCK-MAN!
PSST. HEY, PULVERIZER, HOW'D YOU DO ON YOUR G.E.D.?
GREAT, BEN. THANKS FOR HELPING ME WITH MY ALGEBRA.
I'M GOIN' FOR MY COLLEGE DEGREE NEXT.
GOOD ON YOU. I'LL SAY "HI" TO YER MA.
YEAH! YOU HEARD ME! YOU'RE A DEAD MAN, GRIMM!

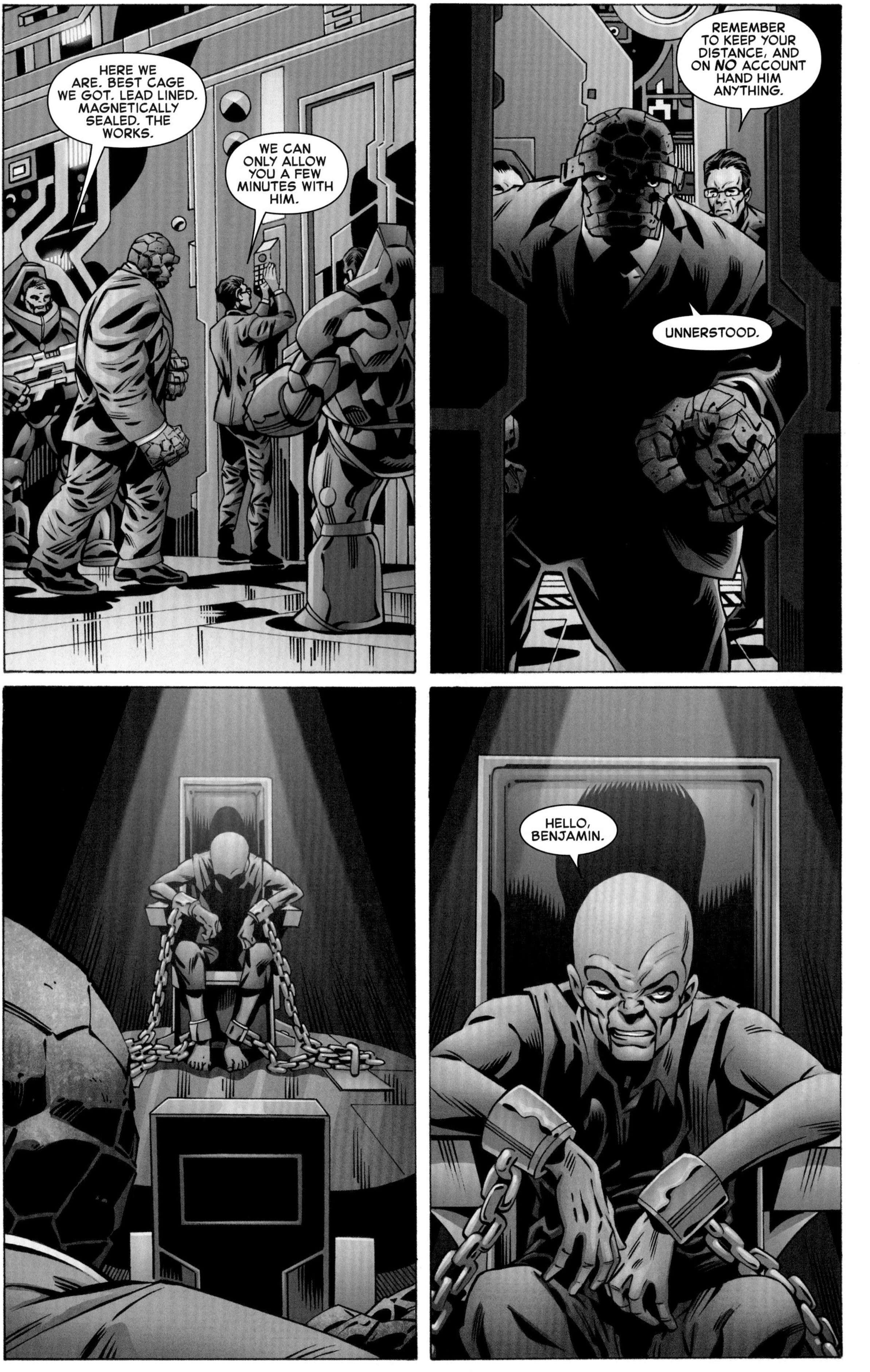
HERE WE ARE. BEST CAGE WE GOT. LEAD LINED. MAGNETICALLY SEALED. THE WORKS.
WE CAN ONLY ALLOW YOU A FEW MINUTES WITH HIM.
REMEMBER TO KEEP YOUR DISTANCE, AND ON NO ACCOUNT HAND HIM ANYTHING.
UNNERSTOOD.
HELLO, BENJAMIN.

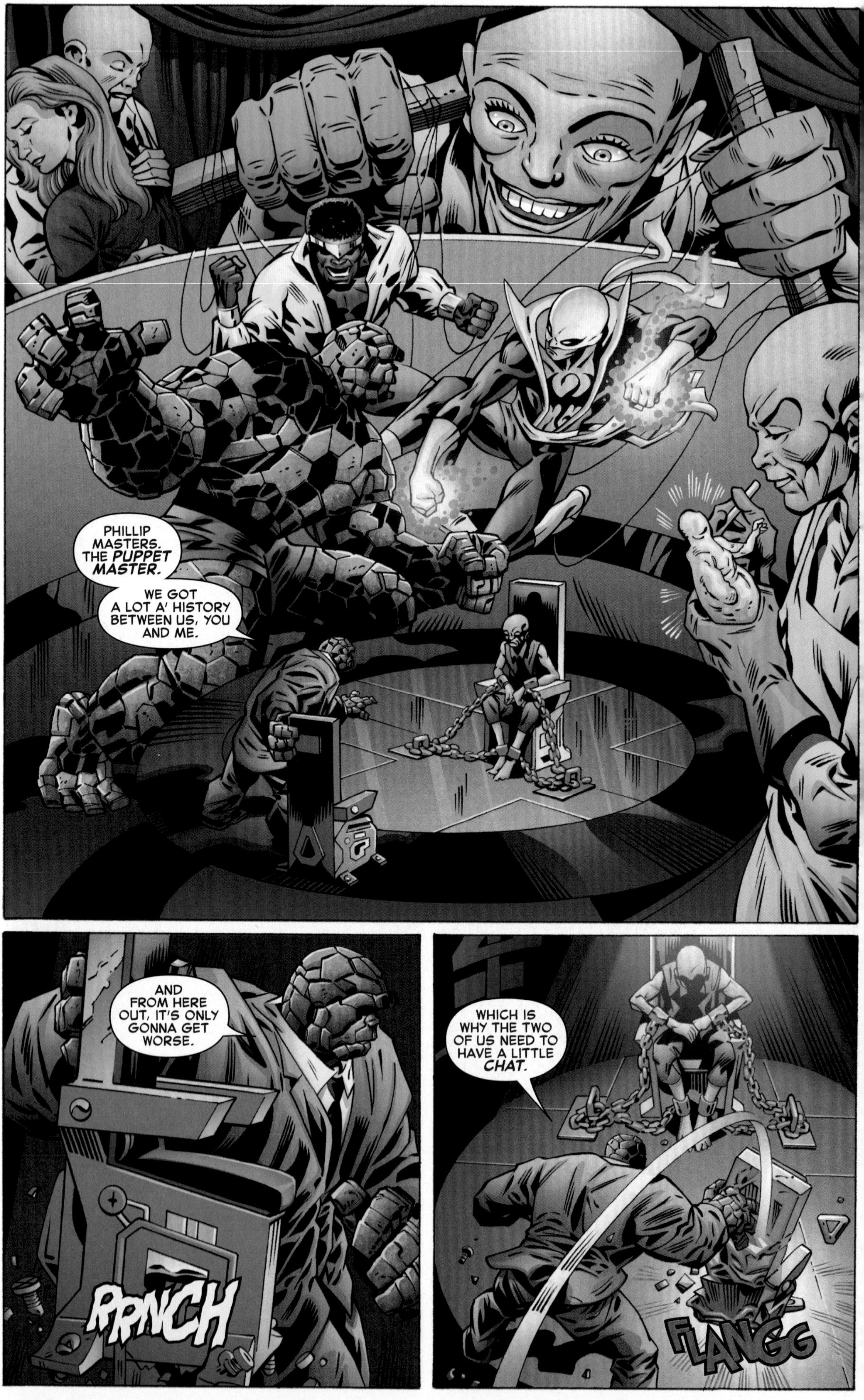
PHILLIP MASTERS. THE *PUPPET MASTER.*
WE GOT A LOT A' HISTORY BETWEEN US, YOU AND ME.
AND FROM HERE OUT, IT'S ONLY GONNA GET WORSE.
RRNCH
WHICH IS WHY THE TWO OF US NEED TO HAVE A LITTLE *CHAT*.
FLANGG

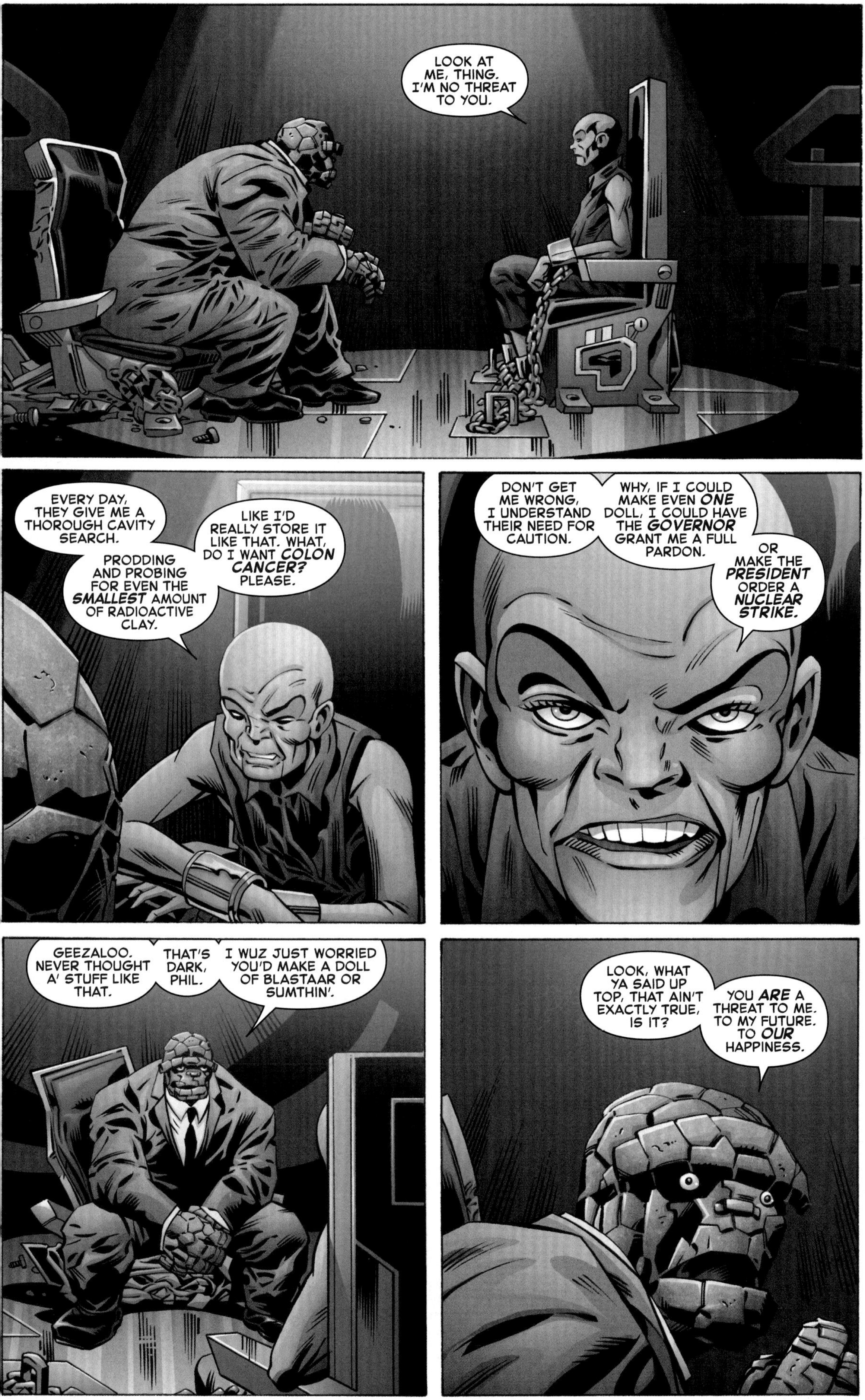
LOOK AT ME, THING. I'M NO THREAT TO YOU.
EVERY DAY, THEY GIVE ME A THOROUGH CAVITY SEARCH.
PRODDING AND PROBING FOR EVEN THE SMALLEST AMOUNT OF RADIOACTIVE CLAY.
LIKE I'D REALLY STORE IT LIKE THAT. WHAT, DO I WANT COLON CANCER? PLEASE.
DON'T GET ME WRONG, I UNDERSTAND THEIR NEED FOR CAUTION.
WHY, IF I COULD MAKE EVEN ONE DOLL, I COULD HAVE THE GOVERNOR GRANT ME A FULL PARDON.
OR MAKE THE PRESIDENT ORDER A NUCLEAR STRIKE.
GEEZALOO. NEVER THOUGHT A' STUFF LIKE THAT.
THAT'S DARK, PHIL.
I WUZ JUST WORRIED YOU'D MAKE A DOLL OF BLASTAAR OR SUMTHIN'.
LOOK, WHAT YA SAID UP TOP, THAT AIN'T EXACTLY TRUE, IS IT?
YOU ARE A THREAT TO ME. TO MY FUTURE. TO OUR HAPPINESS.

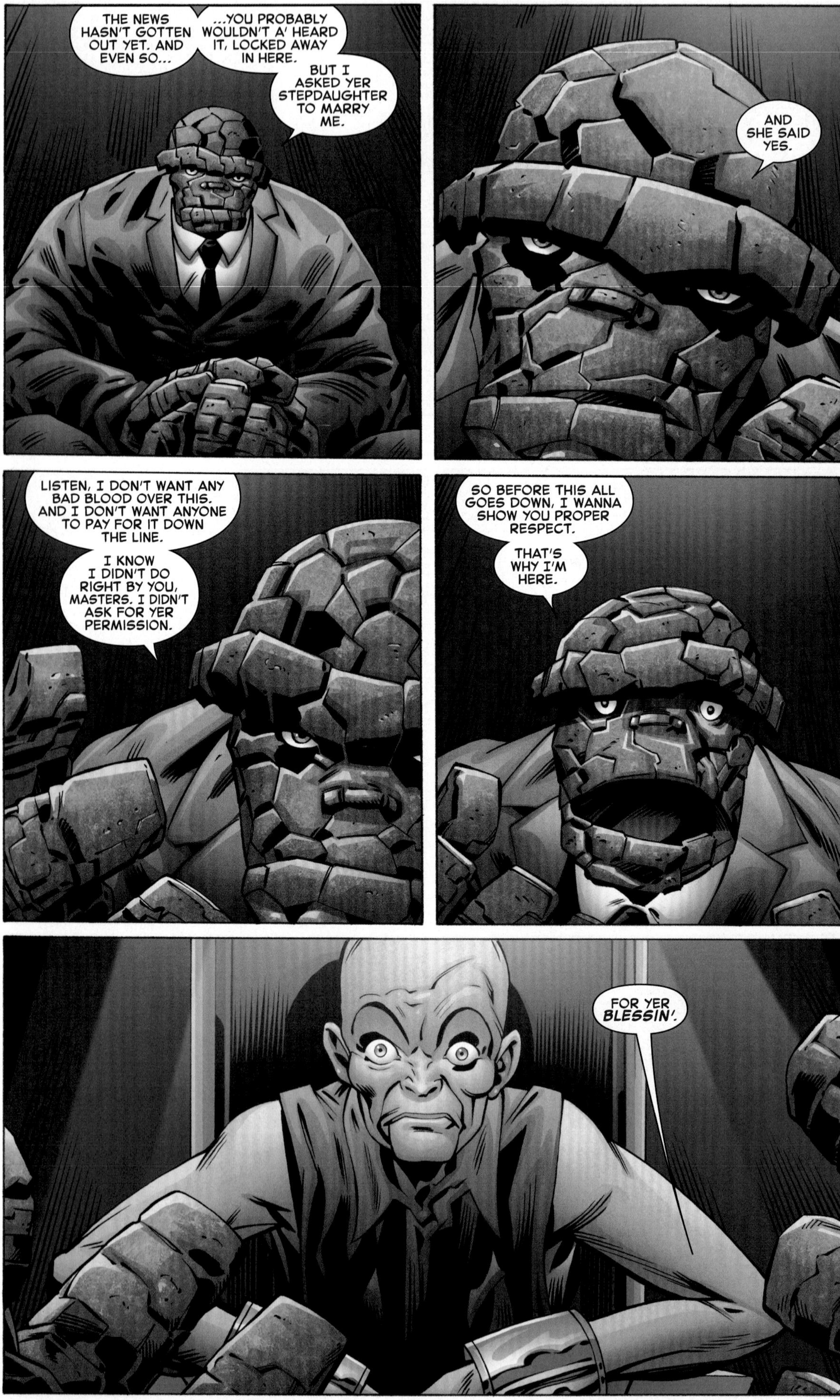
THE NEWS HASN'T GOTTEN OUT YET. AND EVEN SO...
...YOU PROBABLY WOULDN'T A' HEARD IT, LOCKED AWAY IN HERE.
BUT I ASKED YER STEPDAUGHTER TO MARRY ME.
AND SHE SAID YES.
LISTEN, I DON'T WANT ANY BAD BLOOD OVER THIS. AND I DON'T WANT ANYONE TO PAY FOR IT DOWN THE LINE.
I KNOW I DIDN'T DO RIGHT BY YOU, MASTERS. I DIDN'T ASK FOR YER PERMISSION.
SO BEFORE THIS ALL GOES DOWN, I WANNA SHOW YOU PROPER RESPECT.
THAT'S WHY I'M HERE.
FOR YER BLESSIN'.

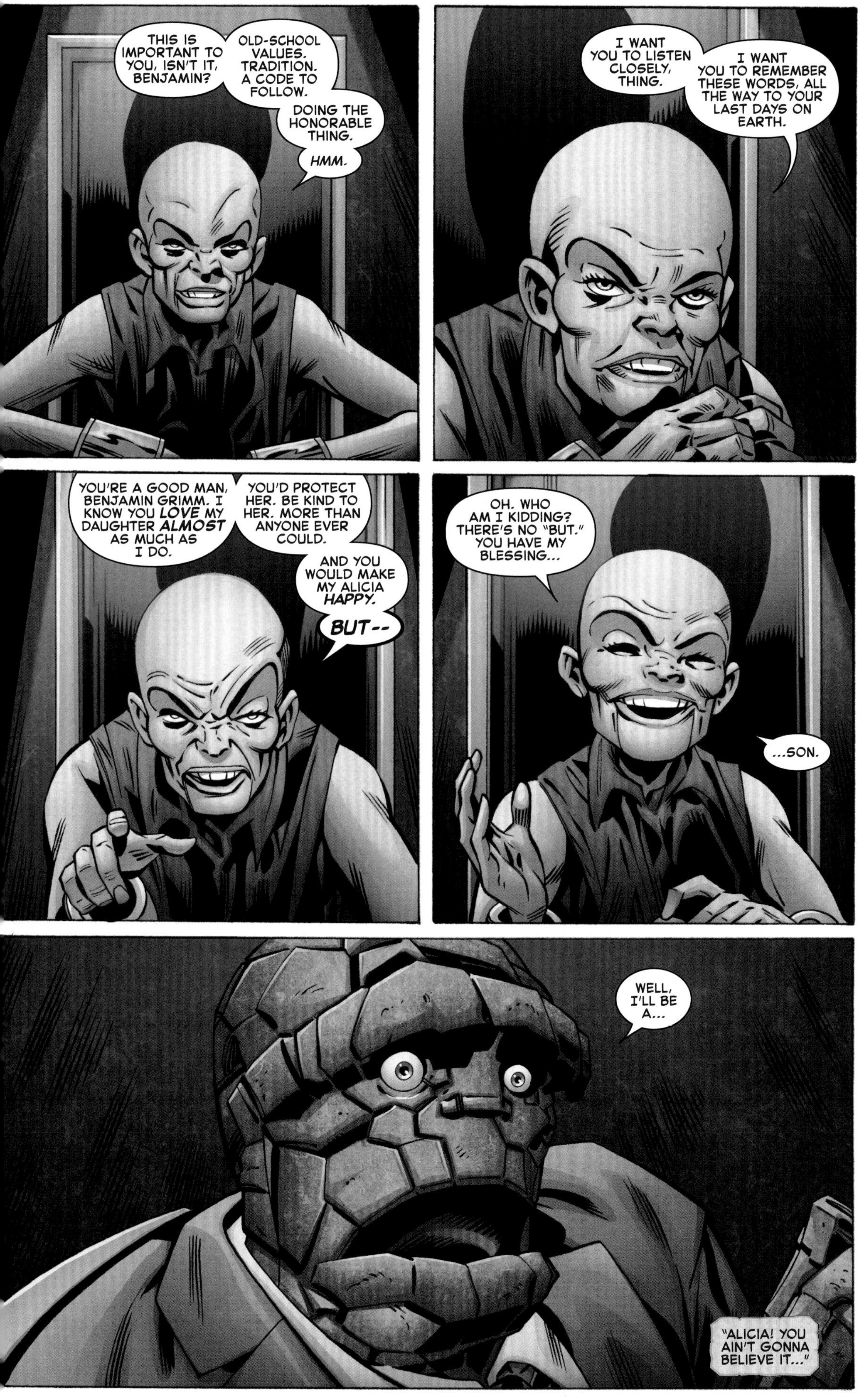
THIS IS IMPORTANT TO YOU, ISN'T IT, BENJAMIN?
OLD-SCHOOL VALUES. TRADITION. A CODE TO FOLLOW.
DOING THE HONORABLE THING.
HMM.
I WANT YOU TO LISTEN CLOSELY, THING.
I WANT YOU TO REMEMBER THESE WORDS, ALL THE WAY TO YOUR LAST DAYS ON EARTH.
YOU'RE A GOOD MAN, BENJAMIN GRIMM. I KNOW YOU LOVE MY DAUGHTER ALMOST AS MUCH AS I DO.
YOU'D PROTECT HER. BE KIND TO HER. MORE THAN ANYONE EVER COULD.
AND YOU WOULD MAKE MY ALICIA HAPPY.
BUT--
OH. WHO AM I KIDDING? THERE'S NO "BUT." YOU HAVE MY BLESSING...
...SON.
WELL, I'LL BE A...
"ALICIA! YOU AIN'T GONNA BELIEVE IT..."

...HE SAID YES!

WHAT?

WHO'DA THUNK IT?! THIS WEDDING SHINDIG OF OURS IS A GO--MORE THAN EVER!

I TOLD YOU. ALL THIS TIME YOU WERE WORRIED OVER NOTHING.

HOT DIGGITY! WE GOTTA CALL THE RABBI! AND UNCLE JAKE AN' AUNT PETUNIA! WOTTA DAY!

YOU COMIN', BUTTERCUP?!

OF COURSE.

BE WITH YOU IN A MINUTE, DEAR.

JUST HAVE TO FINISH TIDYING UP.

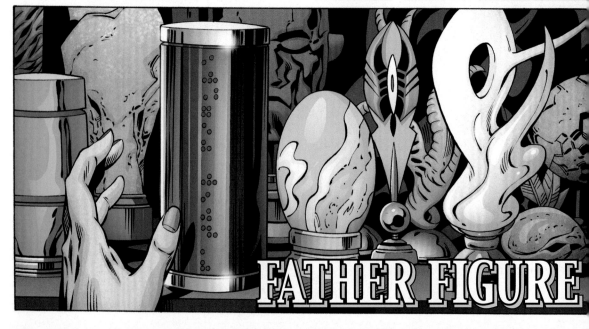

FATHER FIGURE

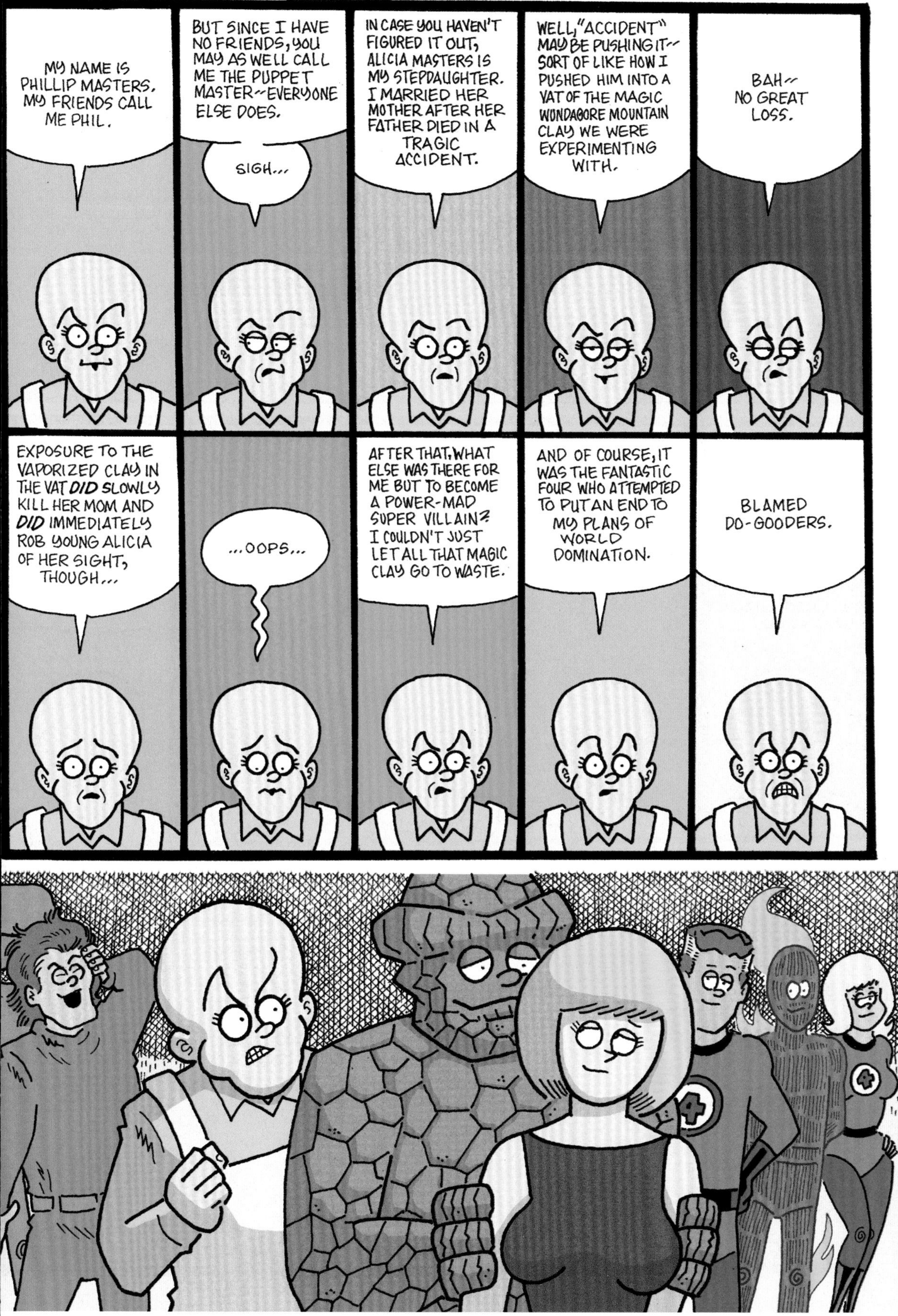
MY NAME IS PHILLIP MASTERS. MY FRIENDS CALL ME PHIL.
BUT SINCE I HAVE NO FRIENDS, YOU MAY AS WELL CALL ME THE PUPPET MASTER--EVERYONE ELSE DOES.
SIGH...
IN CASE YOU HAVEN'T FIGURED IT OUT, ALICIA MASTERS IS MY STEPDAUGHTER. I MARRIED HER MOTHER AFTER HER FATHER DIED IN A TRAGIC ACCIDENT.
WELL, "ACCIDENT" MAY BE PUSHING IT-- SORT OF LIKE HOW I PUSHED HIM INTO A VAT OF THE MAGIC WUNDAGORE MOUNTAIN CLAY WE WERE EXPERIMENTING WITH.
BAH-- NO GREAT LOSS.
EXPOSURE TO THE VAPORIZED CLAY IN THE VAT *DID* SLOWLY KILL HER MOM AND *DID* IMMEDIATELY ROB YOUNG ALICIA OF HER SIGHT, THOUGH...
...OOPS...
AFTER THAT, WHAT ELSE WAS THERE FOR ME BUT TO BECOME A POWER-MAD SUPER VILLAIN? I COULDN'T JUST LET ALL THAT MAGIC CLAY GO TO WASTE.
AND OF COURSE, IT WAS THE FANTASTIC FOUR WHO ATTEMPTED TO PUT AN END TO MY PLANS OF WORLD DOMINATION.
BLAMED DO-GOODERS.

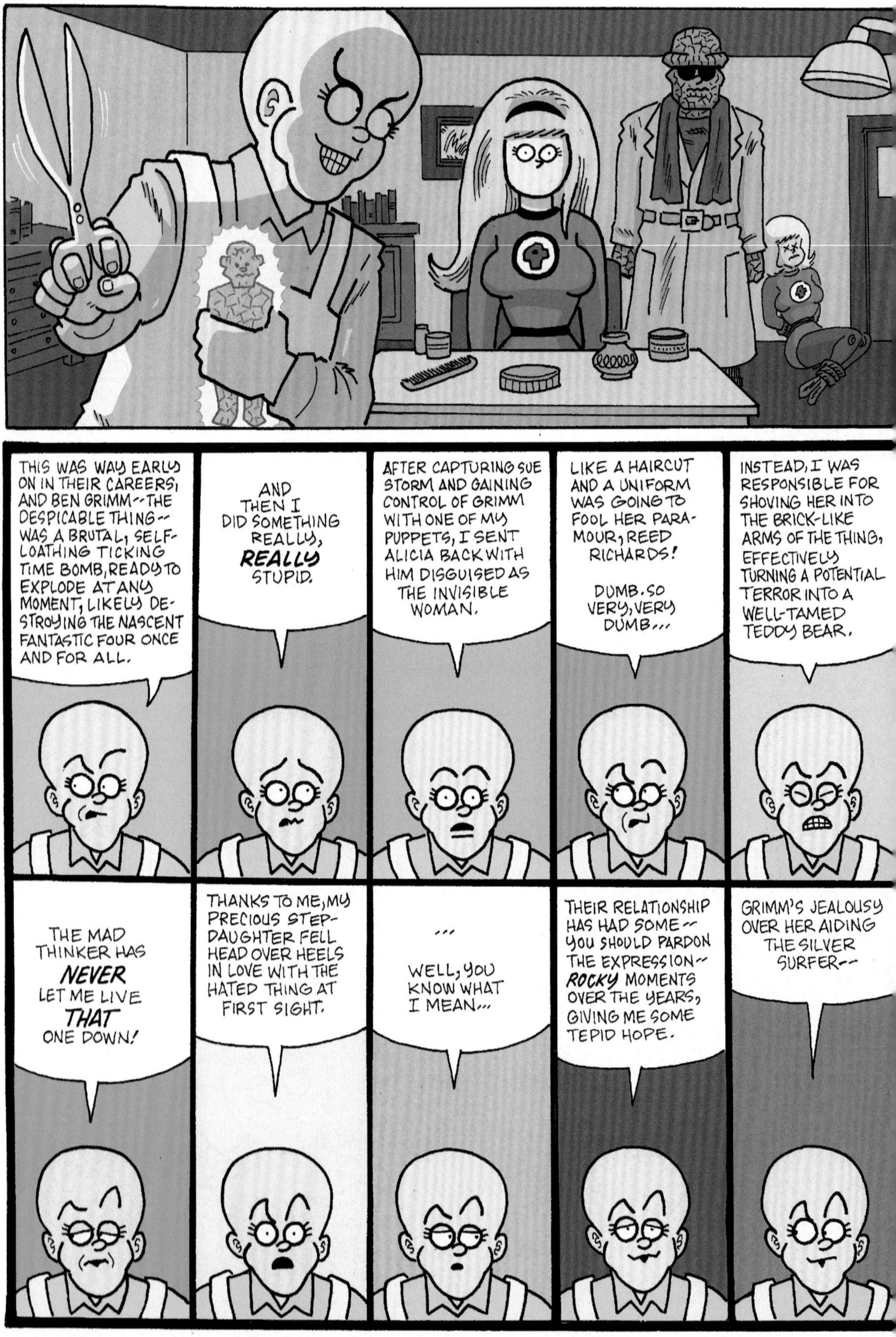
THIS WAS WAY EARLY ON IN THEIR CAREERS, AND BEN GRIMM--THE DESPICABLE THING--WAS A BRUTAL, SELF-LOATHING TICKING TIME BOMB, READY TO EXPLODE AT ANY MOMENT, LIKELY DESTROYING THE NASCENT FANTASTIC FOUR ONCE AND FOR ALL.
AND THEN I DID SOMETHING REALLY, REALLY STUPID.
AFTER CAPTURING SUE STORM AND GAINING CONTROL OF GRIMM WITH ONE OF MY PUPPETS, I SENT ALICIA BACK WITH HIM DISGUISED AS THE INVISIBLE WOMAN.
LIKE A HAIRCUT AND A UNIFORM WAS GOING TO FOOL HER PARAMOUR, REED RICHARDS!
DUMB. SO VERY, VERY DUMB...
INSTEAD, I WAS RESPONSIBLE FOR SHOVING HER INTO THE BRICK-LIKE ARMS OF THE THING, EFFECTIVELY TURNING A POTENTIAL TERROR INTO A WELL-TAMED TEDDY BEAR.
THE MAD THINKER HAS NEVER LET ME LIVE THAT ONE DOWN!
THANKS TO ME, MY PRECIOUS STEP-DAUGHTER FELL HEAD OVER HEELS IN LOVE WITH THE HATED THING AT FIRST SIGHT.
...
WELL, YOU KNOW WHAT I MEAN...
THEIR RELATIONSHIP HAS HAD SOME--YOU SHOULD PARDON THE EXPRESSION--ROCKY MOMENTS OVER THE YEARS, GIVING ME SOME TEPID HOPE.
GRIMM'S JEALOUSY OVER HER AIDING THE SILVER SURFER--

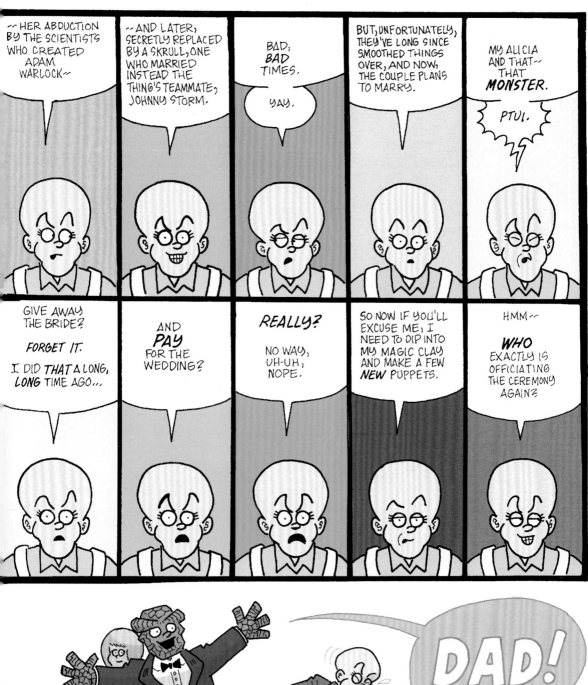

-- HER ABDUCTION BY THE SCIENTISTS WHO CREATED ADAM WARLOCK--

--AND LATER, SECRETLY REPLACED BY A SKRULL, ONE WHO MARRIED INSTEAD THE THING'S TEAMMATE, JOHNNY STORM.

BAD, *BAD* TIMES.

YAY.

BUT, UNFORTUNATELY, THEY'VE LONG SINCE SMOOTHED THINGS OVER, AND NOW, THE COUPLE PLANS TO MARRY.

MY ALICIA AND THAT-- THAT *MONSTER.*

PTUI.

GIVE AWAY THE BRIDE?

FORGET IT.

I DID *THAT* A LONG, *LONG* TIME AGO...

AND *PAY* FOR THE WEDDING?

REALLY?

NO WAY, UH-UH, NOPE.

SO NOW IF YOU'LL EXCUSE ME, I NEED TO DIP INTO MY MAGIC CLAY AND MAKE A FEW *NEW* PUPPETS.

HMM--

WHO EXACTLY IS OFFICIATING THE CEREMONY AGAIN?

DAD!

THE *PUPPET MASTER'S* LAMENT!

by FRED HEMBECK

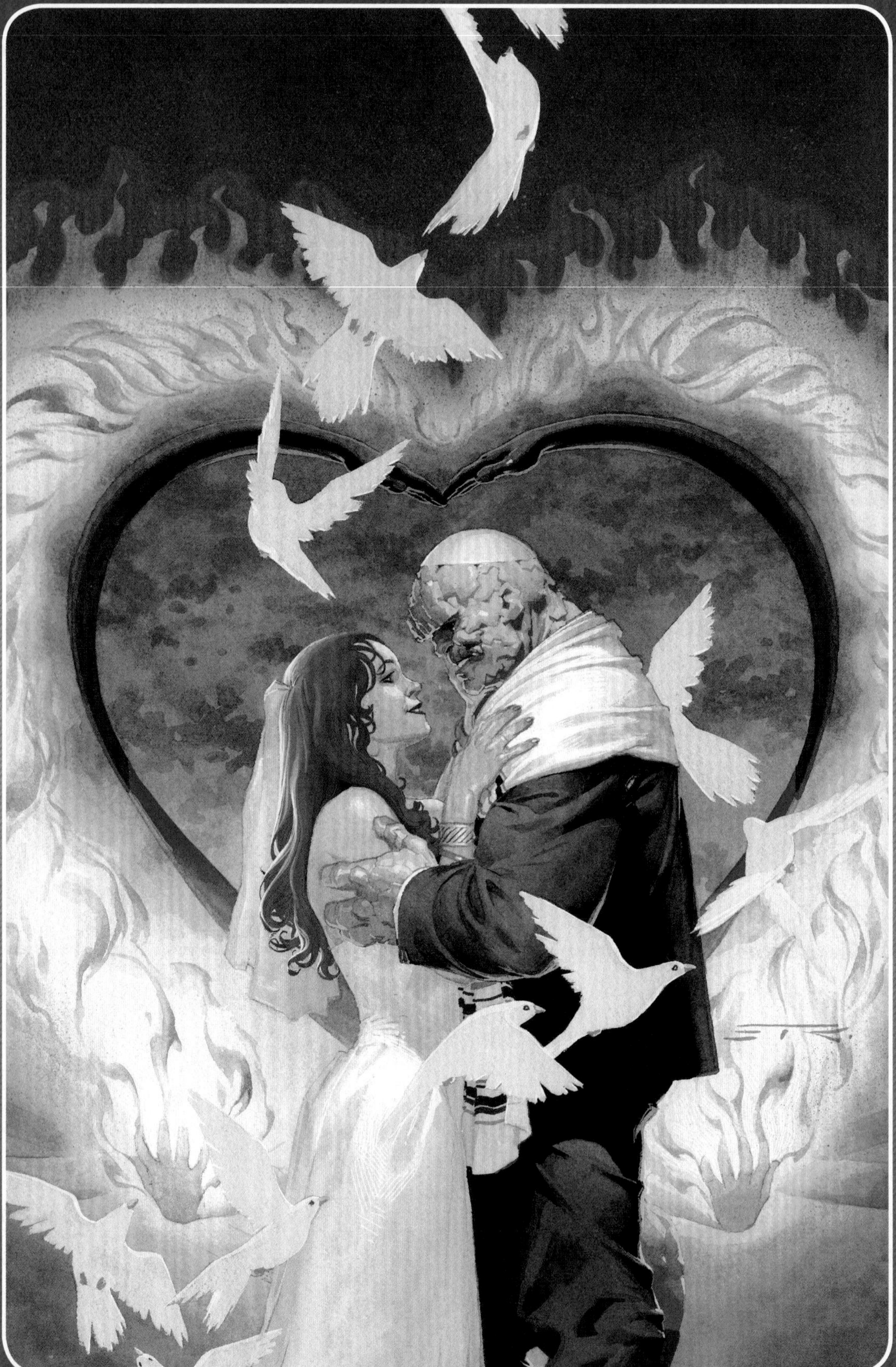

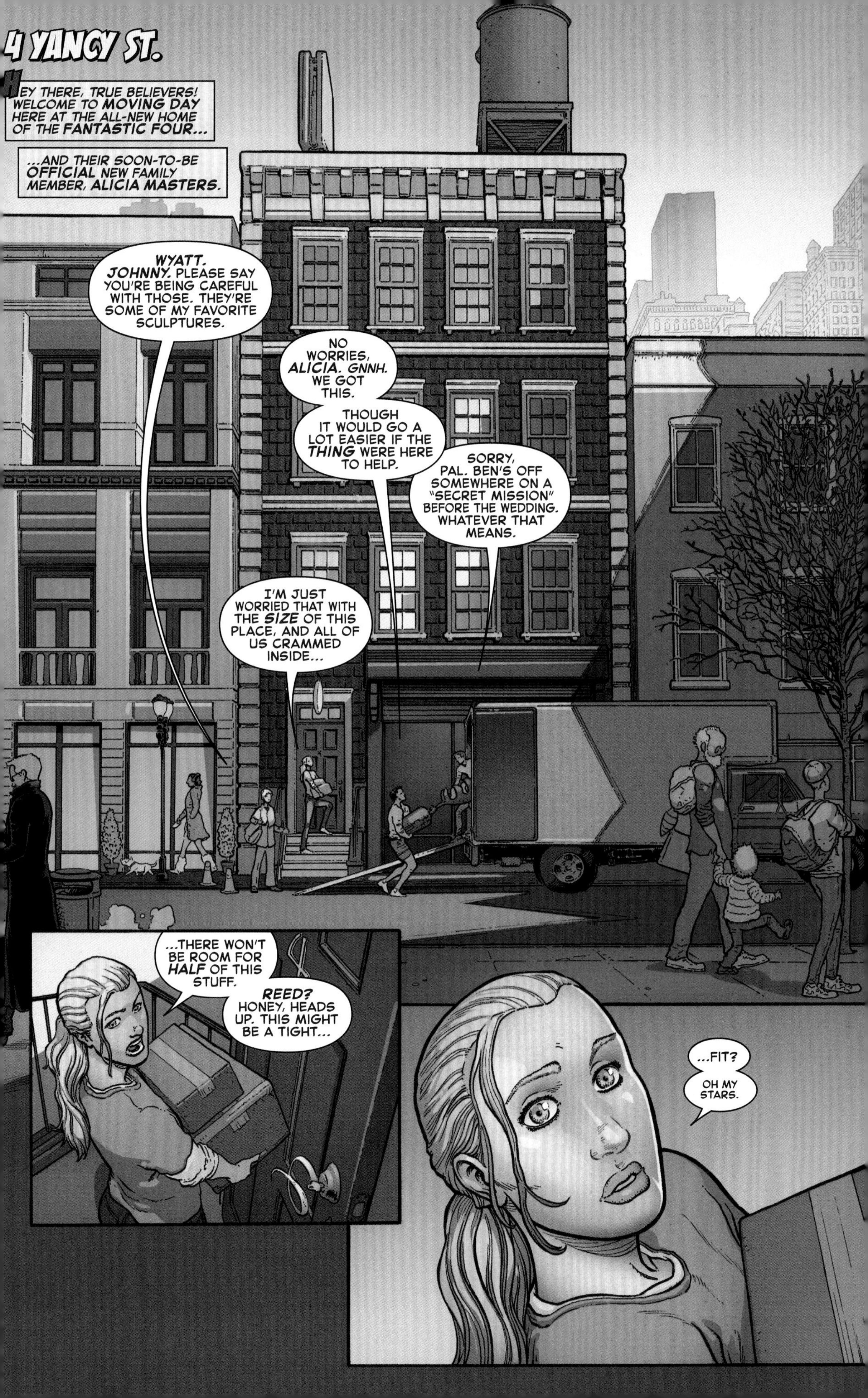
4 YANCY ST.
HEY THERE, TRUE BELIEVERS! WELCOME TO MOVING DAY HERE AT THE ALL-NEW HOME OF THE FANTASTIC FOUR...
...AND THEIR SOON-TO-BE OFFICIAL NEW FAMILY MEMBER, ALICIA MASTERS.
WYATT. JOHNNY. PLEASE SAY YOU'RE BEING CAREFUL WITH THOSE. THEY'RE SOME OF MY FAVORITE SCULPTURES.
NO WORRIES, ALICIA. GNNH. WE GOT THIS.
THOUGH IT WOULD GO A LOT EASIER IF THE THING WERE HERE TO HELP.
SORRY, PAL. BEN'S OFF SOMEWHERE ON A "SECRET MISSION" BEFORE THE WEDDING. WHATEVER THAT MEANS.
I'M JUST WORRIED THAT WITH THE SIZE OF THIS PLACE, AND ALL OF US CRAMMED INSIDE...
...THERE WON'T BE ROOM FOR HALF OF THIS STUFF.
REED? HONEY, HEADS UP. THIS MIGHT BE A TIGHT...
...FIT?
OH MY STARS.

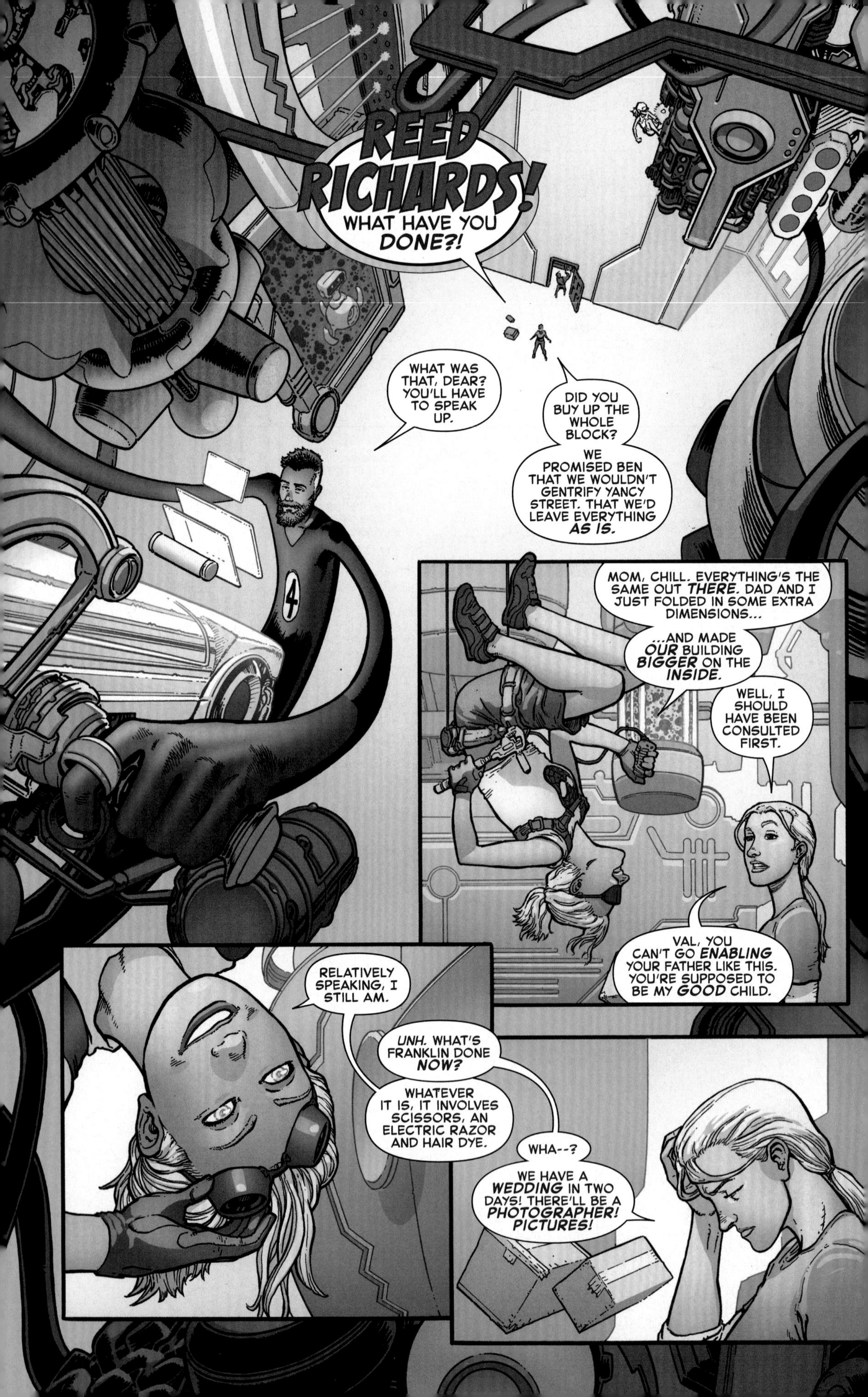
REED RICHARDS! WHAT HAVE YOU DONE?!
WHAT WAS THAT, DEAR? YOU'LL HAVE TO SPEAK UP.
DID YOU BUY UP THE WHOLE BLOCK?
WE PROMISED BEN THAT WE WOULDN'T GENTRIFY YANCY STREET. THAT WE'D LEAVE EVERYTHING AS IS.
MOM, CHILL. EVERYTHING'S THE SAME OUT THERE. DAD AND I JUST FOLDED IN SOME EXTRA DIMENSIONS...
...AND MADE OUR BUILDING BIGGER ON THE INSIDE.
WELL, I SHOULD HAVE BEEN CONSULTED FIRST.
VAL, YOU CAN'T GO ENABLING YOUR FATHER LIKE THIS. YOU'RE SUPPOSED TO BE MY GOOD CHILD.
RELATIVELY SPEAKING, I STILL AM.
UNH. WHAT'S FRANKLIN DONE NOW?
WHATEVER IT IS, IT INVOLVES SCISSORS, AN ELECTRIC RAZOR AND HAIR DYE.
WHA--?
WE HAVE A WEDDING IN TWO DAYS! THERE'LL BE A PHOTOGRAPHER! PICTURES!

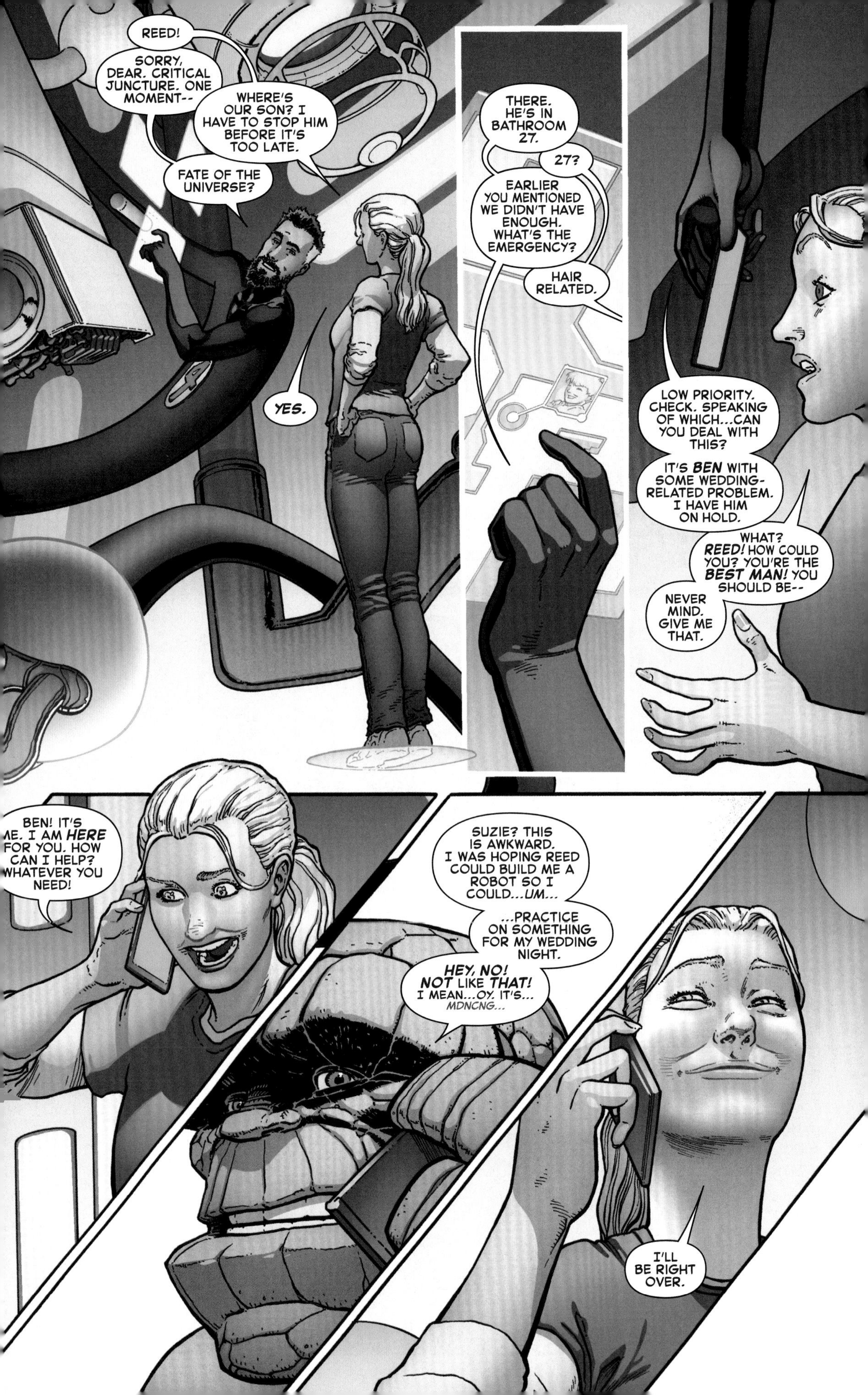
REED!
SORRY, DEAR. CRITICAL JUNCTURE. ONE MOMENT--
WHERE'S OUR SON? I HAVE TO STOP HIM BEFORE IT'S TOO LATE.
FATE OF THE UNIVERSE?
YES.
THERE. HE'S IN BATHROOM 27.
27?
EARLIER YOU MENTIONED WE DIDN'T HAVE ENOUGH. WHAT'S THE EMERGENCY?
HAIR RELATED.
LOW PRIORITY. CHECK. SPEAKING OF WHICH...CAN YOU DEAL WITH THIS?
IT'S BEN WITH SOME WEDDING-RELATED PROBLEM. I HAVE HIM ON HOLD.
WHAT? REED! HOW COULD YOU? YOU'RE THE BEST MAN! YOU SHOULD BE--
NEVER MIND. GIVE ME THAT.
BEN! IT'S ME. I AM HERE FOR YOU. HOW CAN I HELP? WHATEVER YOU NEED!
SUZIE? THIS IS AWKWARD. I WAS HOPING REED COULD BUILD ME A ROBOT SO I COULD...UM...
...PRACTICE ON SOMETHING FOR MY WEDDING NIGHT.
HEY, NO! NOT LIKE THAT! I MEAN...OY, IT'S... MDNCNG...
I'LL BE RIGHT OVER.

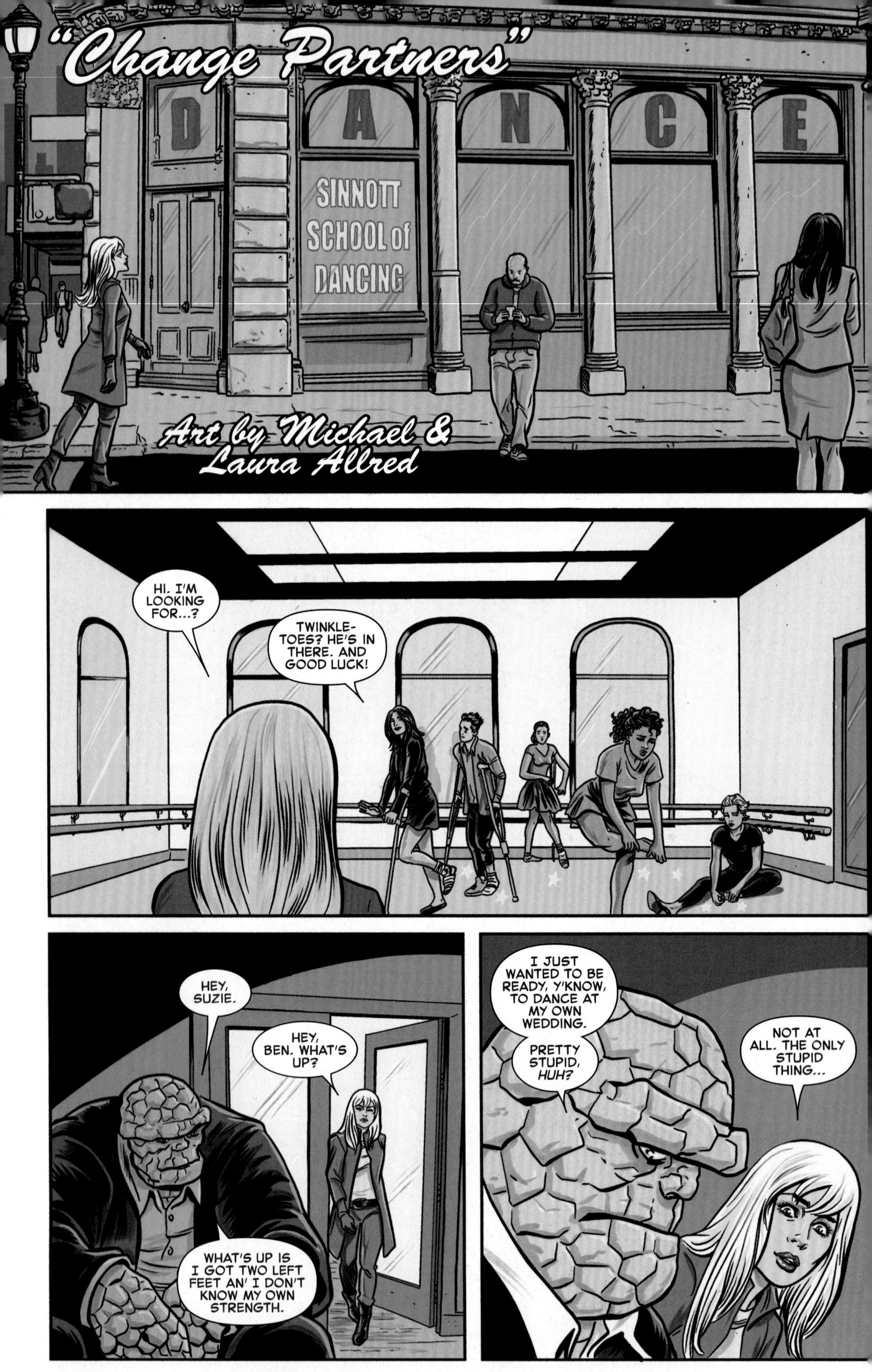
"Change Partners"
DANCE
SINNOTT SCHOOL of DANCING
Art by Michael & Laura Allred
HI. I'M LOOKING FOR...?
TWINKLE-TOES? HE'S IN THERE. AND GOOD LUCK!
HEY, SUZIE.
HEY, BEN. WHAT'S UP?
WHAT'S UP IS I GOT TWO LEFT FEET AN' I DON'T KNOW MY OWN STRENGTH.
I JUST WANTED TO BE READY, Y'KNOW, TO DANCE AT MY OWN WEDDING.
PRETTY STUPID, HUH?
NOT AT ALL. THE ONLY STUPID THING...

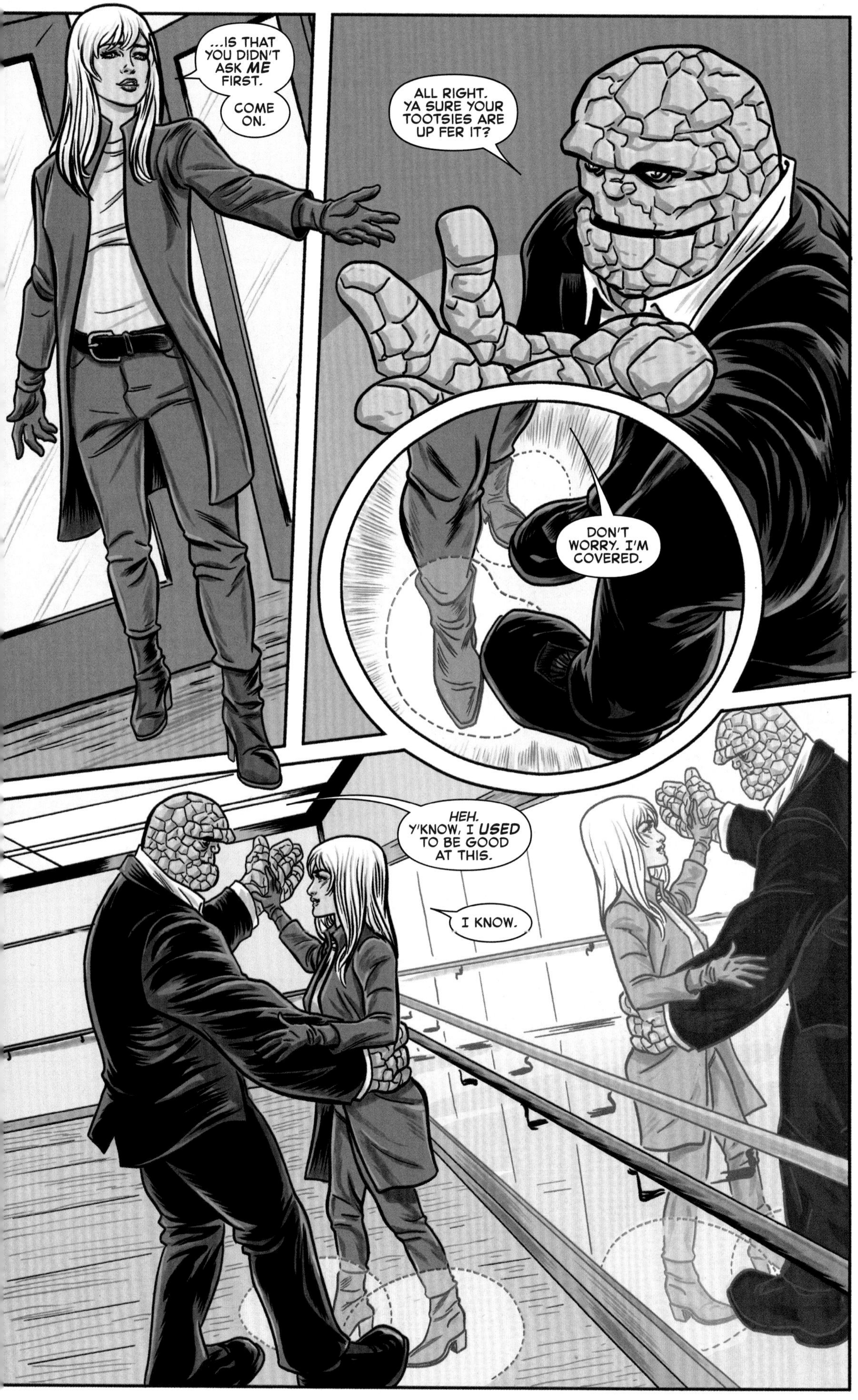
...IS THAT YOU DIDN'T ASK *ME* FIRST.
COME ON.
ALL RIGHT. YA SURE YOUR TOOTSIES ARE UP FER IT?
DON'T WORRY. I'M COVERED.
HEH. Y'KNOW, I *USED* TO BE GOOD AT THIS.
I KNOW.

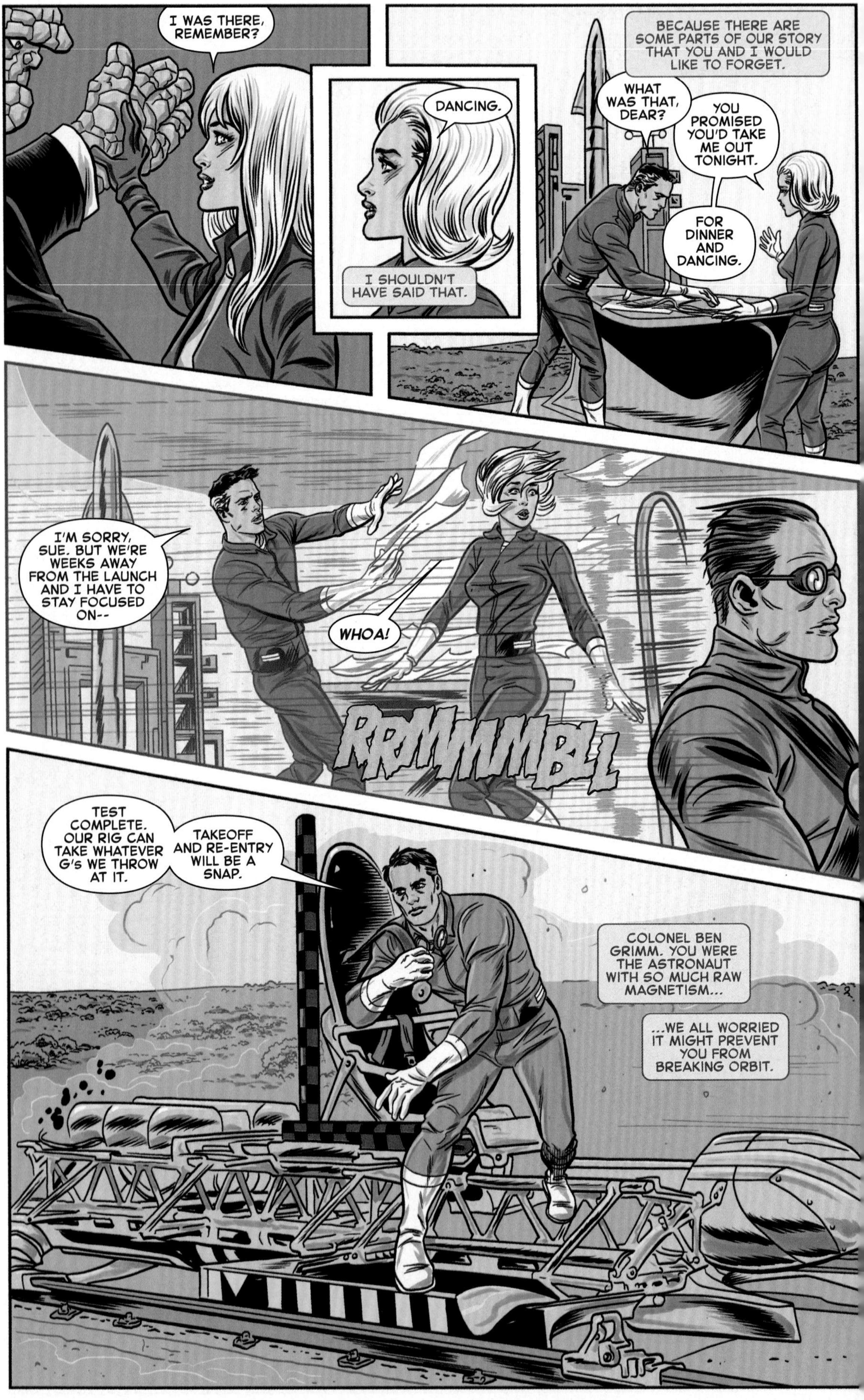
I WAS THERE, REMEMBER?
DANCING.
I SHOULDN'T HAVE SAID THAT.
BECAUSE THERE ARE SOME PARTS OF OUR STORY THAT YOU AND I WOULD LIKE TO FORGET.
WHAT WAS THAT, DEAR?
YOU PROMISED YOU'D TAKE ME OUT TONIGHT.
FOR DINNER AND DANCING.
I'M SORRY, SUE. BUT WE'RE WEEKS AWAY FROM THE LAUNCH AND I HAVE TO STAY FOCUSED ON--
WHOA!
RRMMMBLL
TEST COMPLETE. OUR RIG CAN TAKE WHATEVER G'S WE THROW AT IT.
TAKEOFF AND RE-ENTRY WILL BE A SNAP.
COLONEL BEN GRIMM. YOU WERE THE ASTRONAUT WITH SO MUCH RAW MAGNETISM...
...WE ALL WORRIED IT MIGHT PREVENT YOU FROM BREAKING ORBIT.

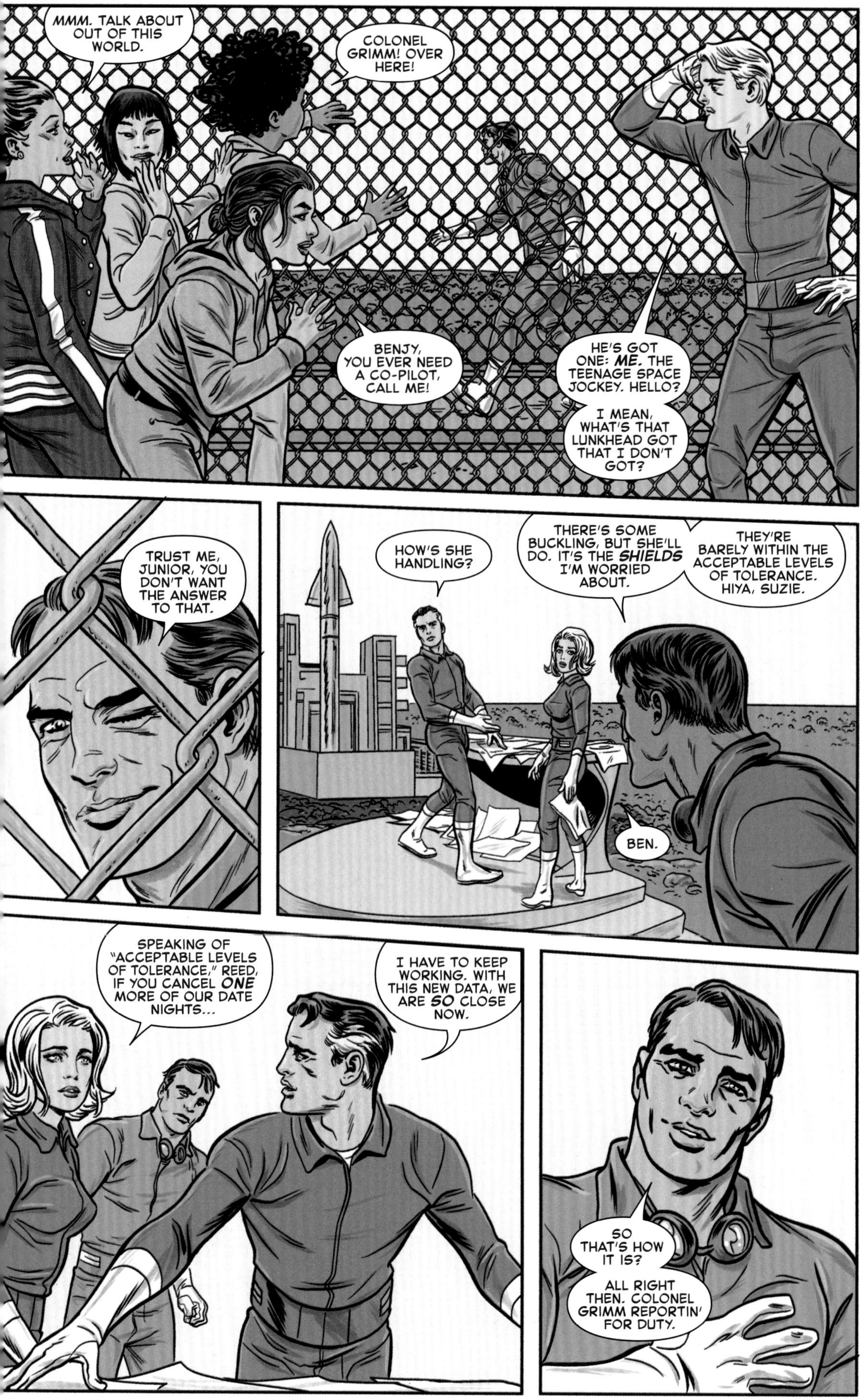
MMM. TALK ABOUT OUT OF THIS WORLD.
COLONEL GRIMM! OVER HERE!
BENJY, YOU EVER NEED A CO-PILOT, CALL ME!
HE'S GOT ONE: ME. THE TEENAGE SPACE JOCKEY. HELLO?
I MEAN, WHAT'S THAT LUNKHEAD GOT THAT I DON'T GOT?
TRUST ME, JUNIOR, YOU DON'T WANT THE ANSWER TO THAT.
HOW'S SHE HANDLING?
THERE'S SOME BUCKLING, BUT SHE'LL DO. IT'S THE SHIELDS I'M WORRIED ABOUT.
THEY'RE BARELY WITHIN THE ACCEPTABLE LEVELS OF TOLERANCE. HIYA, SUZIE.
BEN.
"SPEAKING OF "ACCEPTABLE LEVELS OF TOLERANCE," REED, IF YOU CANCEL ONE MORE OF OUR DATE NIGHTS...
I HAVE TO KEEP WORKING. WITH THIS NEW DATA, WE ARE SO CLOSE NOW.
SO THAT'S HOW IT IS?
ALL RIGHT THEN. COLONEL GRIMM REPORTIN' FOR DUTY.

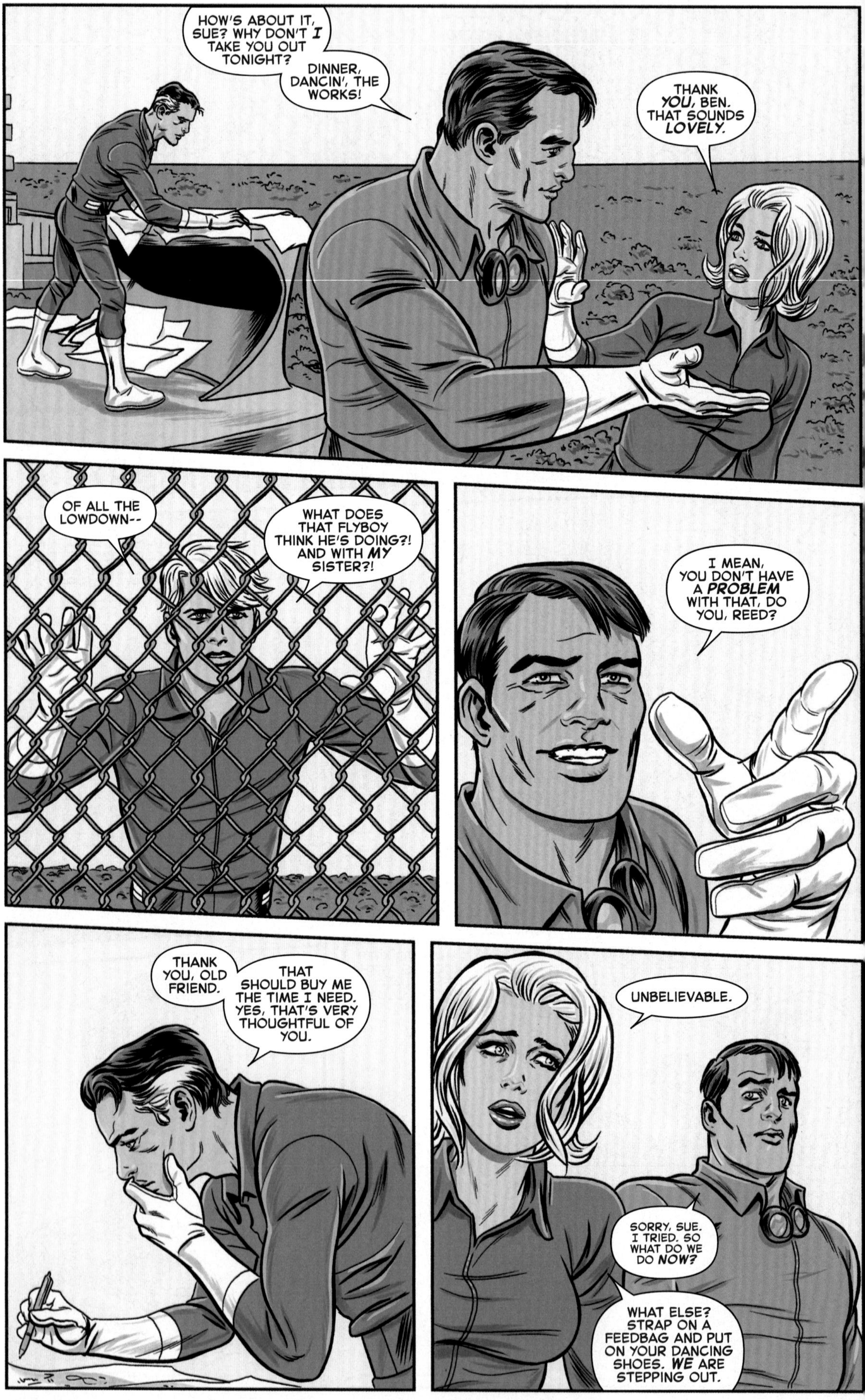
HOW'S ABOUT IT, SUE? WHY DON'T *I* TAKE YOU OUT TONIGHT?
DINNER, DANCIN', THE WORKS!
THANK *YOU*, BEN. THAT SOUNDS *LOVELY*.
OF ALL THE LOWDOWN--
WHAT DOES THAT FLYBOY THINK HE'S DOING?! AND WITH *MY* SISTER?!
I MEAN, YOU DON'T HAVE A *PROBLEM* WITH THAT, DO YOU, REED?
THANK YOU, OLD FRIEND.
THAT SHOULD BUY ME THE TIME I NEED. YES, THAT'S VERY THOUGHTFUL OF YOU.
UNBELIEVABLE.
SORRY, SUE. I TRIED. SO WHAT DO WE DO *NOW?*
WHAT ELSE? STRAP ON A FEEDBAG AND PUT ON YOUR DANCING SHOES. *WE* ARE STEPPING OUT.

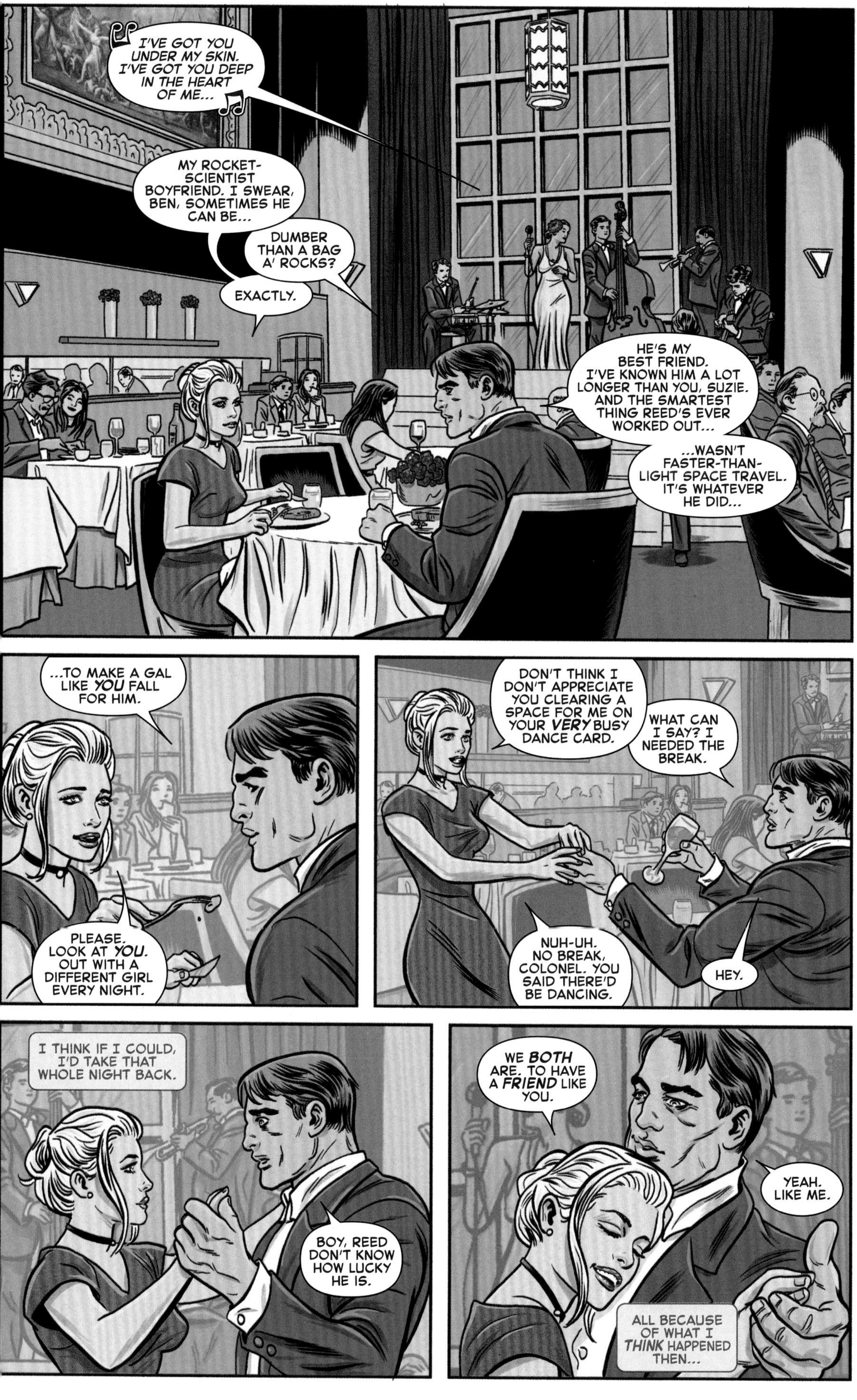
I'VE GOT YOU UNDER MY SKIN. I'VE GOT YOU DEEP IN THE HEART OF ME...
MY ROCKET-SCIENTIST BOYFRIEND. I SWEAR, BEN, SOMETIMES HE CAN BE...
DUMBER THAN A BAG A' ROCKS?
EXACTLY.
HE'S MY BEST FRIEND. I'VE KNOWN HIM A LOT LONGER THAN YOU, SUZIE. AND THE SMARTEST THING REED'S EVER WORKED OUT...
...WASN'T FASTER-THAN-LIGHT SPACE TRAVEL. IT'S WHATEVER HE DID...
...TO MAKE A GAL LIKE YOU FALL FOR HIM.
PLEASE. LOOK AT YOU. OUT WITH A DIFFERENT GIRL EVERY NIGHT.
DON'T THINK I DON'T APPRECIATE YOU CLEARING A SPACE FOR ME ON YOUR VERY BUSY DANCE CARD.
WHAT CAN I SAY? I NEEDED THE BREAK.
NUH-UH. NO BREAK, COLONEL. YOU SAID THERE'D BE DANCING.
HEY.
I THINK IF I COULD, I'D TAKE THAT WHOLE NIGHT BACK.
BOY, REED DON'T KNOW HOW LUCKY HE IS.
WE BOTH ARE. TO HAVE A FRIEND LIKE YOU.
YEAH. LIKE ME.
ALL BECAUSE OF WHAT I THINK HAPPENED THEN...

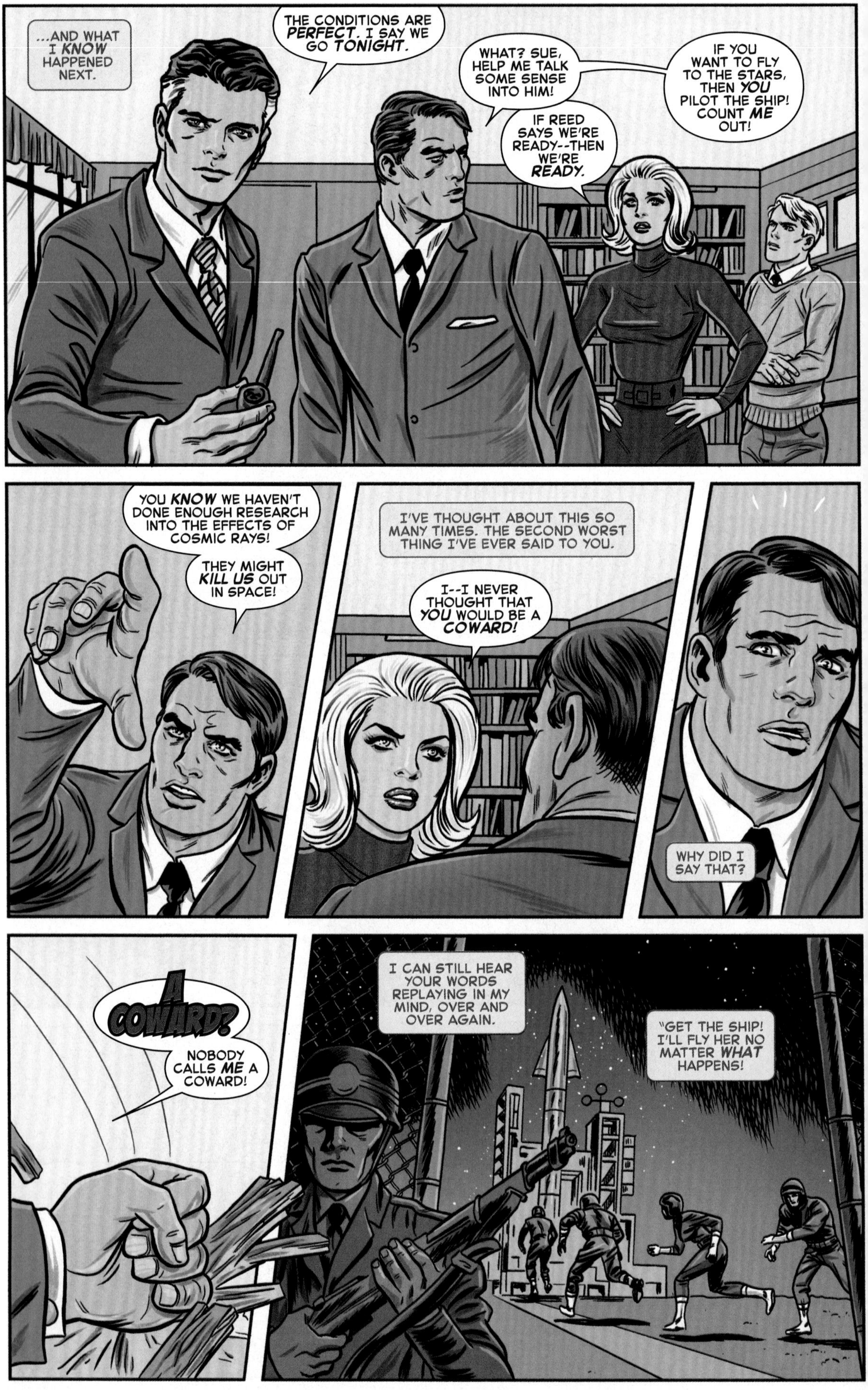
...AND WHAT I KNOW HAPPENED NEXT.
THE CONDITIONS ARE PERFECT. I SAY WE GO TONIGHT.
WHAT? SUE, HELP ME TALK SOME SENSE INTO HIM!
IF YOU WANT TO FLY TO THE STARS, THEN YOU PILOT THE SHIP! COUNT ME OUT!
IF REED SAYS WE'RE READY--THEN WE'RE READY.
YOU KNOW WE HAVEN'T DONE ENOUGH RESEARCH INTO THE EFFECTS OF COSMIC RAYS!
THEY MIGHT KILL US OUT IN SPACE!
I'VE THOUGHT ABOUT THIS SO MANY TIMES. THE SECOND WORST THING I'VE EVER SAID TO YOU.
I--I NEVER THOUGHT THAT YOU WOULD BE A COWARD!
WHY DID I SAY THAT?
A COWARD?
NOBODY CALLS ME A COWARD!
I CAN STILL HEAR YOUR WORDS REPLAYING IN MY MIND, OVER AND OVER AGAIN.
"GET THE SHIP! I'LL FLY HER NO MATTER WHAT HAPPENS!

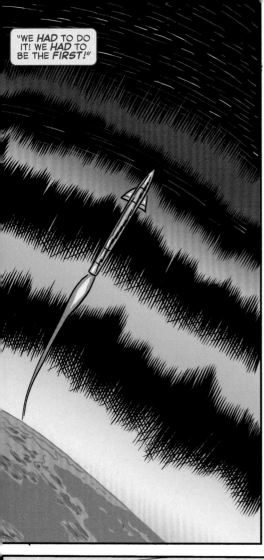

"WE *HAD* TO DO IT! WE *HAD* TO BE THE *FIRST!*"

RAK *TAC TAC TAC TAC*

HEAR *THAT?!* IT'S THE *COSMIC RAYS!* I--I *WARNED* YOU ABOUT 'EM!

THEY'RE PENETRATING THE SHIP! OUR SHIELDING *ISN'T STRONG ENOUGH!*

YOU WERE RIGHT. THE REST OF US WERE WRONG.

AND THAT'S WHAT MADE EVERYTHING THAT FOLLOWED SO UNFAIR...

...AND CRUEL.

OH, REED-- I FEEL SO STRANGE.

SUSAN! LOOK AT SUSAN!

WHAT'S WRONG?

YOU'RE *FADING AWAY!*

OH, NO! *NO!*

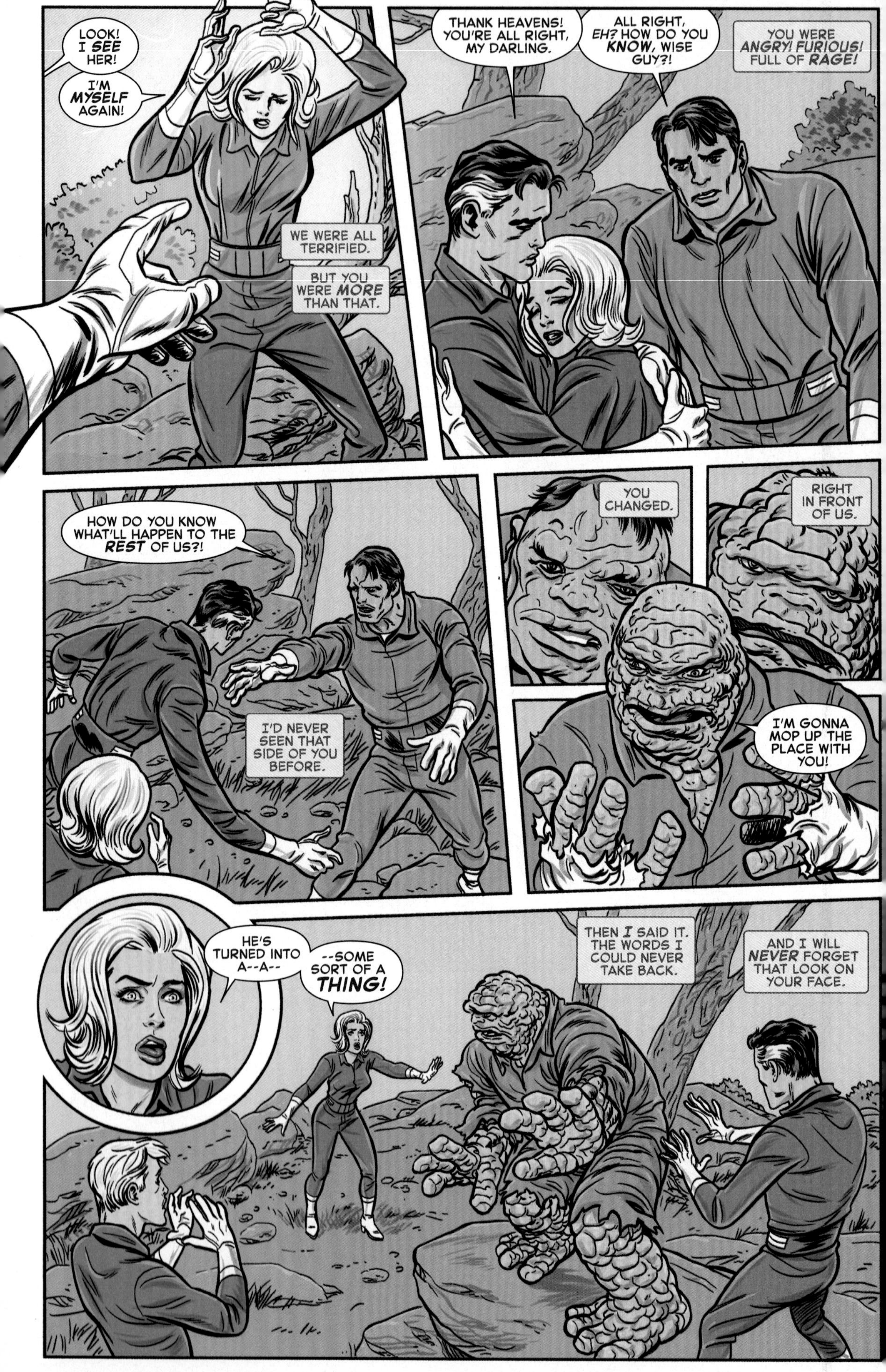

LOOK! I SEE HER!
I'M MYSELF AGAIN!
WE WERE ALL TERRIFIED.
BUT YOU WERE MORE THAN THAT.
THANK HEAVENS! YOU'RE ALL RIGHT, MY DARLING.
ALL RIGHT, EH? HOW DO YOU KNOW, WISE GUY?!
YOU WERE ANGRY! FURIOUS! FULL OF RAGE!
HOW DO YOU KNOW WHAT'LL HAPPEN TO THE REST OF US?!
I'D NEVER SEEN THAT SIDE OF YOU BEFORE.
YOU CHANGED.
RIGHT IN FRONT OF US.
I'M GONNA MOP UP THE PLACE WITH YOU!
HE'S TURNED INTO A--A--
--SOME SORT OF A THING!
THEN I SAID IT. THE WORDS I COULD NEVER TAKE BACK.
AND I WILL NEVER FORGET THAT LOOK ON YOUR FACE.

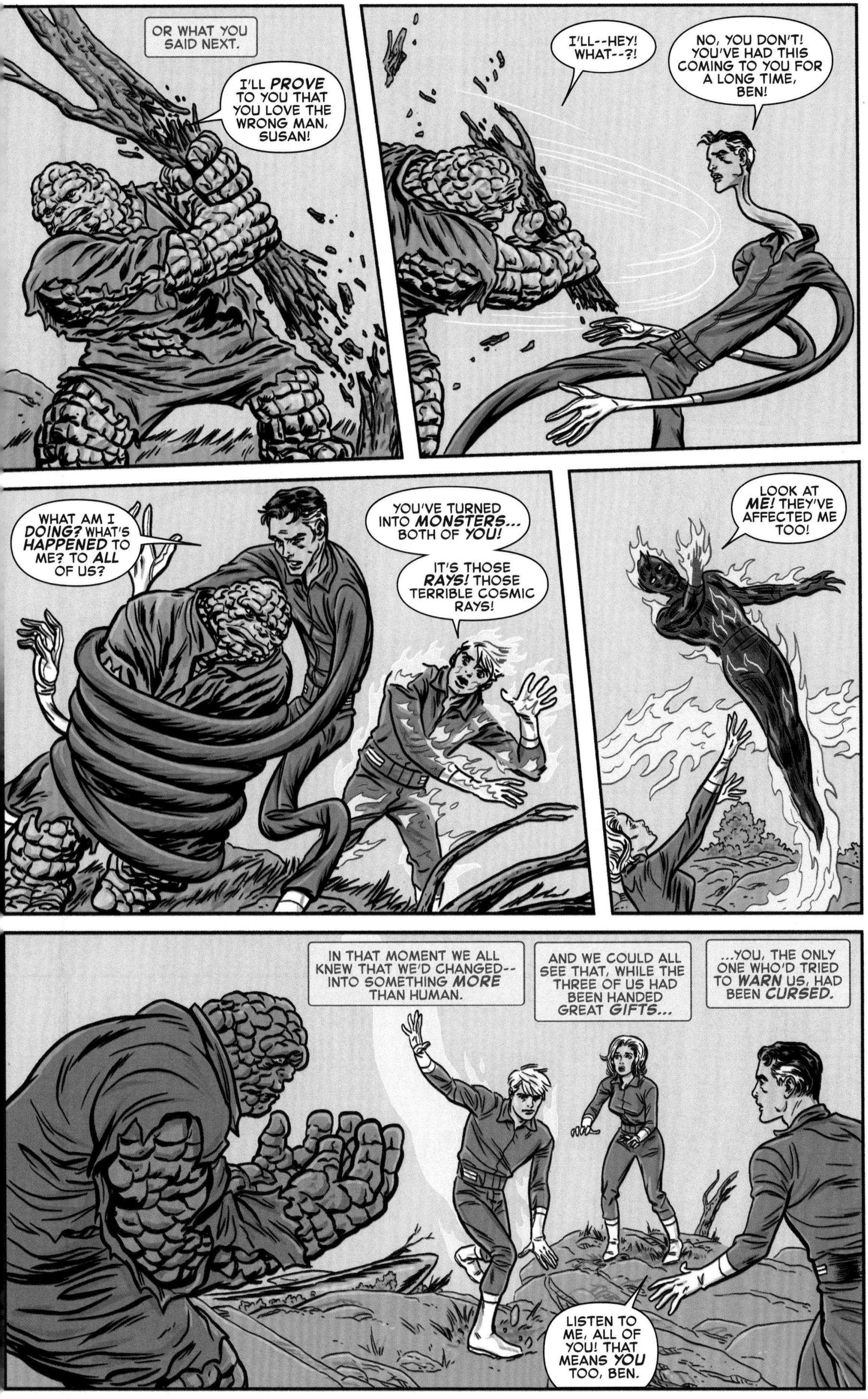
OR WHAT YOU SAID NEXT.
I'LL PROVE TO YOU THAT YOU LOVE THE WRONG MAN, SUSAN!
I'LL--HEY! WHAT--?!
NO, YOU DON'T! YOU'VE HAD THIS COMING TO YOU FOR A LONG TIME, BEN!
WHAT AM I DOING? WHAT'S HAPPENED TO ME? TO ALL OF US?
YOU'VE TURNED INTO MONSTERS... BOTH OF YOU!
IT'S THOSE RAYS! THOSE TERRIBLE COSMIC RAYS!
LOOK AT ME! THEY'VE AFFECTED ME TOO!
IN THAT MOMENT WE ALL KNEW THAT WE'D CHANGED-- INTO SOMETHING MORE THAN HUMAN.
AND WE COULD ALL SEE THAT, WHILE THE THREE OF US HAD BEEN HANDED GREAT GIFTS...
...YOU, THE ONLY ONE WHO'D TRIED TO WARN US, HAD BEEN CURSED.
LISTEN TO ME, ALL OF YOU! THAT MEANS YOU TOO, BEN.

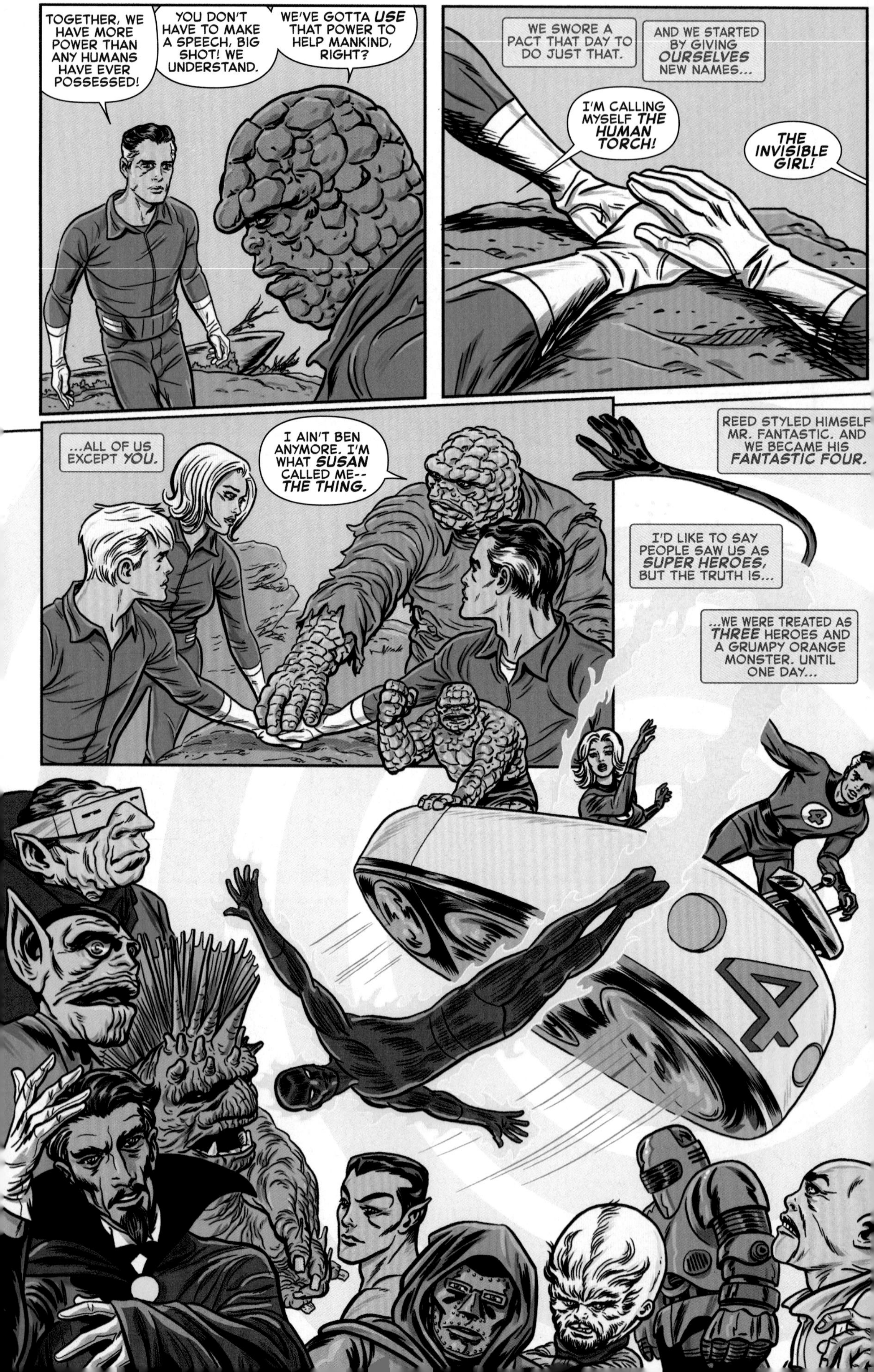
TOGETHER, WE HAVE MORE POWER THAN ANY HUMANS HAVE EVER POSSESSED!
YOU DON'T HAVE TO MAKE A SPEECH, BIG SHOT! WE UNDERSTAND.
WE'VE GOTTA USE THAT POWER TO HELP MANKIND, RIGHT?
WE SWORE A PACT THAT DAY TO DO JUST THAT.
AND WE STARTED BY GIVING OURSELVES NEW NAMES...
I'M CALLING MYSELF THE HUMAN TORCH!
THE INVISIBLE GIRL!
...ALL OF US EXCEPT YOU.
I AIN'T BEN ANYMORE. I'M WHAT SUSAN CALLED ME-- THE THING.
REED STYLED HIMSELF MR. FANTASTIC. AND WE BECAME HIS FANTASTIC FOUR.
I'D LIKE TO SAY PEOPLE SAW US AS SUPER HEROES, BUT THE TRUTH IS...
...WE WERE TREATED AS THREE HEROES AND A GRUMPY ORANGE MONSTER. UNTIL ONE DAY...

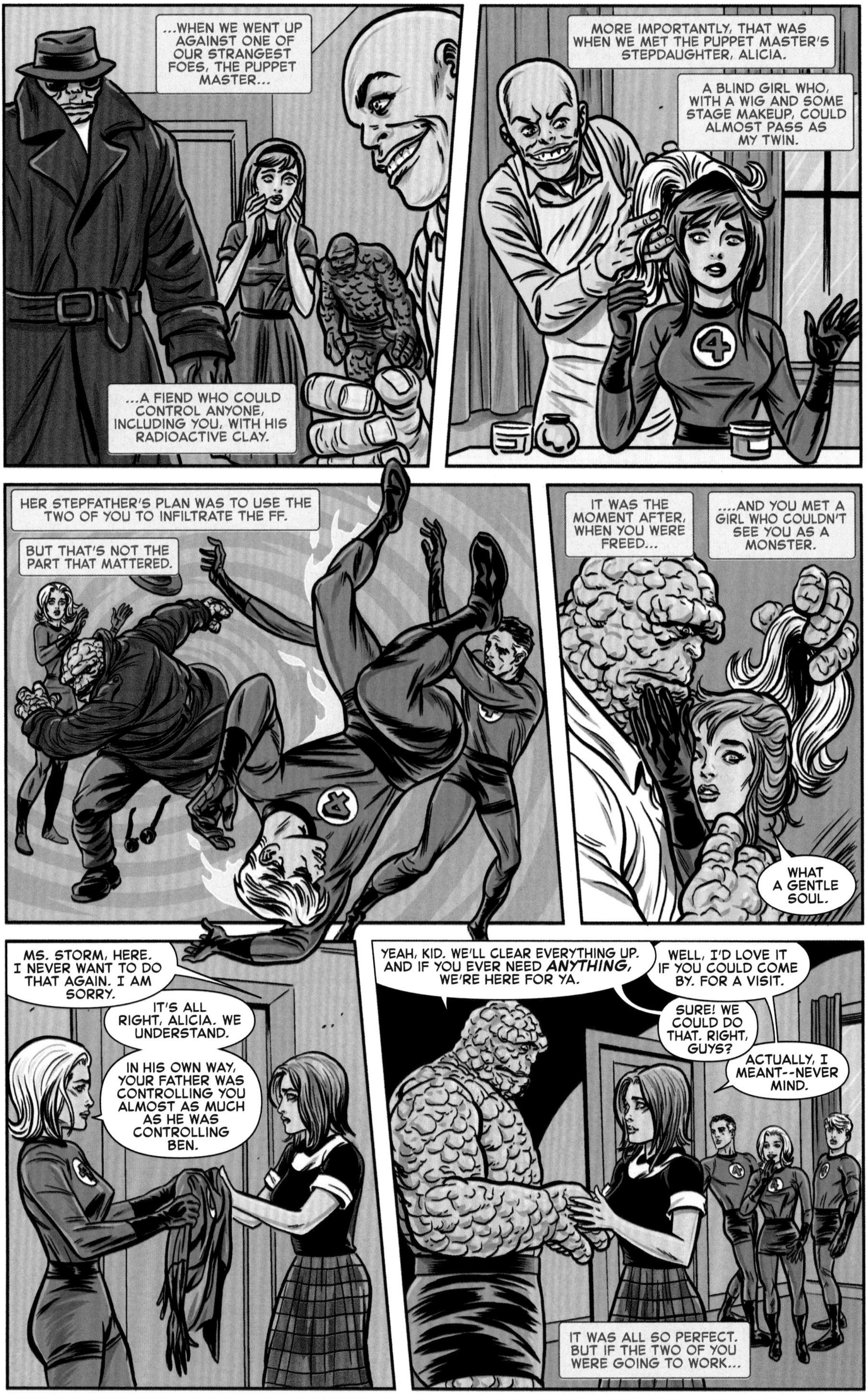
...WHEN WE WENT UP AGAINST ONE OF OUR STRANGEST FOES, THE PUPPET MASTER...
...A FIEND WHO COULD CONTROL ANYONE, INCLUDING YOU, WITH HIS RADIOACTIVE CLAY.
MORE IMPORTANTLY, THAT WAS WHEN WE MET THE PUPPET MASTER'S STEPDAUGHTER, ALICIA.
A BLIND GIRL WHO, WITH A WIG AND SOME STAGE MAKEUP, COULD ALMOST PASS AS MY TWIN.
HER STEPFATHER'S PLAN WAS TO USE THE TWO OF YOU TO INFILTRATE THE FF.
BUT THAT'S NOT THE PART THAT MATTERED.
IT WAS THE MOMENT AFTER, WHEN YOU WERE FREED...
....AND YOU MET A GIRL WHO COULDN'T SEE YOU AS A MONSTER.
WHAT A GENTLE SOUL.
MS. STORM, HERE. I NEVER WANT TO DO THAT AGAIN. I AM SORRY.
IT'S ALL RIGHT, ALICIA. WE UNDERSTAND.
IN HIS OWN WAY, YOUR FATHER WAS CONTROLLING YOU ALMOST AS MUCH AS HE WAS CONTROLLING BEN.
YEAH, KID. WE'LL CLEAR EVERYTHING UP. AND IF YOU EVER NEED ***ANYTHING,*** WE'RE HERE FOR YA.
WELL, I'D LOVE IT IF YOU COULD COME BY. FOR A VISIT.
SURE! WE COULD DO THAT. RIGHT, GUYS?
ACTUALLY, I MEANT--NEVER MIND.
IT WAS ALL SO PERFECT. BUT IF THE TWO OF YOU WERE GOING TO WORK...

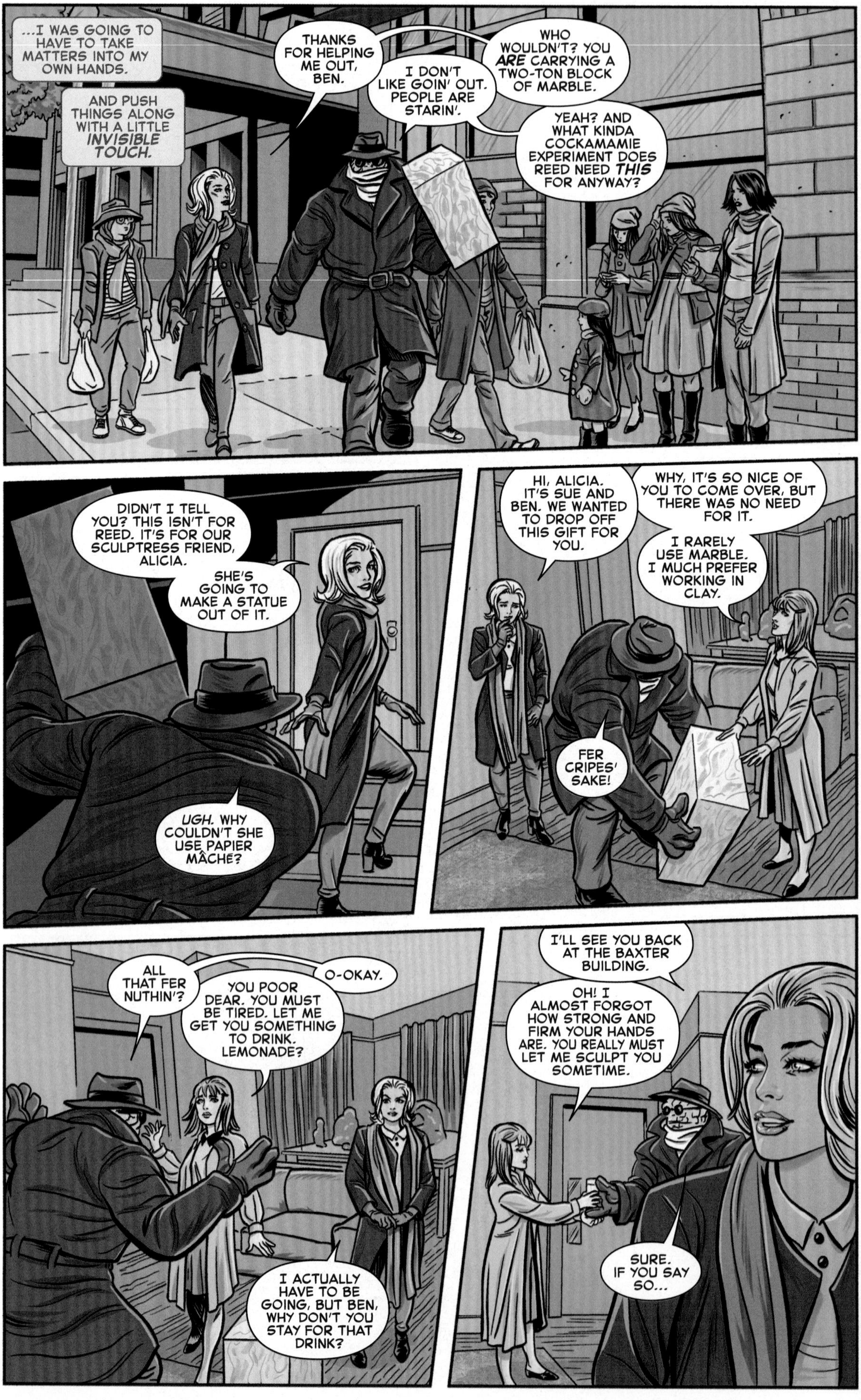
...I WAS GOING TO HAVE TO TAKE MATTERS INTO MY OWN HANDS.
AND PUSH THINGS ALONG WITH A LITTLE *INVISIBLE TOUCH.*
THANKS FOR HELPING ME OUT, BEN.
WHO WOULDN'T? YOU *ARE* CARRYING A TWO-TON BLOCK OF MARBLE.
I DON'T LIKE GOIN' OUT. PEOPLE ARE STARIN'.
YEAH? AND WHAT KINDA COCKAMAMIE EXPERIMENT DOES REED NEED *THIS* FOR ANYWAY?
DIDN'T I TELL YOU? THIS ISN'T FOR REED. IT'S FOR OUR SCULPTRESS FRIEND, ALICIA.
SHE'S GOING TO MAKE A STATUE OUT OF IT.
UGH. WHY COULDN'T SHE USE PAPIER MÂCHÉ?
HI, ALICIA. IT'S SUE AND BEN. WE WANTED TO DROP OFF THIS GIFT FOR YOU.
WHY, IT'S SO NICE OF YOU TO COME OVER, BUT THERE WAS NO NEED FOR IT.
I RARELY USE MARBLE. I MUCH PREFER WORKING IN CLAY.
FER CRIPES' SAKE!
ALL THAT FER NUTHIN'?
YOU POOR DEAR. YOU MUST BE TIRED. LET ME GET YOU SOMETHING TO DRINK. LEMONADE?
O-OKAY.
I ACTUALLY HAVE TO BE GOING, BUT BEN, WHY DON'T YOU STAY FOR THAT DRINK?
I'LL SEE YOU BACK AT THE BAXTER BUILDING.
OH! I ALMOST FORGOT HOW STRONG AND FIRM YOUR HANDS ARE. YOU REALLY MUST LET ME SCULPT YOU SOMETIME.
SURE. IF YOU SAY SO...

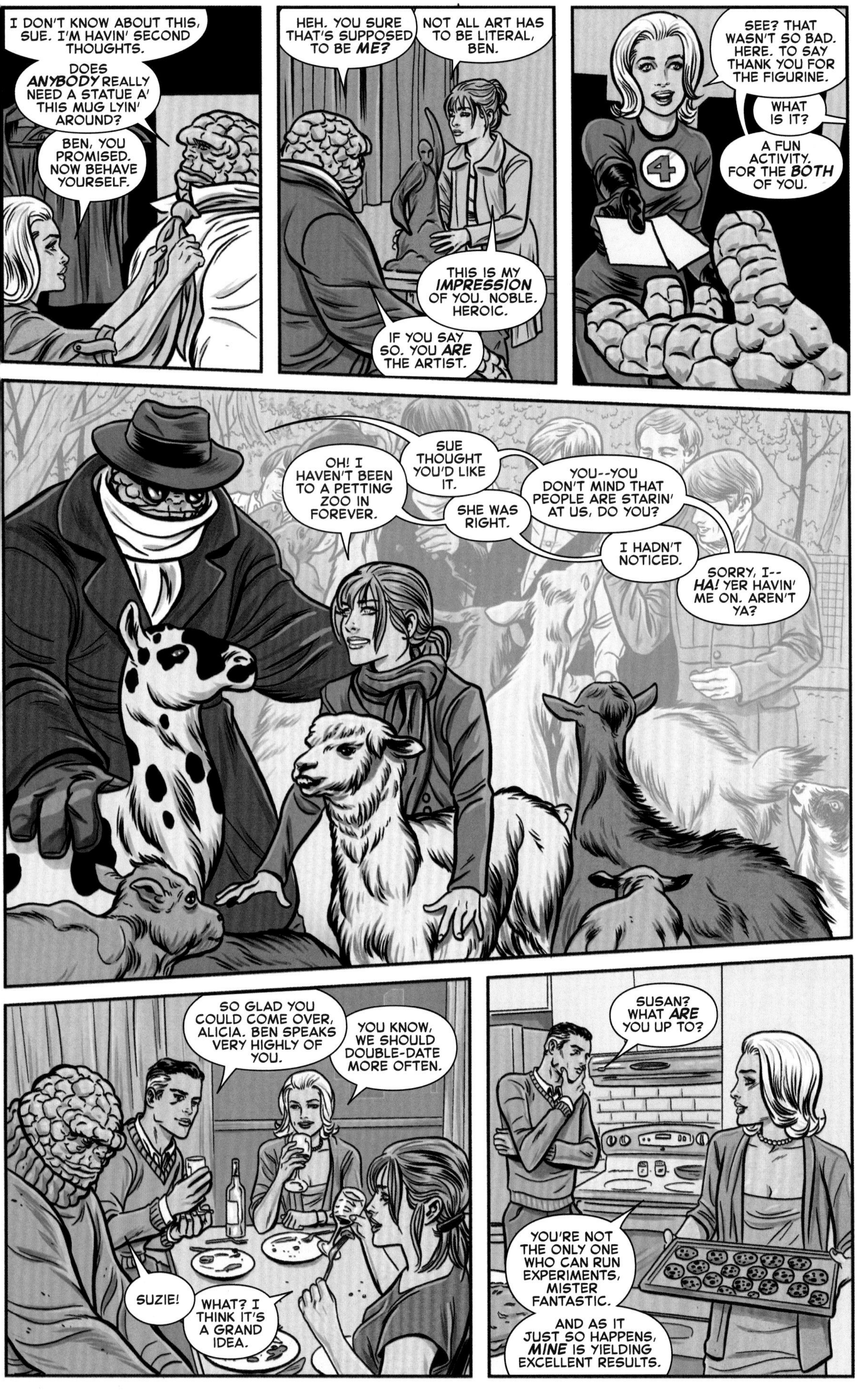

I DON'T KNOW ABOUT THIS, SUE. I'M HAVIN' SECOND THOUGHTS.
DOES ANYBODY REALLY NEED A STATUE A' THIS MUG LYIN' AROUND?
BEN, YOU PROMISED. NOW BEHAVE YOURSELF.
HEH. YOU SURE THAT'S SUPPOSED TO BE ME?
NOT ALL ART HAS TO BE LITERAL, BEN.
THIS IS MY IMPRESSION OF YOU. NOBLE. HEROIC.
IF YOU SAY SO. YOU ARE THE ARTIST.
SEE? THAT WASN'T SO BAD. HERE. TO SAY THANK YOU FOR THE FIGURINE.
WHAT IS IT?
A FUN ACTIVITY. FOR THE BOTH OF YOU.
OH! I HAVEN'T BEEN TO A PETTING ZOO IN FOREVER.
SUE THOUGHT YOU'D LIKE IT.
SHE WAS RIGHT.
YOU--YOU DON'T MIND THAT PEOPLE ARE STARIN' AT US, DO YOU?
I HADN'T NOTICED.
SORRY, I-- HA! YER HAVIN' ME ON. AREN'T YA?
SO GLAD YOU COULD COME OVER, ALICIA. BEN SPEAKS VERY HIGHLY OF YOU.
YOU KNOW, WE SHOULD DOUBLE-DATE MORE OFTEN.
SUZIE!
WHAT? I THINK IT'S A GRAND IDEA.
SUSAN? WHAT ARE YOU UP TO?
YOU'RE NOT THE ONLY ONE WHO CAN RUN EXPERIMENTS, MISTER FANTASTIC.
AND AS IT JUST SO HAPPENS, MINE IS YIELDING EXCELLENT RESULTS.

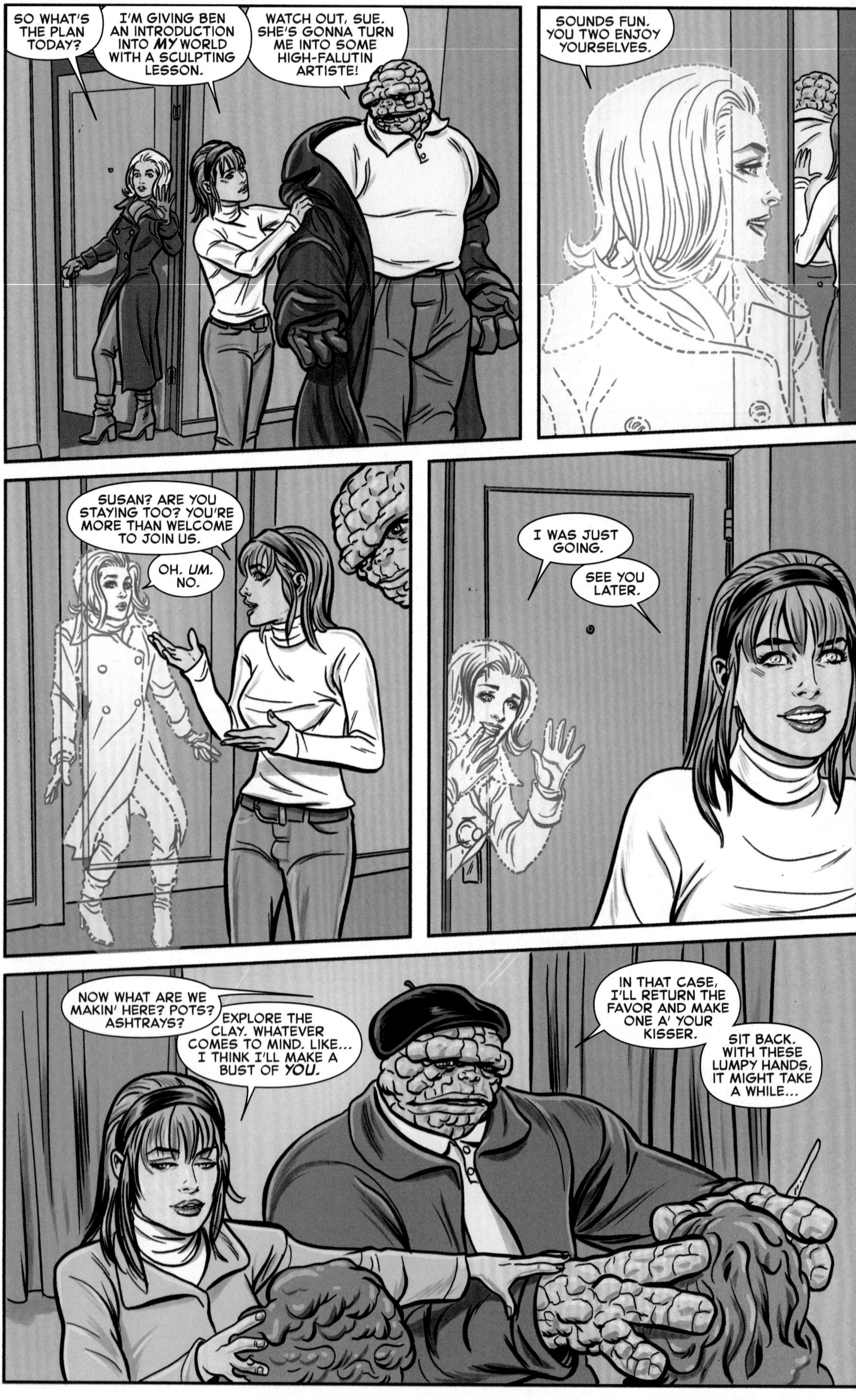
SO WHAT'S THE PLAN TODAY?
I'M GIVING BEN AN INTRODUCTION INTO MY WORLD WITH A SCULPTING LESSON.
WATCH OUT, SUE. SHE'S GONNA TURN ME INTO SOME HIGH-FALUTIN ARTISTE!
SOUNDS FUN. YOU TWO ENJOY YOURSELVES.
SUSAN? ARE YOU STAYING TOO? YOU'RE MORE THAN WELCOME TO JOIN US.
OH. UM. NO.
I WAS JUST GOING.
SEE YOU LATER.
NOW WHAT ARE WE MAKIN' HERE? POTS? ASHTRAYS?
EXPLORE THE CLAY. WHATEVER COMES TO MIND. LIKE... I THINK I'LL MAKE A BUST OF YOU.
IN THAT CASE, I'LL RETURN THE FAVOR AND MAKE ONE A' YOUR KISSER.
SIT BACK. WITH THESE LUMPY HANDS, IT MIGHT TAKE A WHILE...

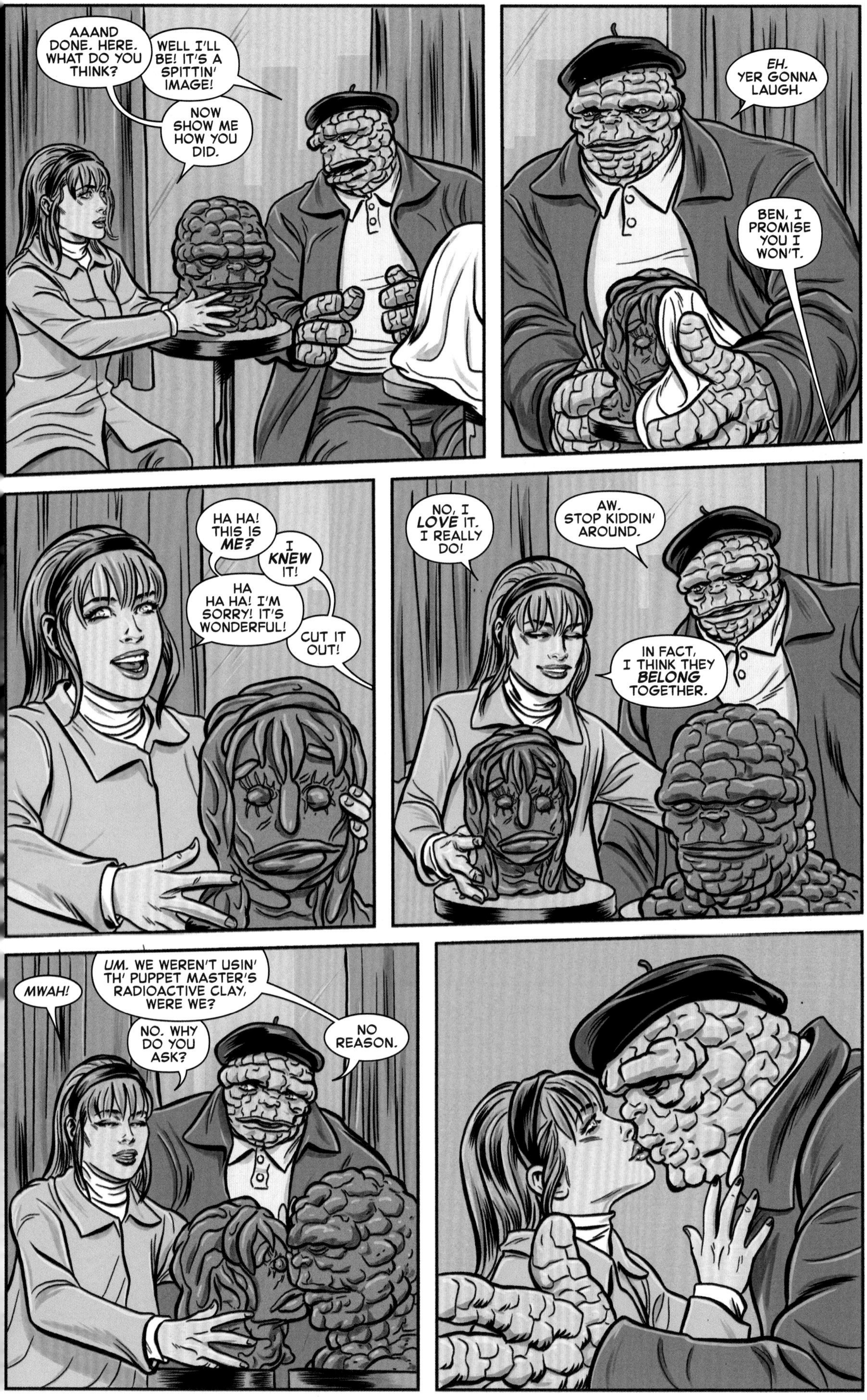
AAAND DONE. HERE. WHAT DO YOU THINK?
WELL I'LL BE! IT'S A SPITTIN' IMAGE!
NOW SHOW ME HOW YOU DID.
EH. YER GONNA LAUGH.
BEN, I PROMISE YOU I WON'T.
HA HA! THIS IS ***ME?***
I ***KNEW*** IT!
HA HA HA! I'M SORRY! IT'S WONDERFUL!
CUT IT OUT!
NO, I ***LOVE*** IT. I REALLY DO!
AW. STOP KIDDIN' AROUND.
IN FACT, I THINK THEY ***BELONG*** TOGETHER.
MWAH!
UM. WE WEREN'T USIN' TH' PUPPET MASTER'S RADIOACTIVE CLAY, WERE WE?
NO. WHY DO YOU ASK?
NO REASON.

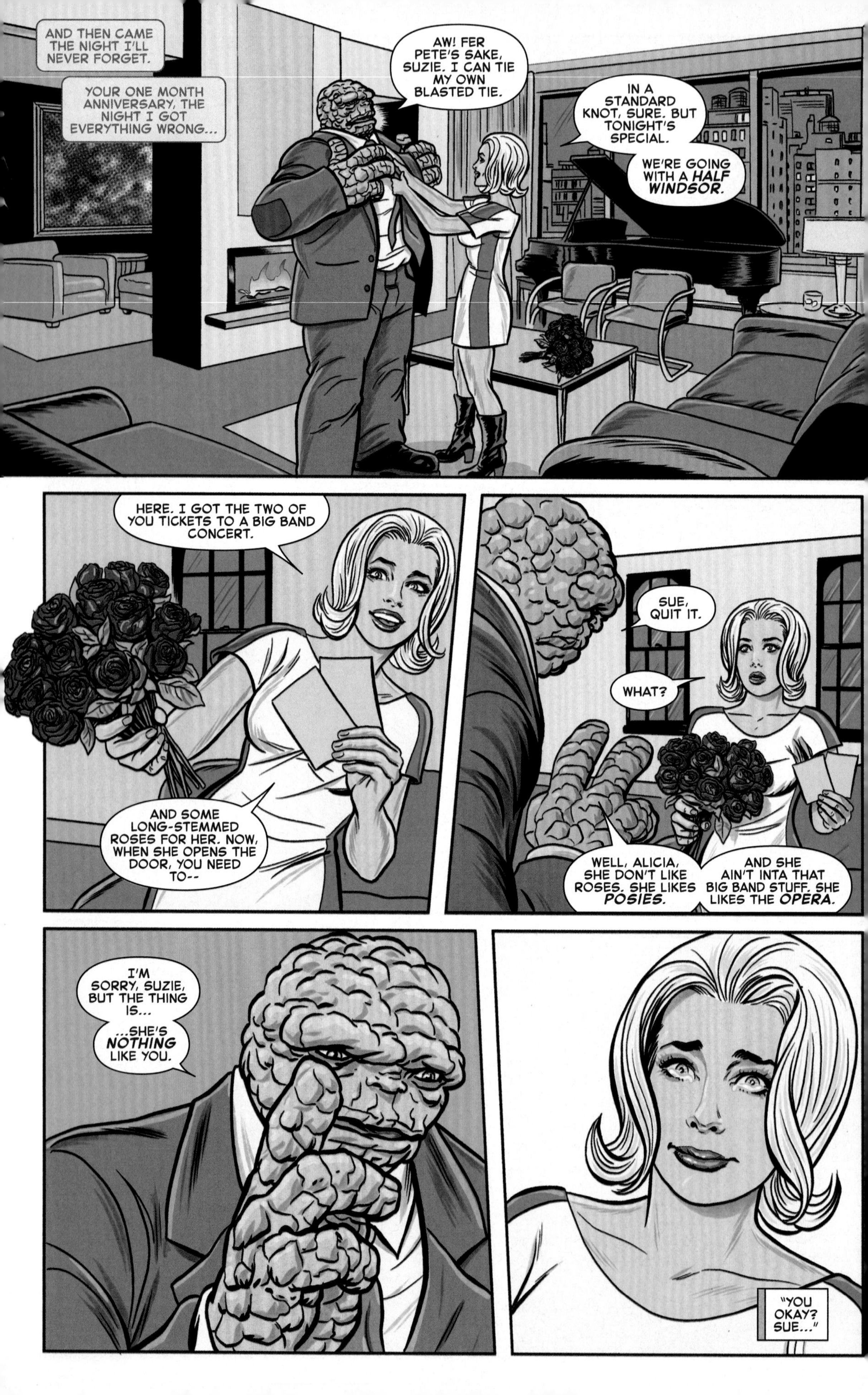
AND THEN CAME THE NIGHT I'LL NEVER FORGET.
YOUR ONE MONTH ANNIVERSARY, THE NIGHT I GOT EVERYTHING WRONG...
AW! FER PETE'S SAKE, SUZIE. I CAN TIE MY OWN BLASTED TIE.
IN A STANDARD KNOT, SURE. BUT TONIGHT'S SPECIAL.
WE'RE GOING WITH A *HALF WINDSOR*.
HERE. I GOT THE TWO OF YOU TICKETS TO A BIG BAND CONCERT.
AND SOME LONG-STEMMED ROSES FOR HER. NOW, WHEN SHE OPENS THE DOOR, YOU NEED TO--
SUE, QUIT IT.
WHAT?
WELL, ALICIA, SHE DON'T LIKE ROSES. SHE LIKES *POSIES.*
AND SHE AIN'T INTA THAT BIG BAND STUFF. SHE LIKES THE *OPERA.*
I'M SORRY, SUZIE, BUT THE THING IS...
...SHE'S *NOTHING* LIKE YOU.
"YOU OKAY? SUE..."

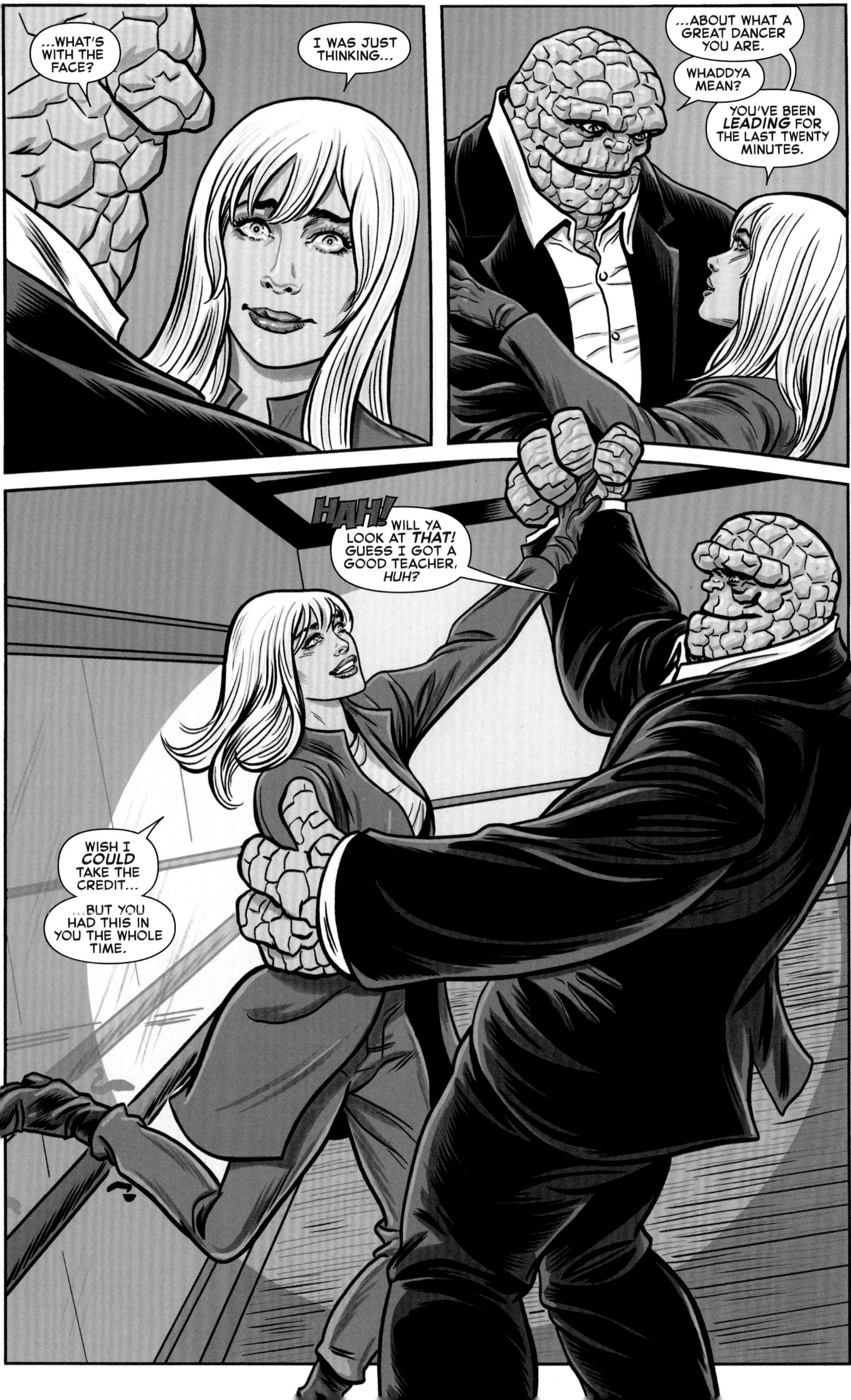

...WHAT'S WITH THE FACE?
I WAS JUST THINKING...
...ABOUT WHAT A GREAT DANCER YOU ARE.
WHADDYA MEAN?
YOU'VE BEEN LEADING FOR THE LAST TWENTY MINUTES.
HAH!
WILL YA LOOK AT THAT! GUESS I GOT A GOOD TEACHER, HUH?
WISH I COULD TAKE THE CREDIT...
...BUT YOU HAD THIS IN YOU THE WHOLE TIME.

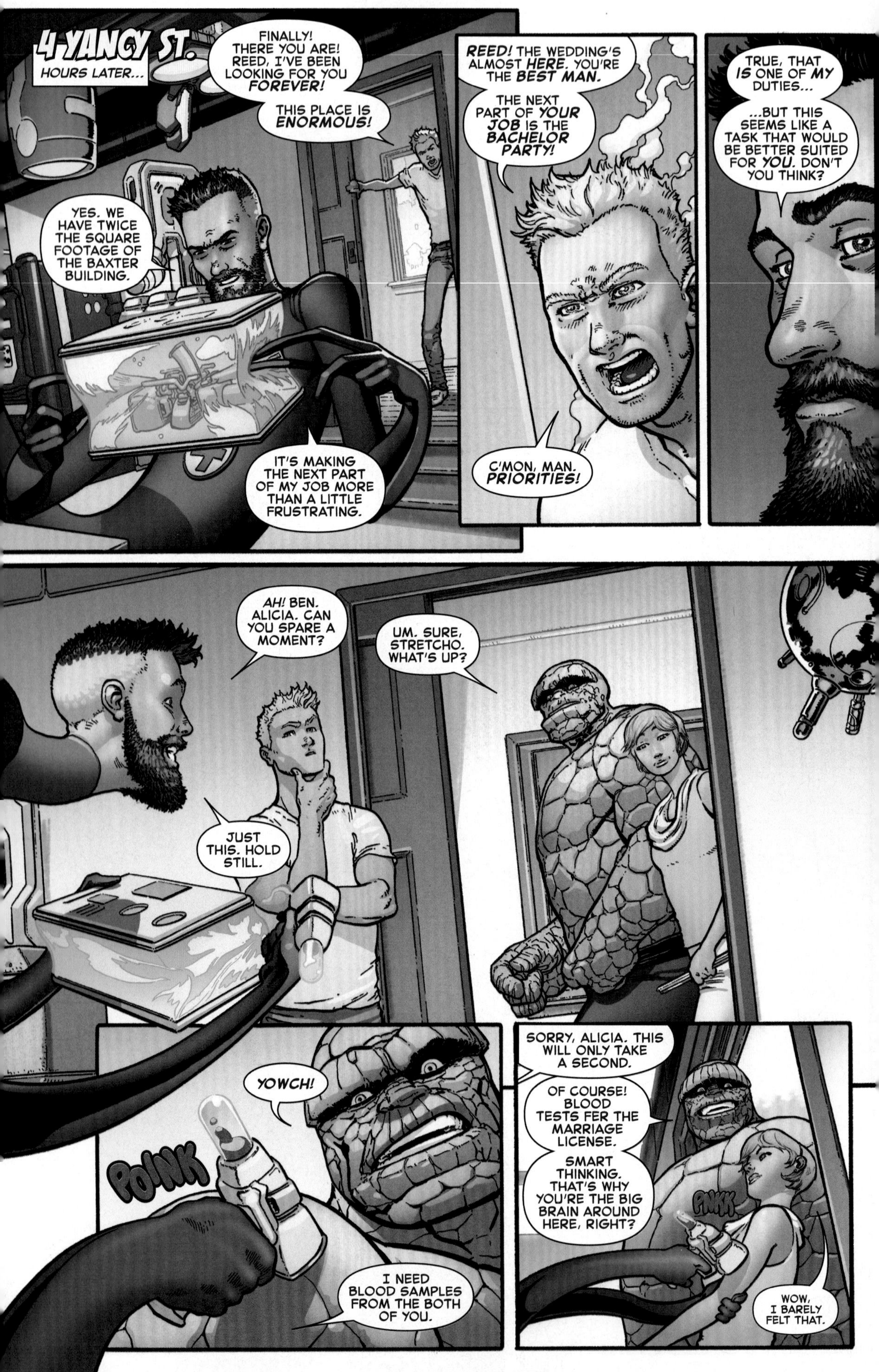
4 YANCY ST.
HOURS LATER...
FINALLY! THERE YOU ARE! REED, I'VE BEEN LOOKING FOR YOU FOREVER!
THIS PLACE IS ENORMOUS!
YES. WE HAVE TWICE THE SQUARE FOOTAGE OF THE BAXTER BUILDING.
IT'S MAKING THE NEXT PART OF MY JOB MORE THAN A LITTLE FRUSTRATING.
REED! THE WEDDING'S ALMOST HERE. YOU'RE THE BEST MAN.
THE NEXT PART OF YOUR JOB IS THE BACHELOR PARTY!
C'MON, MAN. PRIORITIES!
TRUE, THAT IS ONE OF MY DUTIES...
...BUT THIS SEEMS LIKE A TASK THAT WOULD BE BETTER SUITED FOR YOU. DON'T YOU THINK?
AH! BEN. ALICIA. CAN YOU SPARE A MOMENT?
UM. SURE, STRETCHO. WHAT'S UP?
JUST THIS. HOLD STILL.
YOWCH!
POINK
I NEED BLOOD SAMPLES FROM THE BOTH OF YOU.
SORRY, ALICIA. THIS WILL ONLY TAKE A SECOND.
OF COURSE! BLOOD TESTS FER THE MARRIAGE LICENSE.
SMART THINKING. THAT'S WHY YOU'RE THE BIG BRAIN AROUND HERE, RIGHT?
PINKK
WOW, I BARELY FELT THAT.

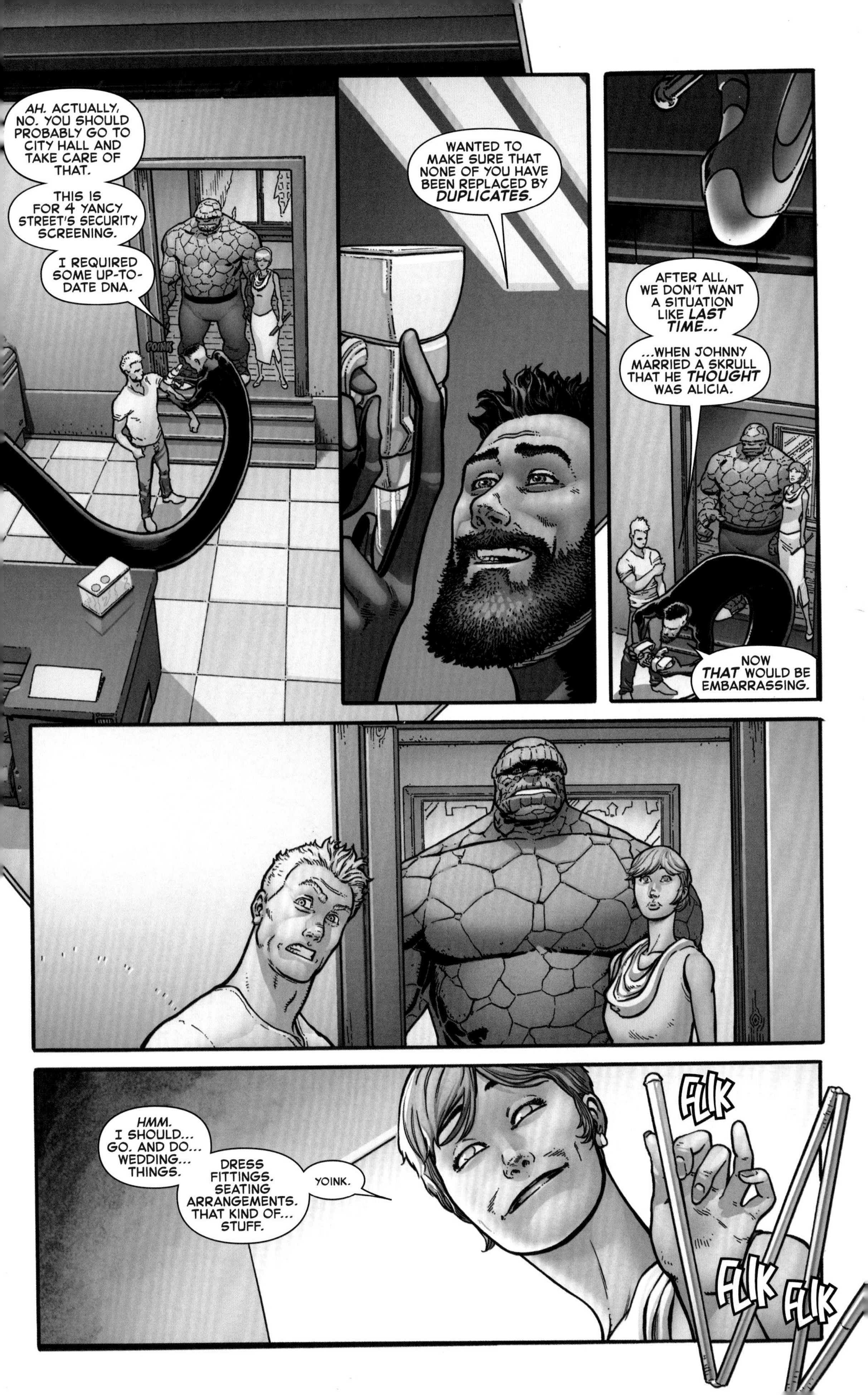
AH. ACTUALLY, NO. YOU SHOULD PROBABLY GO TO CITY HALL AND TAKE CARE OF THAT.
THIS IS FOR 4 YANCY STREET'S SECURITY SCREENING.
I REQUIRED SOME UP-TO-DATE DNA.
POINK
WANTED TO MAKE SURE THAT NONE OF YOU HAVE BEEN REPLACED BY DUPLICATES.
AFTER ALL, WE DON'T WANT A SITUATION LIKE LAST TIME...
...WHEN JOHNNY MARRIED A SKRULL THAT HE THOUGHT WAS ALICIA.
NOW THAT WOULD BE EMBARRASSING.
HMM. I SHOULD... GO. AND DO... WEDDING... THINGS.
DRESS FITTINGS. SEATING ARRANGEMENTS. THAT KIND OF... STUFF.
YOINK.
FLIK
FLIK
FLIK

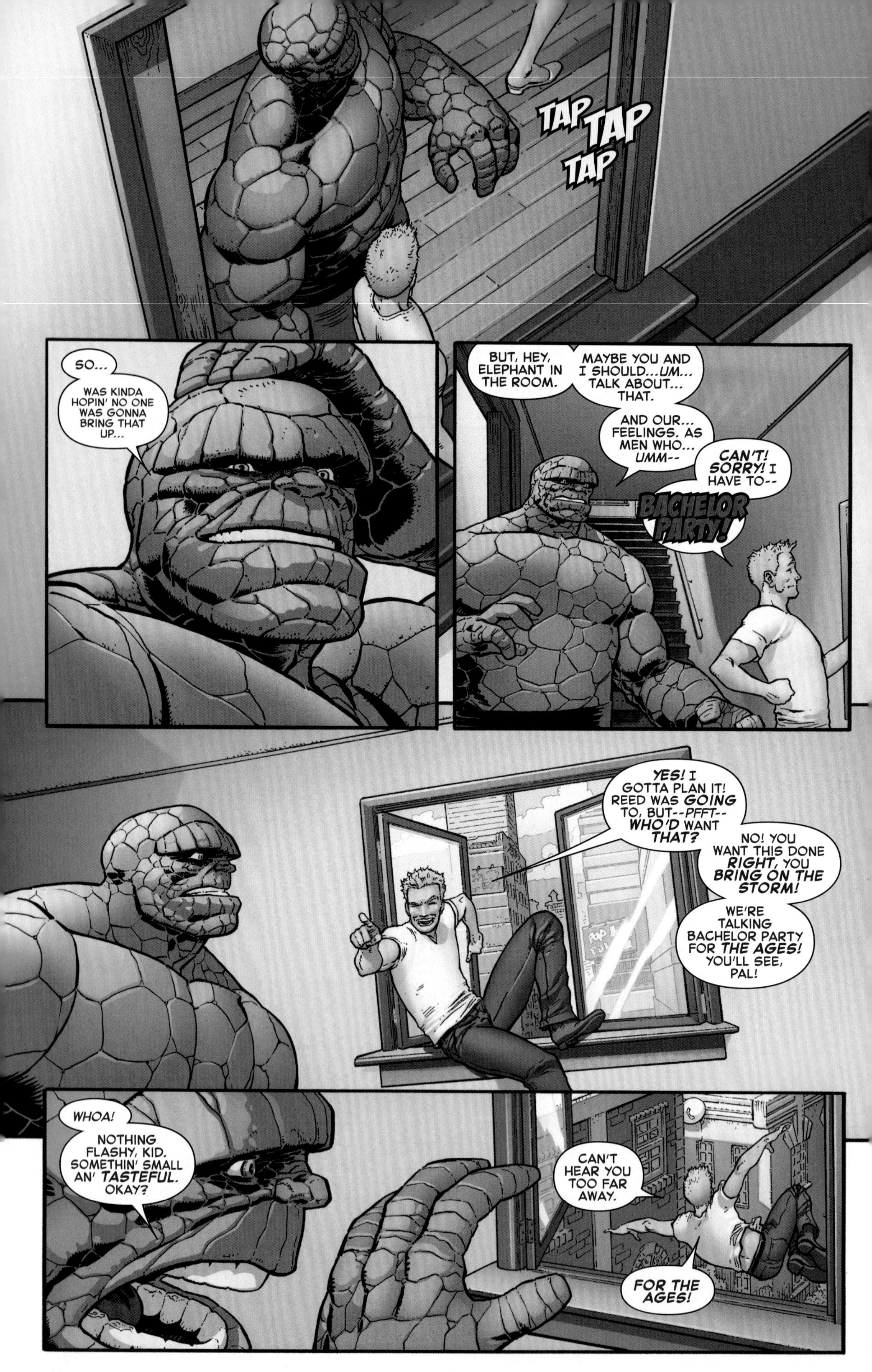
TAP TAP TAP
SO...
WAS KINDA HOPIN' NO ONE WAS GONNA BRING THAT UP...
BUT, HEY, ELEPHANT IN THE ROOM.
MAYBE YOU AND I SHOULD...UM... TALK ABOUT... THAT.
AND OUR... FEELINGS. AS MEN WHO... UMM--
CAN'T! SORRY! I HAVE TO--
BACHELOR PARTY!
YES! I GOTTA PLAN IT! REED WAS GOING TO, BUT--PFFT-- WHO'D WANT THAT?
NO! YOU WANT THIS DONE RIGHT, YOU BRING ON THE STORM!
WE'RE TALKING BACHELOR PARTY FOR THE AGES! YOU'LL SEE, PAL!
WHOA!
NOTHING FLASHY, KID. SOMETHIN' SMALL AN' TASTEFUL. OKAY?
CAN'T HEAR YOU TOO FAR AWAY.
FOR THE AGES!

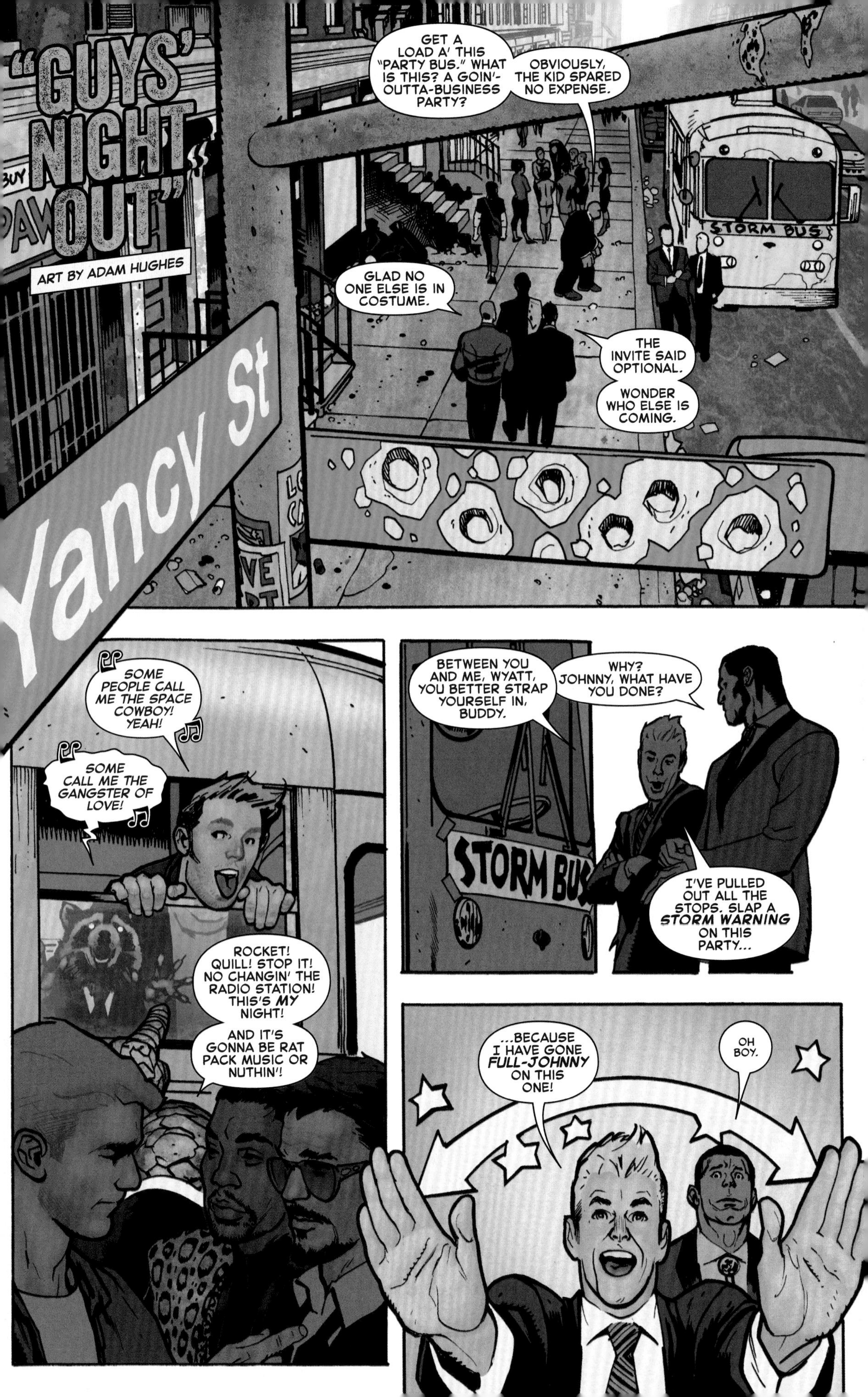
"GUYS' NIGHT OUT"
ART BY ADAM HUGHES
BUY
PAW
GET A LOAD A' THIS "PARTY BUS." WHAT IS THIS? A GOIN'-OUTTA-BUSINESS PARTY?
OBVIOUSLY, THE KID SPARED NO EXPENSE.
STORM BUS
GLAD NO ONE ELSE IS IN COSTUME.
THE INVITE SAID OPTIONAL.
WONDER WHO ELSE IS COMING.
Yancy St
SOME PEOPLE CALL ME THE SPACE COWBOY! YEAH!
SOME CALL ME THE GANGSTER OF LOVE!
ROCKET! QUILL! STOP IT! NO CHANGIN' THE RADIO STATION! THIS'S MY NIGHT!
AND IT'S GONNA BE RAT PACK MUSIC OR NUTHIN'!
BETWEEN YOU AND ME, WYATT, YOU BETTER STRAP YOURSELF IN, BUDDY.
WHY? JOHNNY, WHAT HAVE YOU DONE?
STORM BUS
I'VE PULLED OUT ALL THE STOPS. SLAP A STORM WARNING ON THIS PARTY...
...BECAUSE I HAVE GONE FULL-JOHNNY ON THIS ONE!
OH BOY.

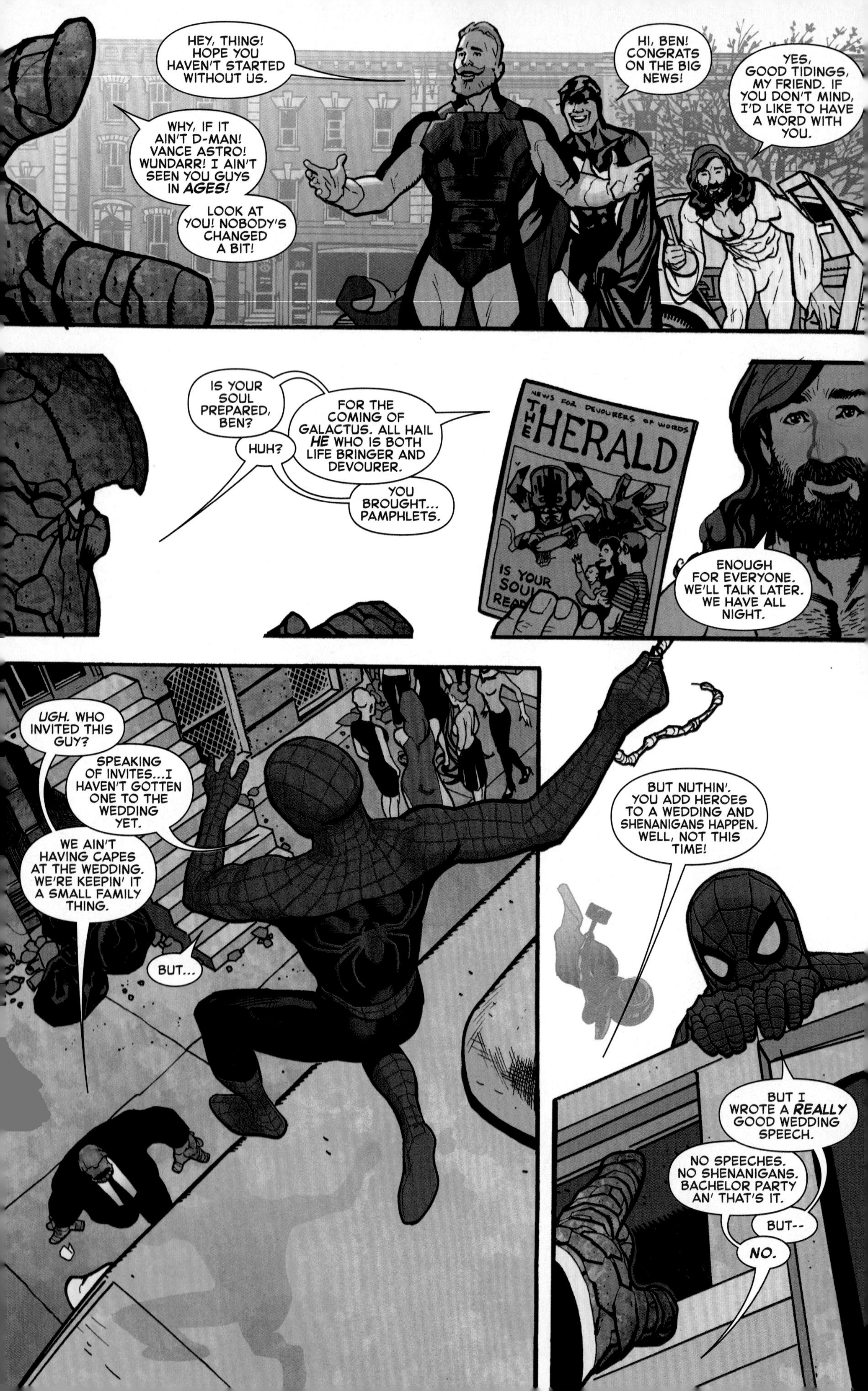
HEY, THING! HOPE YOU HAVEN'T STARTED WITHOUT US.
WHY, IF IT AIN'T D-MAN! VANCE ASTRO! WUNDARR! I AIN'T SEEN YOU GUYS IN AGES!
LOOK AT YOU! NOBODY'S CHANGED A BIT!
HI, BEN! CONGRATS ON THE BIG NEWS!
YES, GOOD TIDINGS, MY FRIEND. IF YOU DON'T MIND, I'D LIKE TO HAVE A WORD WITH YOU.
IS YOUR SOUL PREPARED, BEN?
HUH?
FOR THE COMING OF GALACTUS. ALL HAIL HE WHO IS BOTH LIFE BRINGER AND DEVOURER.
YOU BROUGHT... PAMPHLETS.
NEWS FOR DEVOURERS OF WORDS
THE HERALD
IS YOUR SOUL REA
ENOUGH FOR EVERYONE. WE'LL TALK LATER. WE HAVE ALL NIGHT.
UGH. WHO INVITED THIS GUY?
SPEAKING OF INVITES...I HAVEN'T GOTTEN ONE TO THE WEDDING YET.
WE AIN'T HAVING CAPES AT THE WEDDING. WE'RE KEEPIN' IT A SMALL FAMILY THING.
BUT...
BUT NUTHIN'. YOU ADD HEROES TO A WEDDING AND SHENANIGANS HAPPEN. WELL, NOT THIS TIME!
BUT I WROTE A REALLY GOOD WEDDING SPEECH.
NO SPEECHES. NO SHENANIGANS. BACHELOR PARTY AN' THAT'S IT.
BUT--
NO.

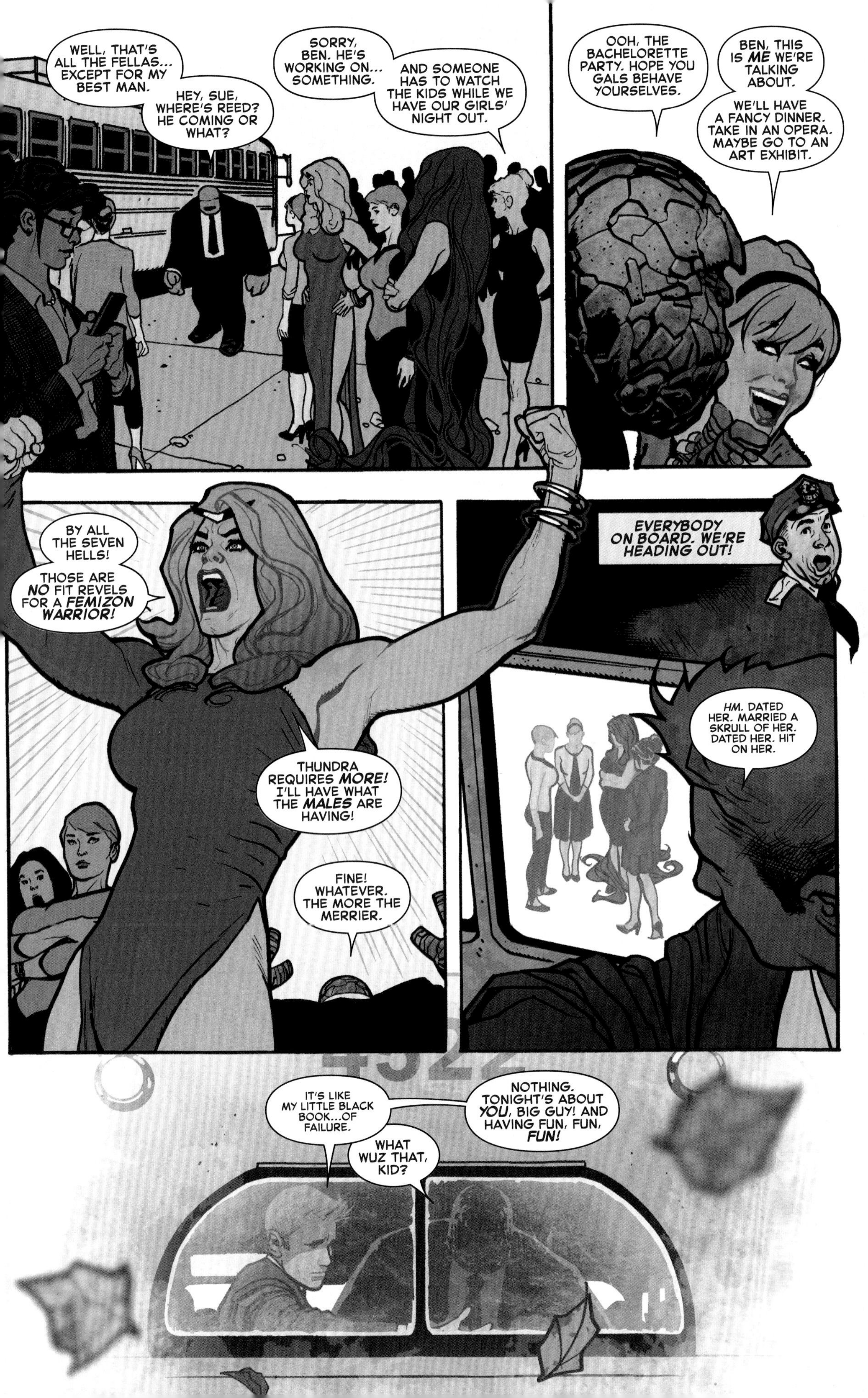

WELL, THAT'S ALL THE FELLAS... EXCEPT FOR MY BEST MAN.
HEY, SUE, WHERE'S REED? HE COMING OR WHAT?
SORRY, BEN. HE'S WORKING ON... SOMETHING.
AND SOMEONE HAS TO WATCH THE KIDS WHILE WE HAVE OUR GIRLS' NIGHT OUT.
OOH, THE BACHELORETTE PARTY. HOPE YOU GALS BEHAVE YOURSELVES.
BEN, THIS IS ME WE'RE TALKING ABOUT.
WE'LL HAVE A FANCY DINNER. TAKE IN AN OPERA. MAYBE GO TO AN ART EXHIBIT.
BY ALL THE SEVEN HELLS!
THOSE ARE NO FIT REVELS FOR A FEMIZON WARRIOR!
THUNDRA REQUIRES MORE! I'LL HAVE WHAT THE MALES ARE HAVING!
FINE! WHATEVER. THE MORE THE MERRIER.
EVERYBODY ON BOARD. WE'RE HEADING OUT!
HM. DATED HER. MARRIED A SKRULL OF HER. DATED HER. HIT ON HER.
IT'S LIKE MY LITTLE BLACK BOOK...OF FAILURE.
WHAT WUZ THAT, KID?
NOTHING. TONIGHT'S ABOUT YOU, BIG GUY! AND HAVING FUN, FUN, FUN!

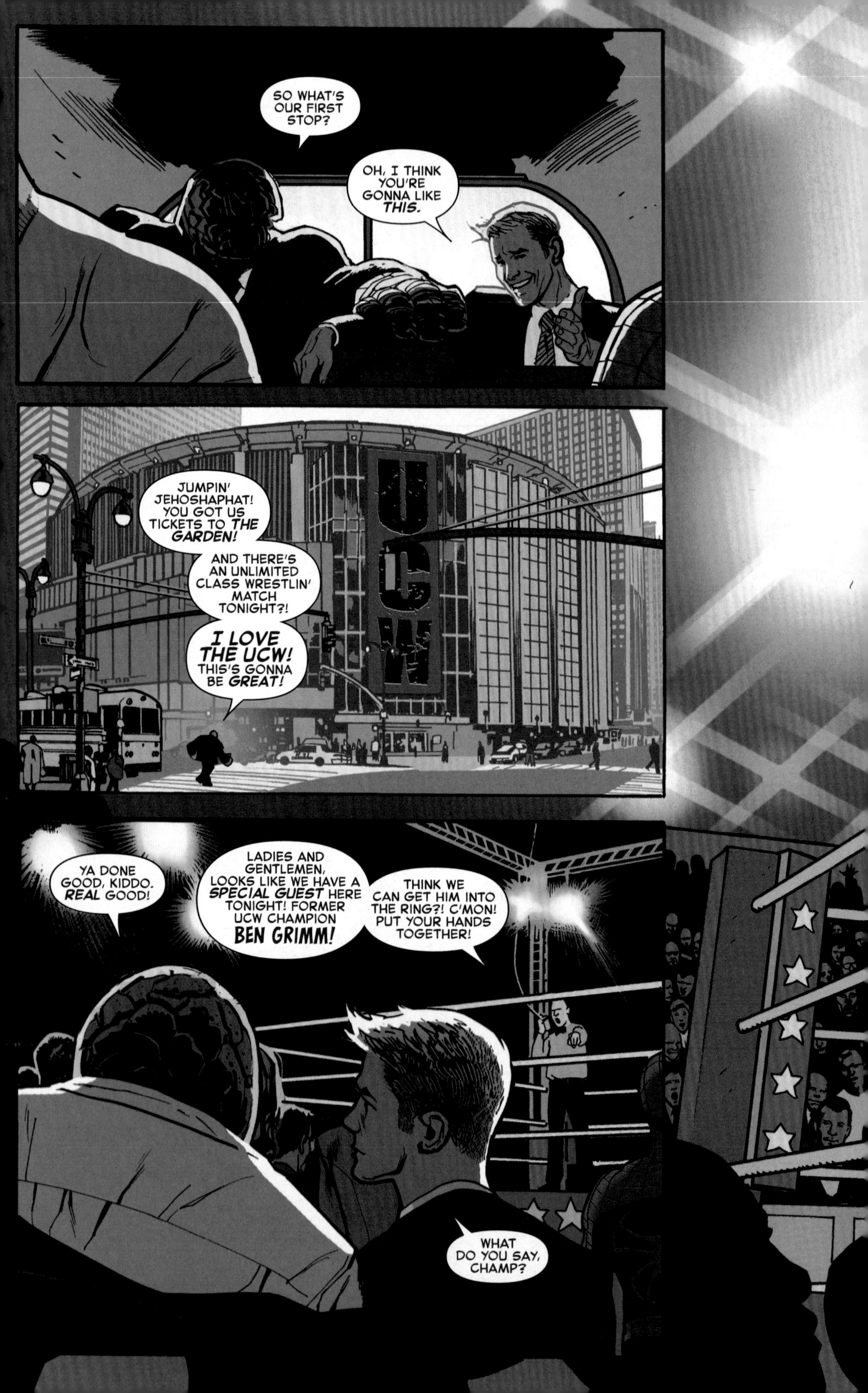
SO WHAT'S OUR FIRST STOP?
OH, I THINK YOU'RE GONNA LIKE THIS.
JUMPIN' JEHOSHAPHAT! YOU GOT US TICKETS TO THE GARDEN!
AND THERE'S AN UNLIMITED CLASS WRESTLIN' MATCH TONIGHT?!
I LOVE THE UCW! THIS'S GONNA BE GREAT!
UCW
YA DONE GOOD, KIDDO. REAL GOOD!
LADIES AND GENTLEMEN, LOOKS LIKE WE HAVE A SPECIAL GUEST HERE TONIGHT! FORMER UCW CHAMPION BEN GRIMM!
THINK WE CAN GET HIM INTO THE RING?! C'MON! PUT YOUR HANDS TOGETHER!
WHAT DO YOU SAY, CHAMP?

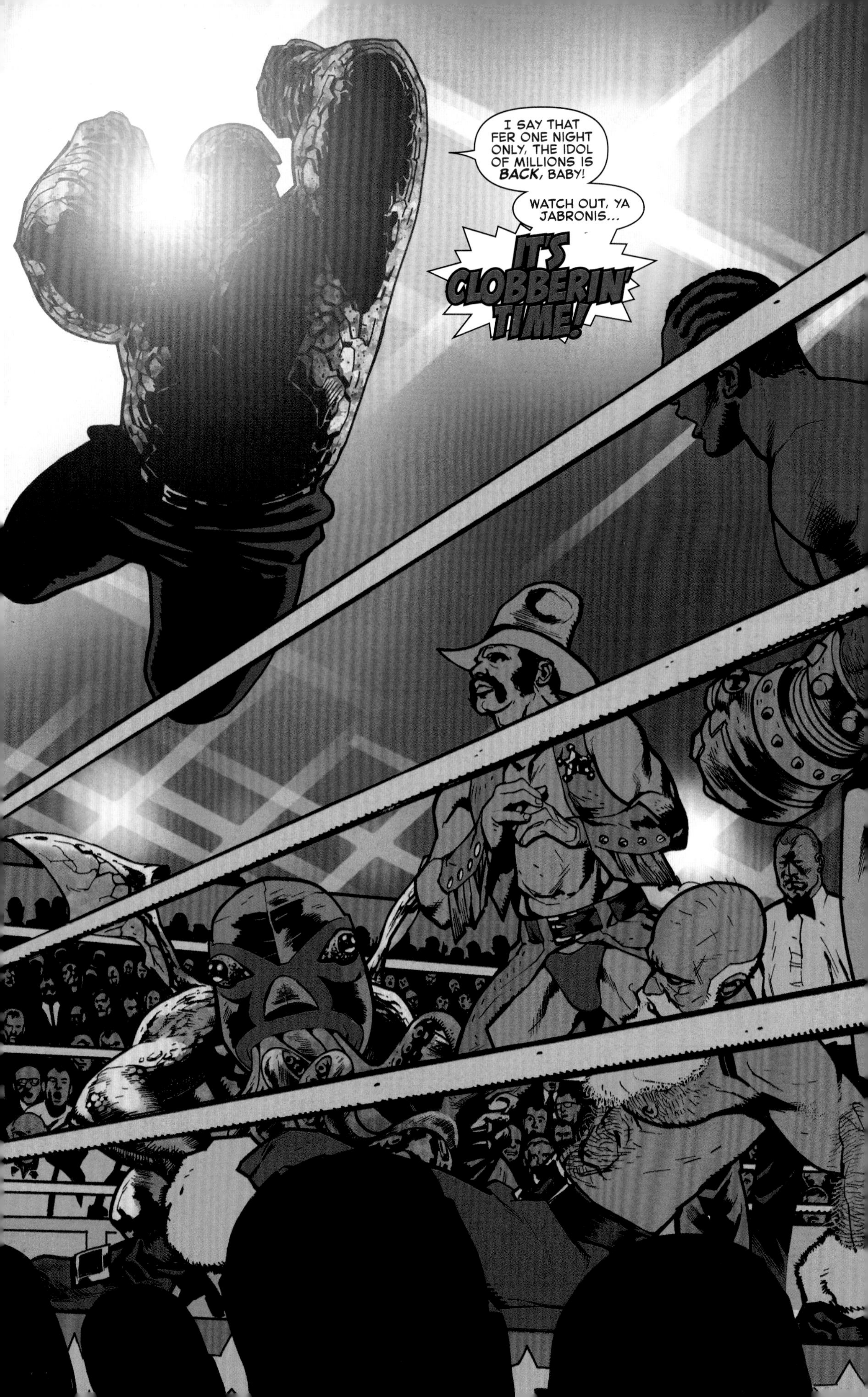
I SAY THAT FER ONE NIGHT ONLY, THE IDOL OF MILLIONS IS BACK, BABY!
WATCH OUT, YA JABRONIS...
IT'S CLOBBERIN' TIME!

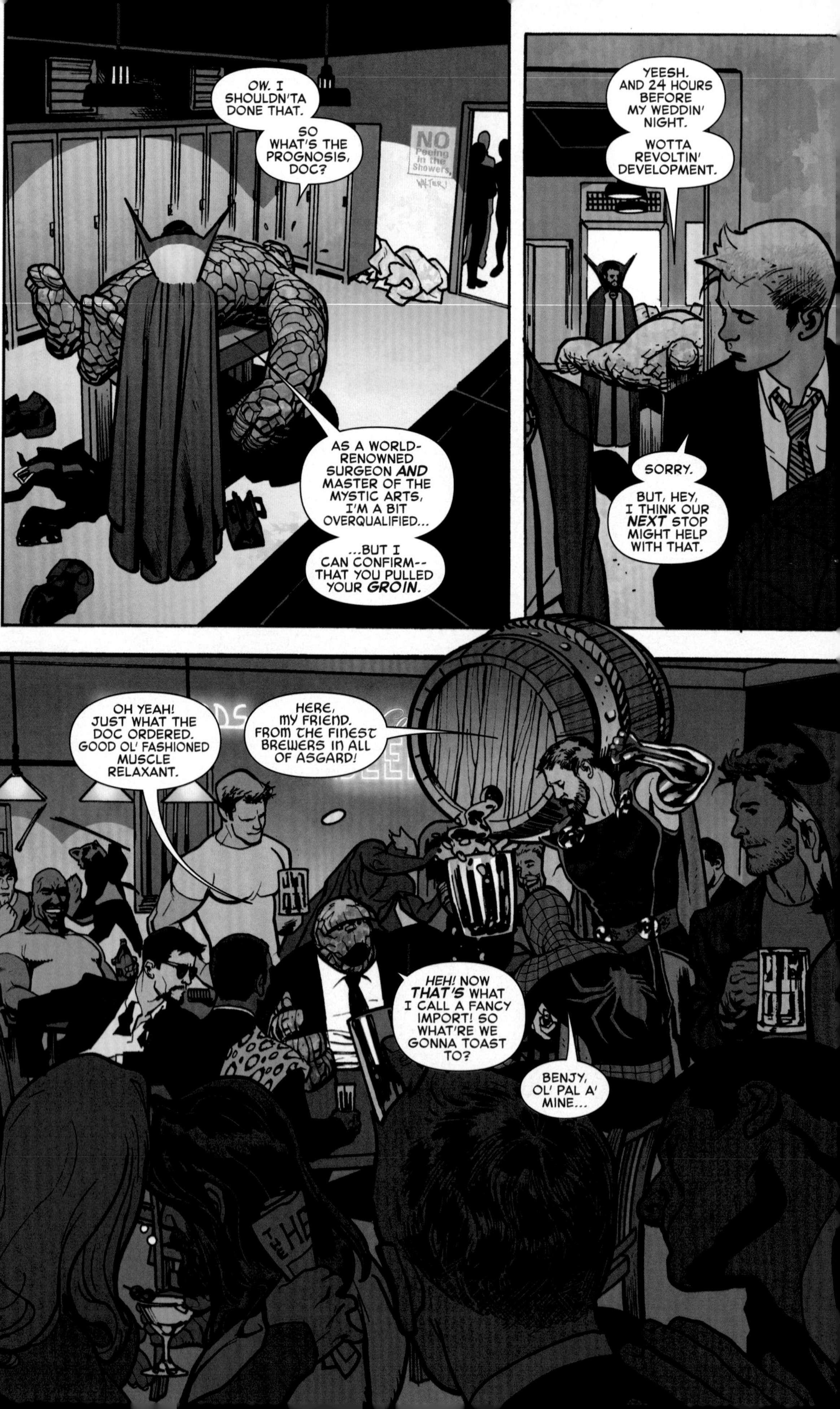
OW. I SHOULDN'TA DONE THAT.
SO WHAT'S THE PROGNOSIS, DOC?
NO Peeing in the Showers, WALTER!
AS A WORLD-RENOWNED SURGEON AND MASTER OF THE MYSTIC ARTS, I'M A BIT OVERQUALIFIED...
...BUT I CAN CONFIRM--THAT YOU PULLED YOUR GROIN.
YEESH. AND 24 HOURS BEFORE MY WEDDIN' NIGHT.
WOTTA REVOLTIN' DEVELOPMENT.
SORRY.
BUT, HEY, I THINK OUR NEXT STOP MIGHT HELP WITH THAT.
OH YEAH! JUST WHAT THE DOC ORDERED. GOOD OL' FASHIONED MUSCLE RELAXANT.
HERE, MY FRIEND. FROM THE FINEST BREWERS IN ALL OF ASGARD!
HEH! NOW THAT'S WHAT I CALL A FANCY IMPORT! SO WHAT'RE WE GONNA TOAST TO?
BENJY, OL' PAL A' MINE...

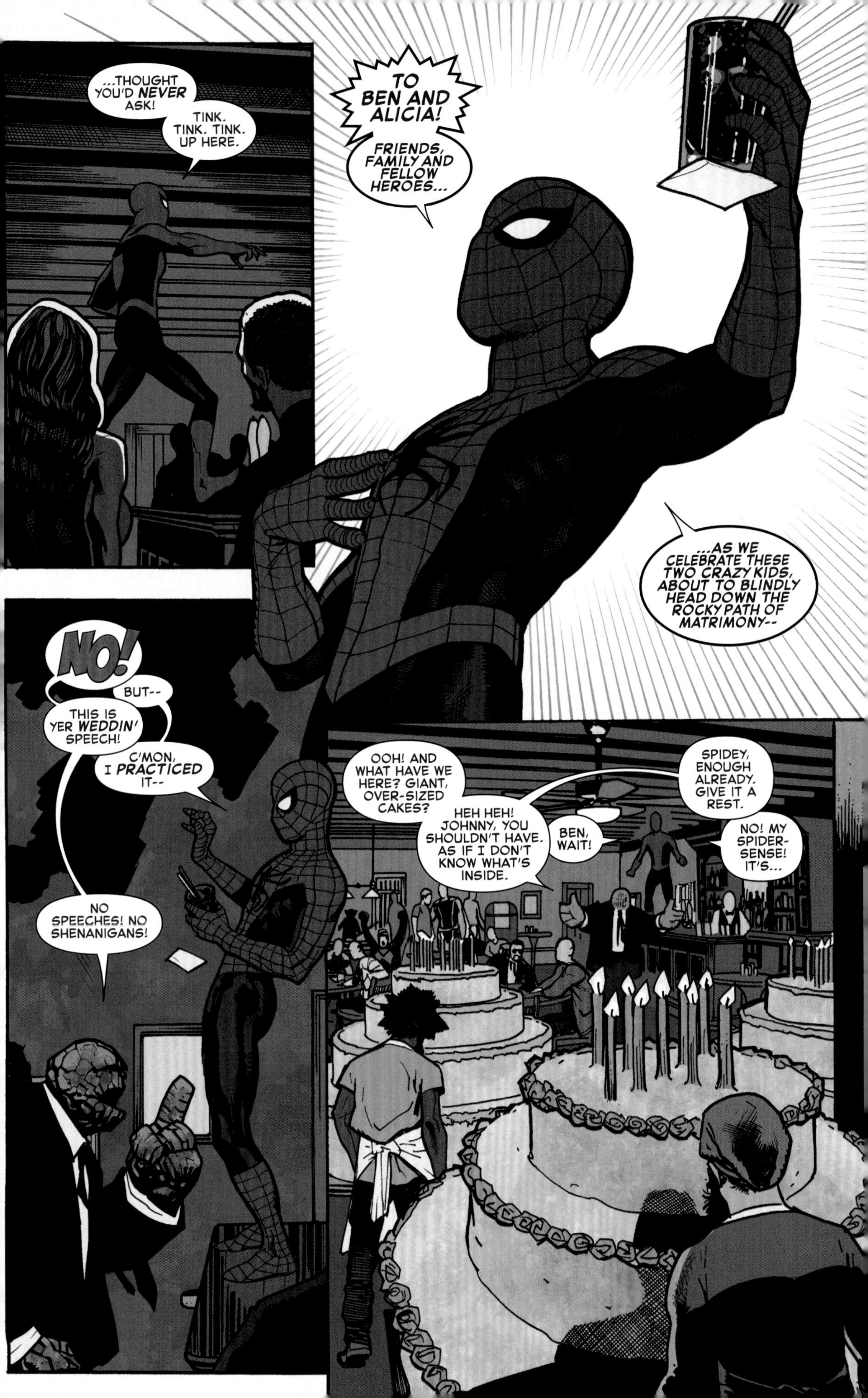
...THOUGHT YOU'D NEVER ASK!
TINK. TINK. TINK. UP HERE.
TO BEN AND ALICIA!
FRIENDS, FAMILY AND FELLOW HEROES...
...AS WE CELEBRATE THESE TWO CRAZY KIDS, ABOUT TO BLINDLY HEAD DOWN THE ROCKY PATH OF MATRIMONY--
NO!
BUT--
THIS IS YER WEDDIN' SPEECH!
C'MON, I PRACTICED IT--
NO SPEECHES! NO SHENANIGANS!
OOH! AND WHAT HAVE WE HERE? GIANT, OVER-SIZED CAKES?
HEH HEH! JOHNNY, YOU SHOULDN'T HAVE. AS IF I DON'T KNOW WHAT'S INSIDE.
BEN, WAIT!
SPIDEY, ENOUGH ALREADY. GIVE IT A REST.
NO! MY SPIDER-SENSE! IT'S...

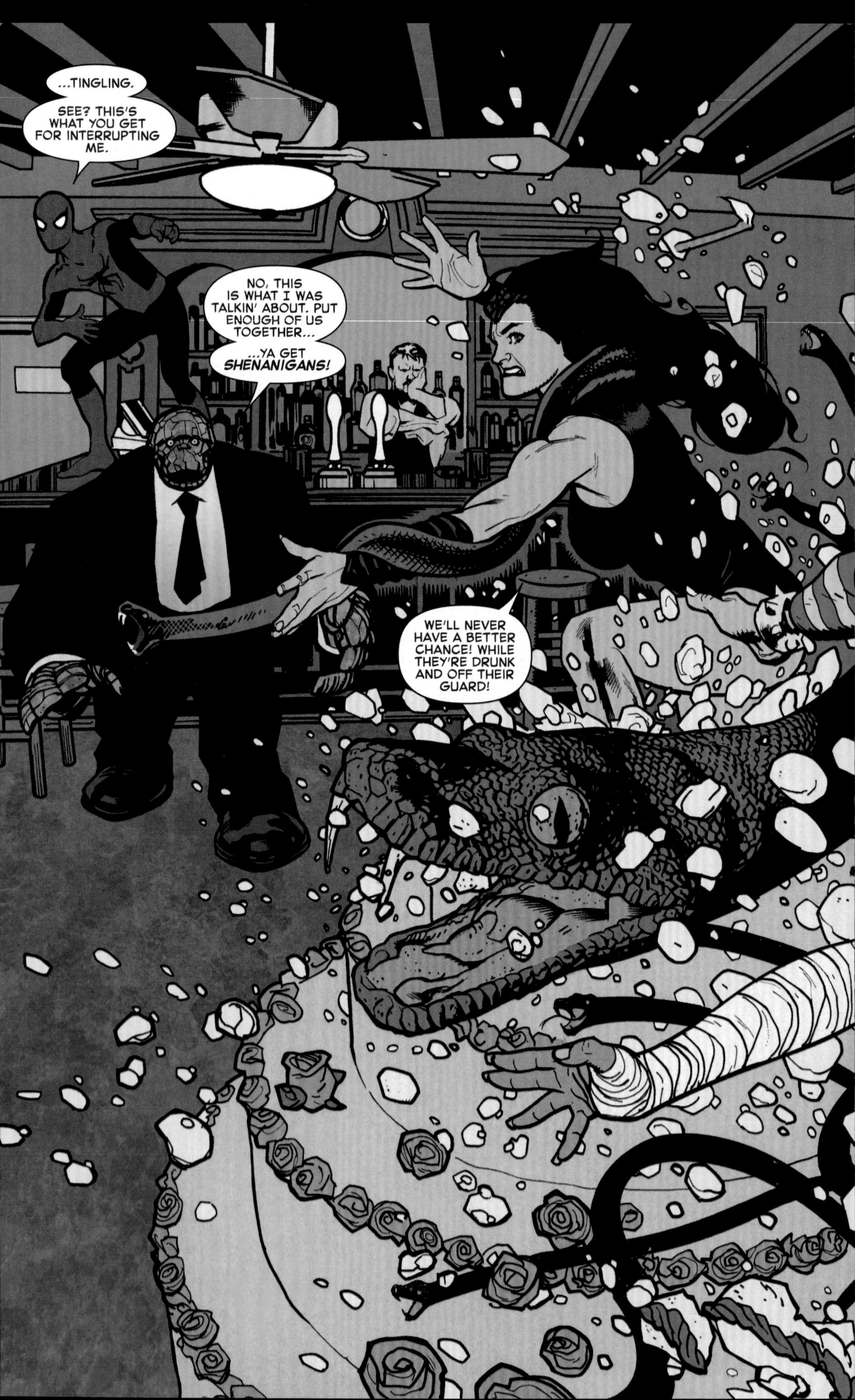
...TINGLING.
SEE? THIS'S WHAT YOU GET FOR INTERRUPTING ME.
NO, THIS IS WHAT I WAS TALKIN' ABOUT. PUT ENOUGH OF US TOGETHER...
...YA GET SHENANIGANS!
WE'LL NEVER HAVE A BETTER CHANCE! WHILE THEY'RE DRUNK AND OFF THEIR GUARD!

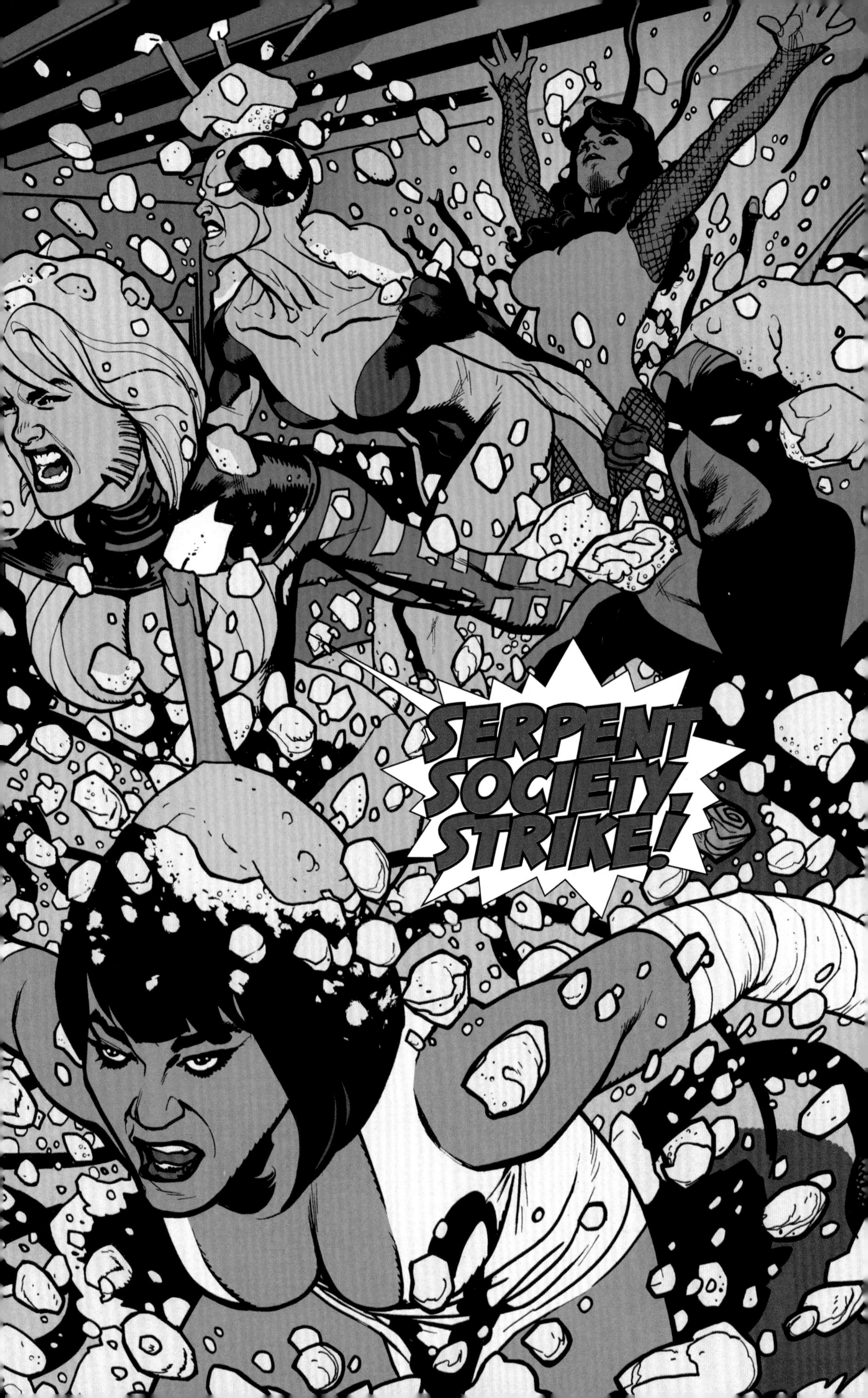
SERPENT SOCIETY, STRIKE!

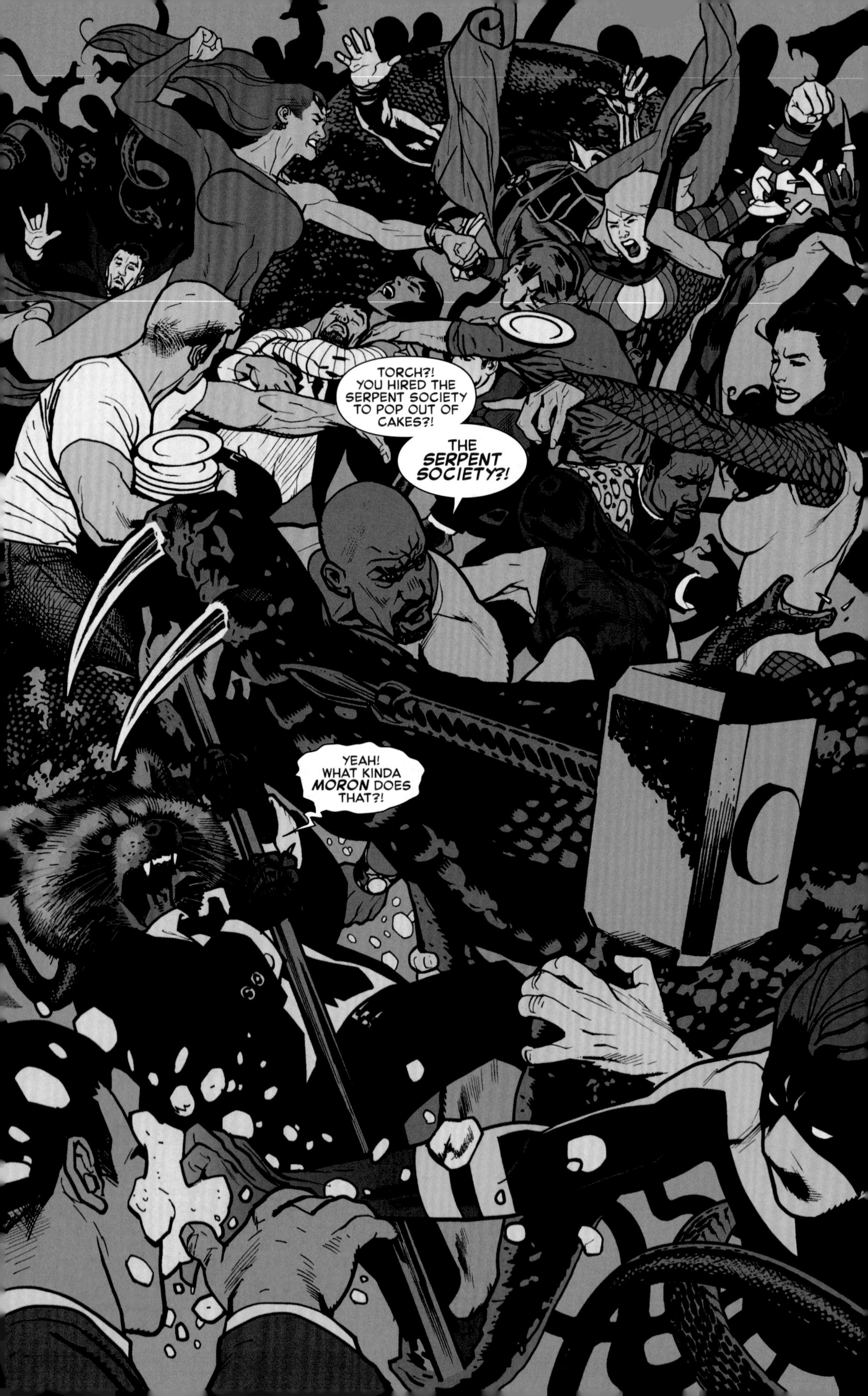
TORCH?! YOU HIRED THE SERPENT SOCIETY TO POP OUT OF CAKES?!
THE *SERPENT SOCIETY?!*
YEAH! WHAT KINDA *MORON* DOES THAT?!

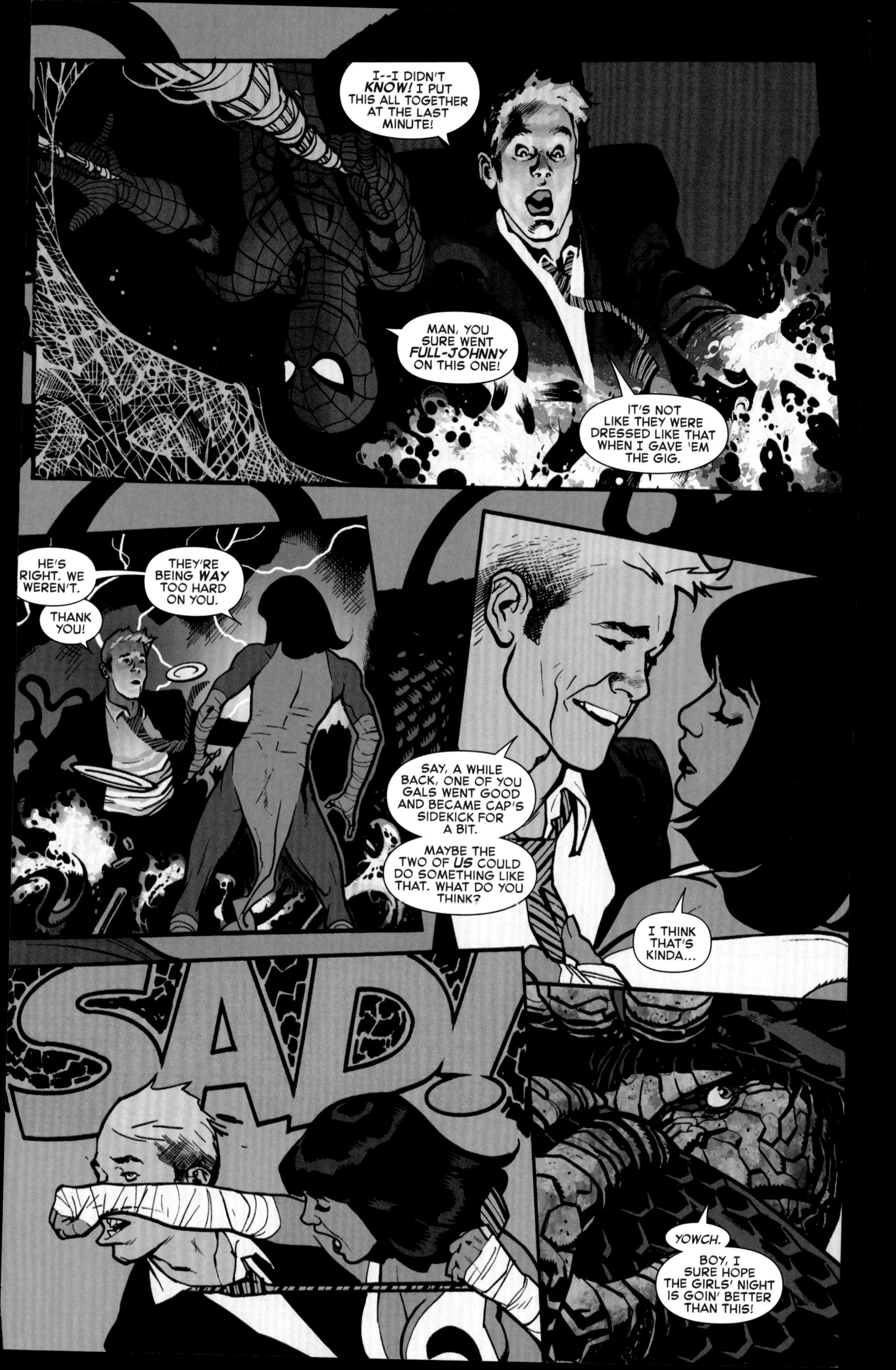
I--I DIDN'T KNOW! I PUT THIS ALL TOGETHER AT THE LAST MINUTE!
MAN, YOU SURE WENT FULL-JOHNNY ON THIS ONE!
IT'S NOT LIKE THEY WERE DRESSED LIKE THAT WHEN I GAVE 'EM THE GIG.
HE'S RIGHT. WE WEREN'T.
THEY'RE BEING WAY TOO HARD ON YOU.
THANK YOU!
SAY, A WHILE BACK, ONE OF YOU GALS WENT GOOD AND BECAME CAP'S SIDEKICK FOR A BIT.
MAYBE THE TWO OF US COULD DO SOMETHING LIKE THAT. WHAT DO YOU THINK?
I THINK THAT'S KINDA...
SAD!
YOWCH.
BOY, I SURE HOPE THE GIRLS' NIGHT IS GOIN' BETTER THAN THIS!

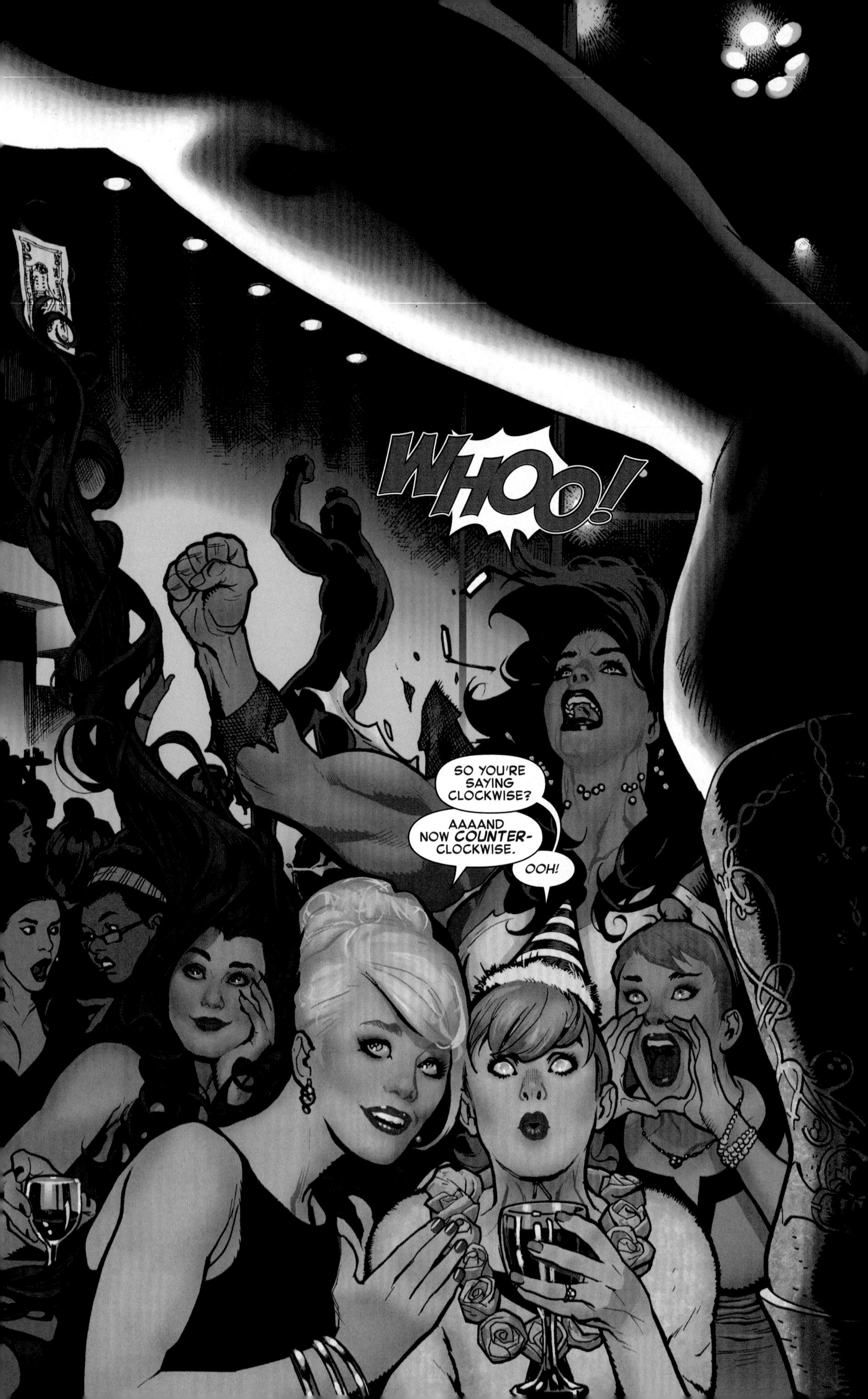
WHOO!
SO YOU'RE SAYING CLOCKWISE?
AAAAND NOW COUNTER-CLOCKWISE.
OOH!

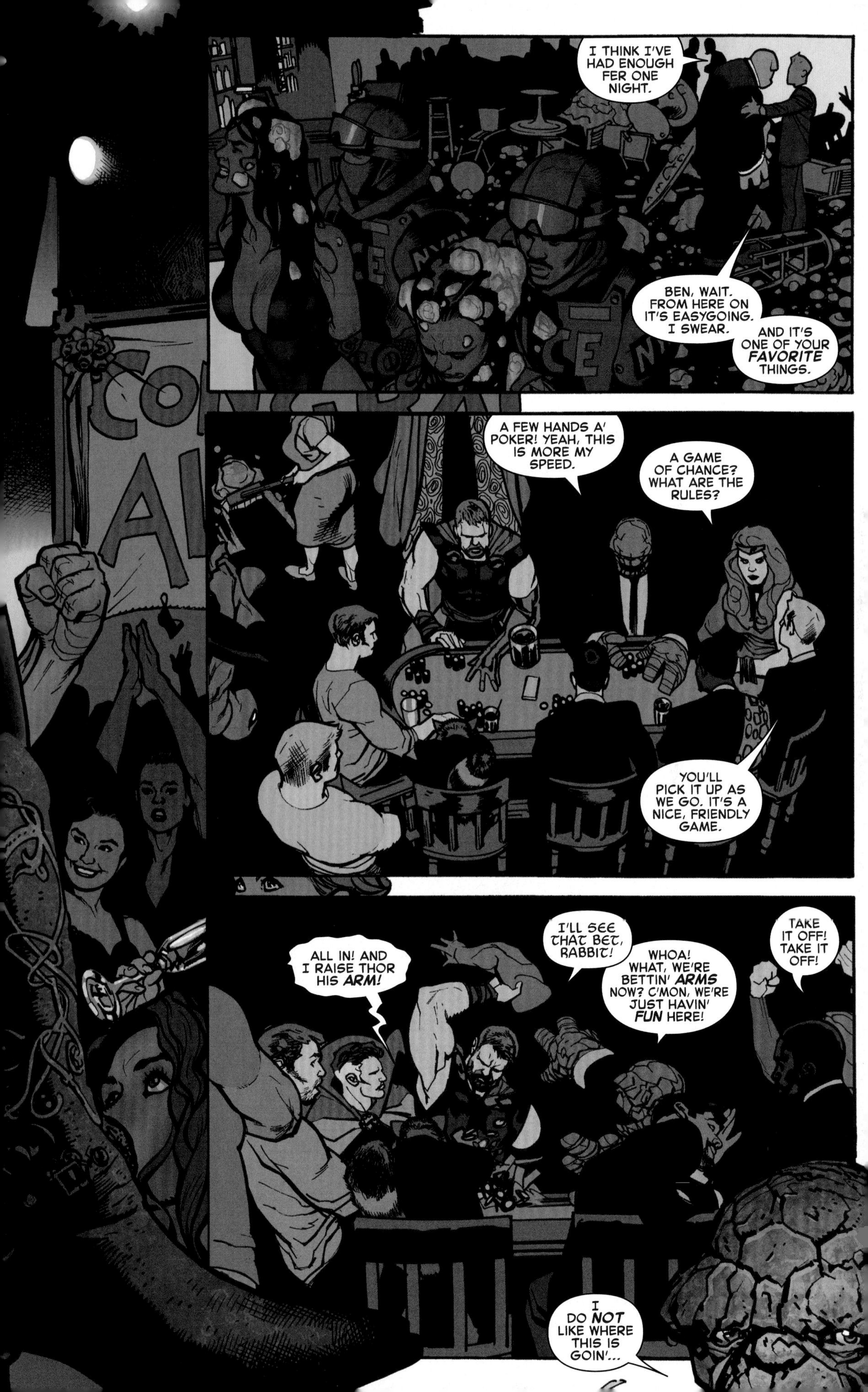
I THINK I'VE HAD ENOUGH FER ONE NIGHT.
BEN, WAIT. FROM HERE ON IT'S EASYGOING. I SWEAR.
AND IT'S ONE OF YOUR *FAVORITE* THINGS.
A FEW HANDS A' POKER! YEAH, THIS IS MORE MY SPEED.
A GAME OF CHANCE? WHAT ARE THE RULES?
YOU'LL PICK IT UP AS WE GO. IT'S A NICE, FRIENDLY GAME.
ALL IN! AND I RAISE THOR HIS *ARM!*
I'LL SEE THAT BET, RABBIT!
WHOA! WHAT, WE'RE BETTIN' *ARMS* NOW? C'MON, WE'RE JUST HAVIN' *FUN* HERE!
TAKE IT OFF! TAKE IT OFF!
I DO *NOT* LIKE WHERE THIS IS GOIN'...

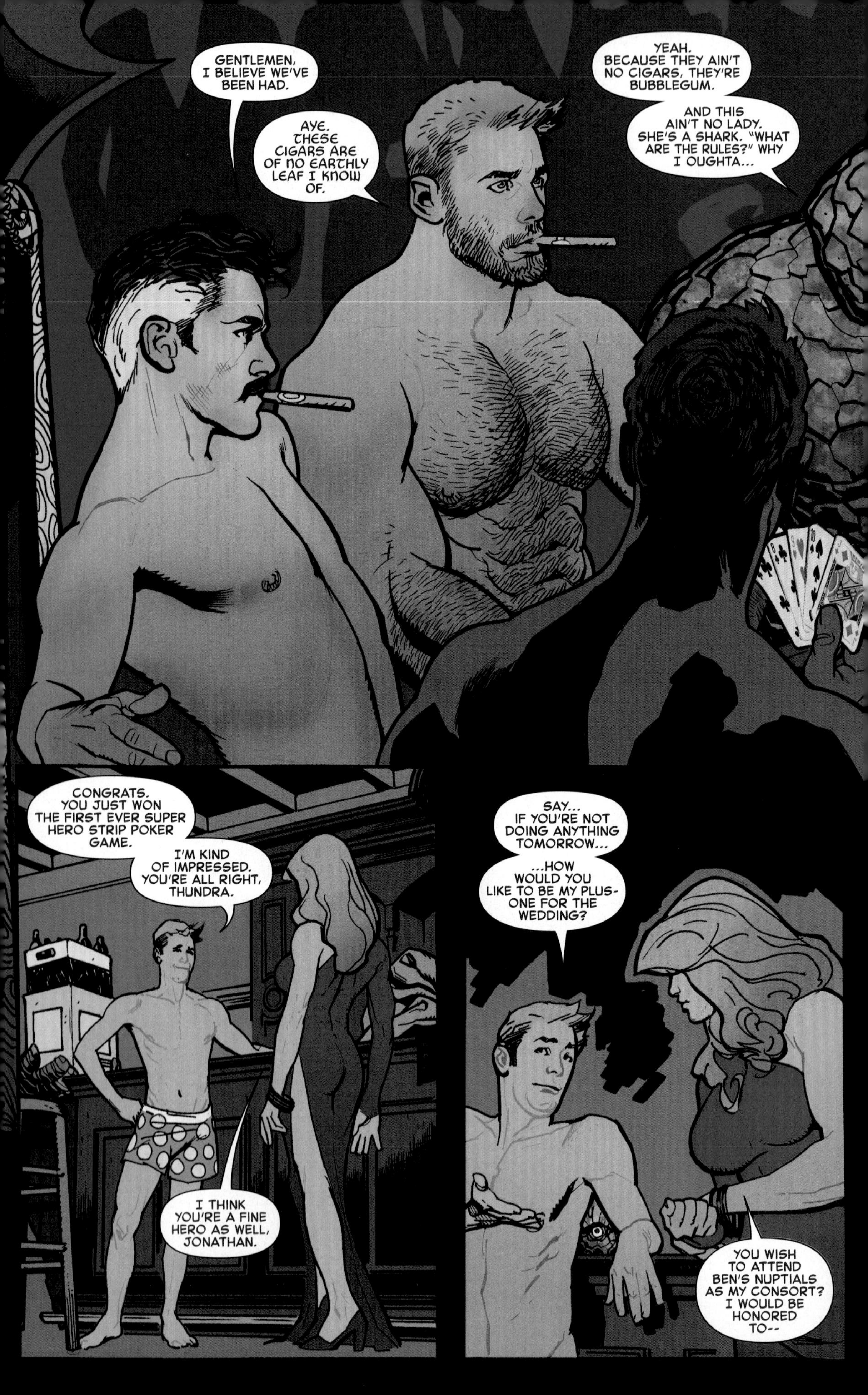
GENTLEMEN, I BELIEVE WE'VE BEEN HAD.
AYE. THESE CIGARS ARE OF NO EARTHLY LEAF I KNOW OF.
YEAH. BECAUSE THEY AIN'T NO CIGARS, THEY'RE BUBBLEGUM.
AND THIS AIN'T NO LADY. SHE'S A SHARK. "WHAT ARE THE RULES?" WHY I OUGHTA...
CONGRATS. YOU JUST WON THE FIRST EVER SUPER HERO STRIP POKER GAME.
I'M KIND OF IMPRESSED. YOU'RE ALL RIGHT, THUNDRA.
I THINK YOU'RE A FINE HERO AS WELL, JONATHAN.
SAY... IF YOU'RE NOT DOING ANYTHING TOMORROW...
...HOW WOULD YOU LIKE TO BE MY PLUS-ONE FOR THE WEDDING?
YOU WISH TO ATTEND BEN'S NUPTIALS AS MY CONSORT? I WOULD BE HONORED TO--

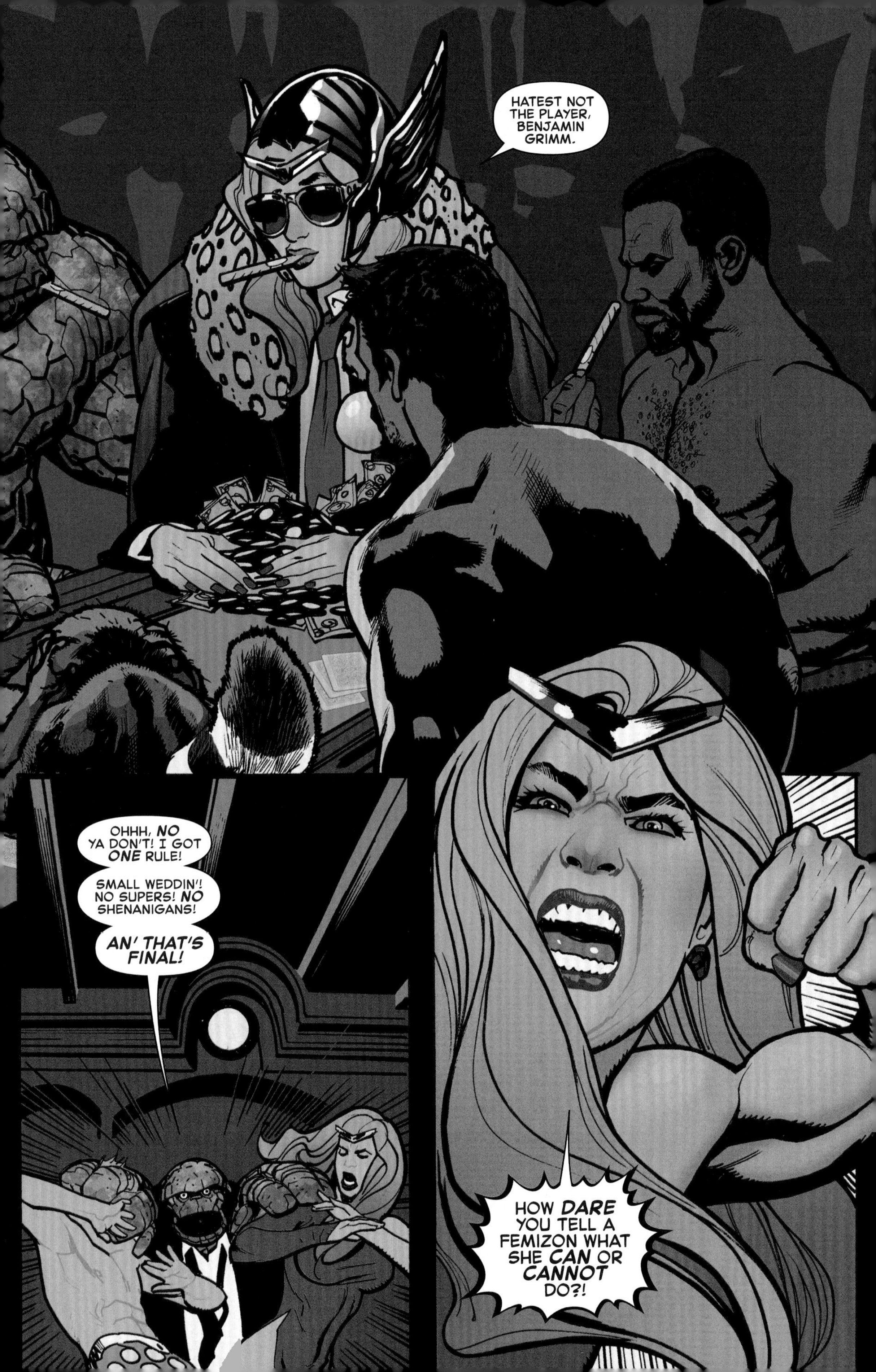
HATEST NOT THE PLAYER, BENJAMIN GRIMM.
OHHH, NO YA DON'T! I GOT ONE RULE!
SMALL WEDDIN'! NO SUPERS! NO SHENANIGANS!
AN' THAT'S FINAL!
HOW DARE YOU TELL A FEMIZON WHAT SHE CAN OR CANNOT DO?!

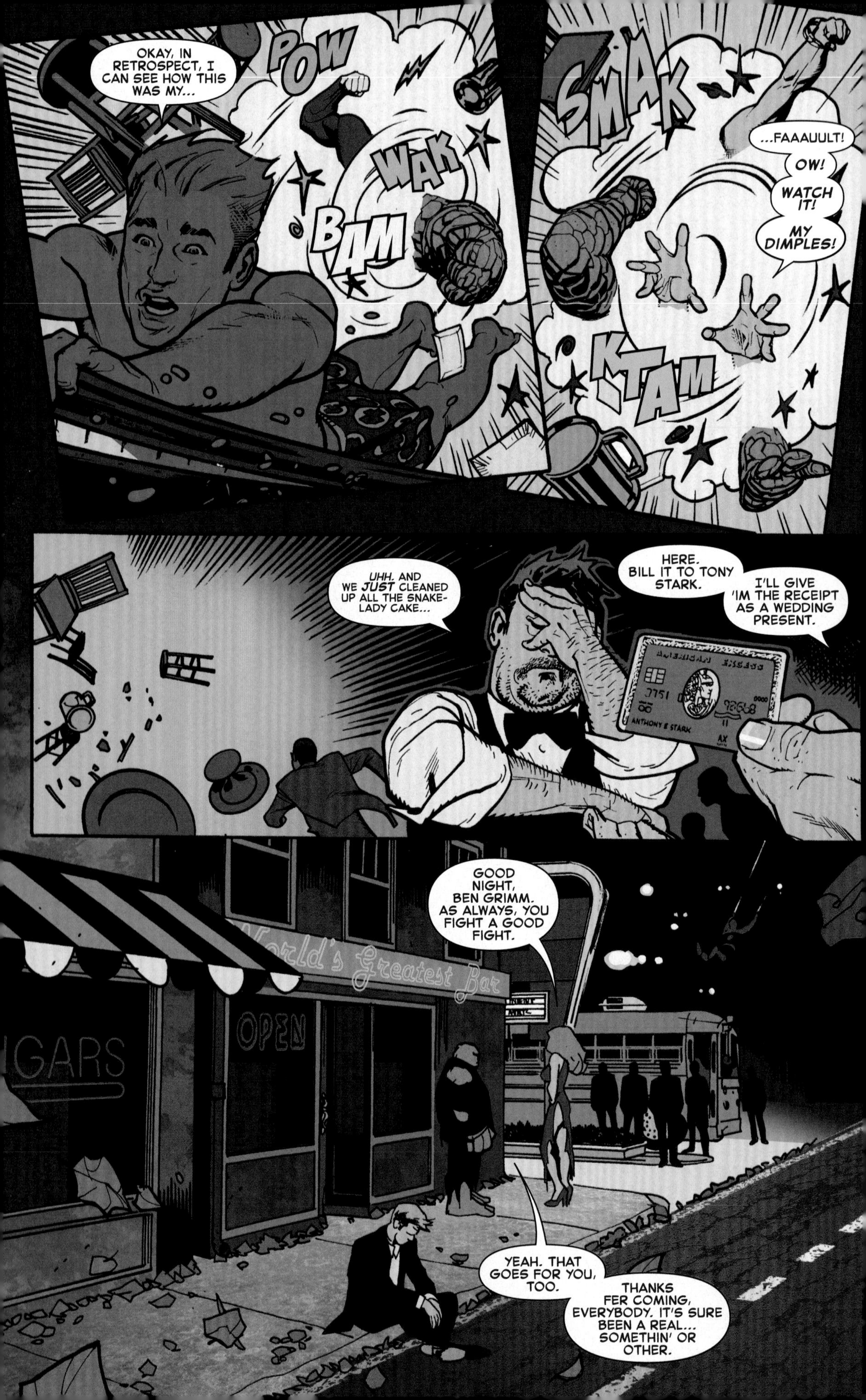
OKAY, IN RETROSPECT, I CAN SEE HOW THIS WAS MY...
POW
WAK
BAM
SMAK
...FAAAUULT!
OW!
WATCH IT!
MY DIMPLES!
KTAM
UHH. AND WE JUST CLEANED UP ALL THE SNAKE-LADY CAKE...
HERE. BILL IT TO TONY STARK.
I'LL GIVE 'IM THE RECEIPT AS A WEDDING PRESENT.
AMERICAN EXPRESS
ANTHONY E STARK
World's Greatest Bar
OPEN
GARS
GOOD NIGHT, BEN GRIMM. AS ALWAYS, YOU FIGHT A GOOD FIGHT.
YEAH. THAT GOES FOR YOU, TOO.
THANKS FER COMING, EVERYBODY. IT'S SURE BEEN A REAL... SOMETHIN' OR OTHER.

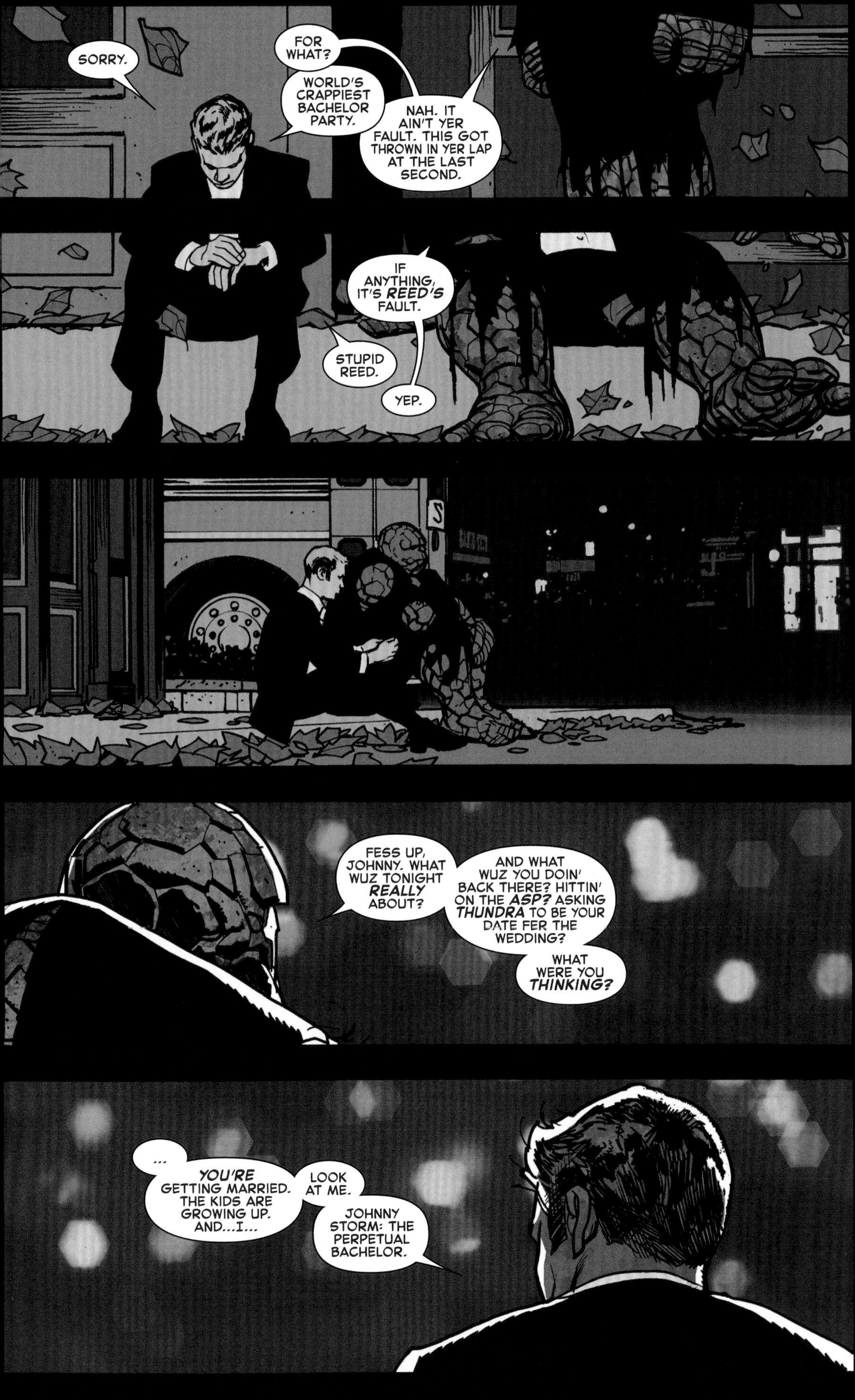
SORRY.
FOR WHAT?
WORLD'S CRAPPIEST BACHELOR PARTY.
NAH. IT AIN'T YER FAULT. THIS GOT THROWN IN YER LAP AT THE LAST SECOND.
IF ANYTHING, IT'S REED'S FAULT.
STUPID REED.
YEP.
FESS UP, JOHNNY. WHAT WUZ TONIGHT REALLY ABOUT?
AND WHAT WUZ YOU DOIN' BACK THERE? HITTIN' ON THE ASP? ASKING THUNDRA TO BE YOUR DATE FER THE WEDDING?
WHAT WERE YOU THINKING?
...
YOU'RE GETTING MARRIED. THE KIDS ARE GROWING UP. AND...I...
LOOK AT ME.
JOHNNY STORM: THE PERPETUAL BACHELOR.

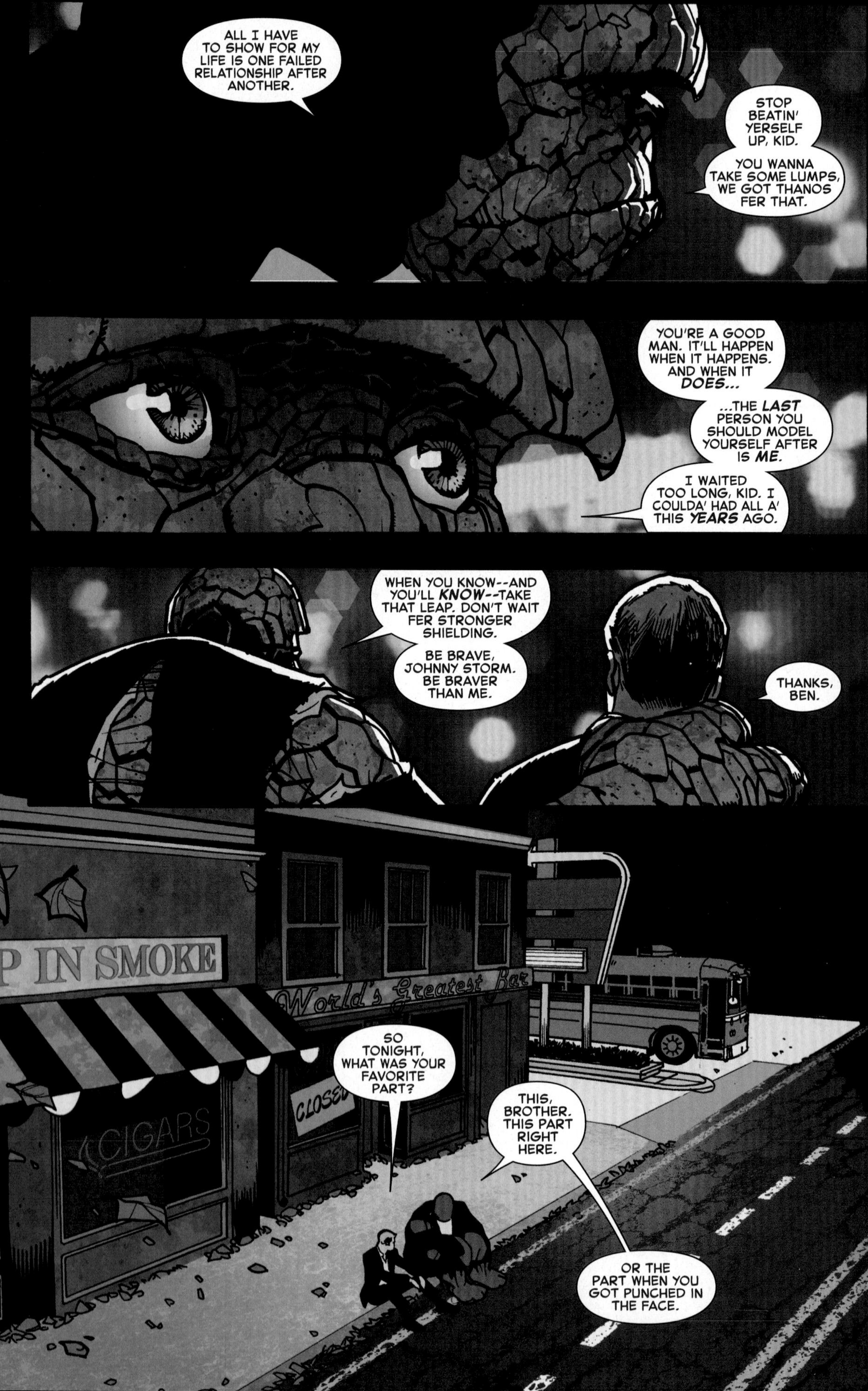
ALL I HAVE TO SHOW FOR MY LIFE IS ONE FAILED RELATIONSHIP AFTER ANOTHER.
STOP BEATIN' YERSELF UP, KID.
YOU WANNA TAKE SOME LUMPS, WE GOT THANOS FER THAT.
YOU'RE A GOOD MAN. IT'LL HAPPEN WHEN IT HAPPENS. AND WHEN IT DOES...
...THE LAST PERSON YOU SHOULD MODEL YOURSELF AFTER IS ME.
I WAITED TOO LONG, KID. I COULDA' HAD ALL A' THIS YEARS AGO.
WHEN YOU KNOW--AND YOU'LL KNOW--TAKE THAT LEAP. DON'T WAIT FER STRONGER SHIELDING.
BE BRAVE, JOHNNY STORM. BE BRAVER THAN ME.
THANKS, BEN.
P IN SMOKE
World's Greatest Bar
CIGARS
CLOSED
SO TONIGHT, WHAT WAS YOUR FAVORITE PART?
THIS, BROTHER. THIS PART RIGHT HERE.
OR THE PART WHEN YOU GOT PUNCHED IN THE FACE.

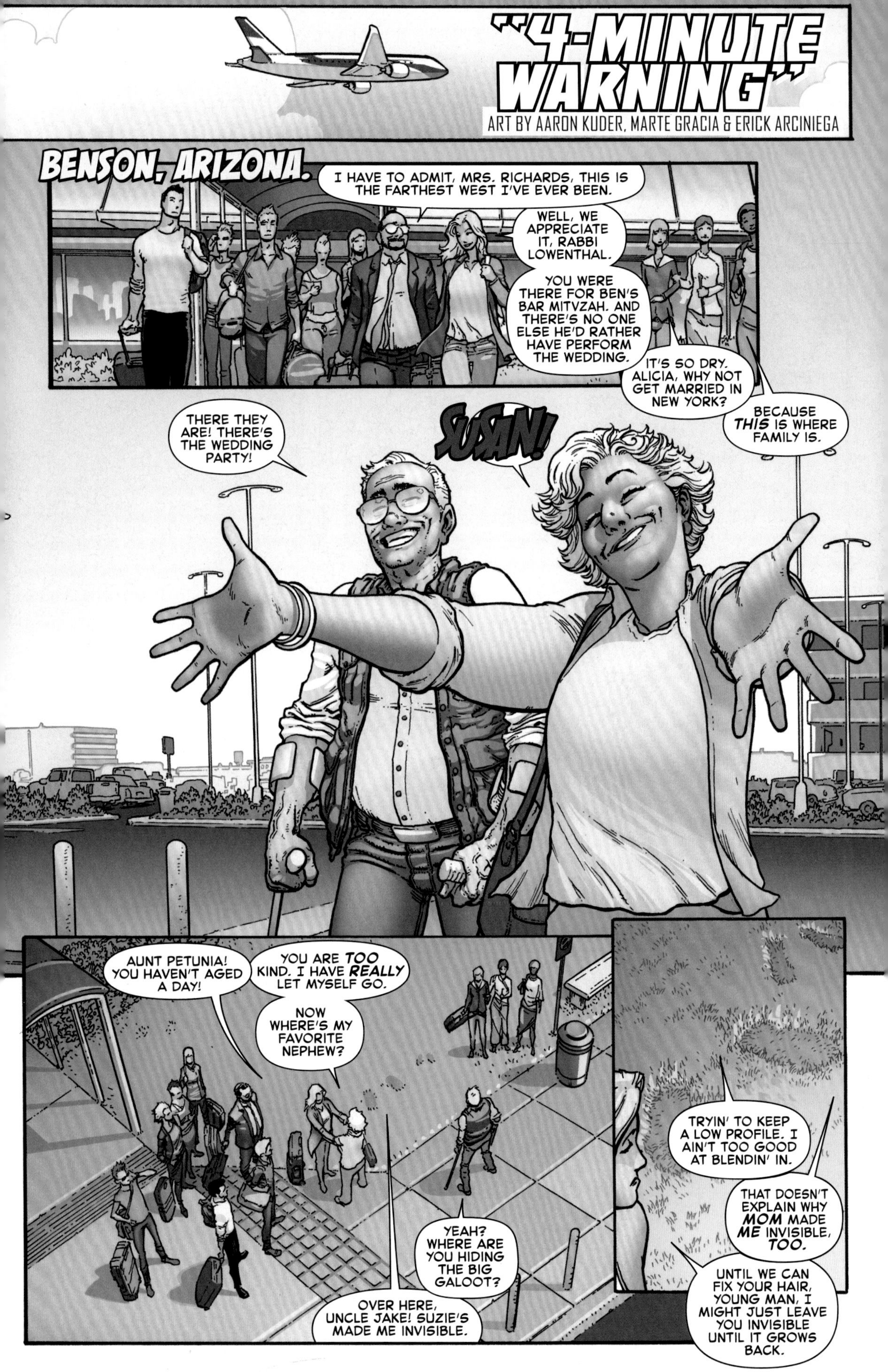
"4-MINUTE WARNING"
ART BY AARON KUDER, MARTE GRACIA & ERICK ARCINIEGA
BENSON, ARIZONA.
I HAVE TO ADMIT, MRS. RICHARDS, THIS IS THE FARTHEST WEST I'VE EVER BEEN.
WELL, WE APPRECIATE IT, RABBI LOWENTHAL.
YOU WERE THERE FOR BEN'S BAR MITVZAH. AND THERE'S NO ONE ELSE HE'D RATHER HAVE PERFORM THE WEDDING.
IT'S SO DRY. ALICIA, WHY NOT GET MARRIED IN NEW YORK?
BECAUSE *THIS* IS WHERE FAMILY IS.
THERE THEY ARE! THERE'S THE WEDDING PARTY!
SUSAN!
AUNT PETUNIA! YOU HAVEN'T AGED A DAY!
YOU ARE *TOO* KIND. I HAVE *REALLY* LET MYSELF GO.
NOW WHERE'S MY FAVORITE NEPHEW?
YEAH? WHERE ARE YOU HIDING THE BIG GALOOT?
OVER HERE, UNCLE JAKE! SUZIE'S MADE ME INVISIBLE.
TRYIN' TO KEEP A LOW PROFILE. I AIN'T TOO GOOD AT BLENDIN' IN.
THAT DOESN'T EXPLAIN WHY *MOM* MADE *ME* INVISIBLE, *TOO.*
UNTIL WE CAN FIX YOUR HAIR, YOUNG MAN, I MIGHT JUST LEAVE YOU INVISIBLE UNTIL IT GROWS BACK.

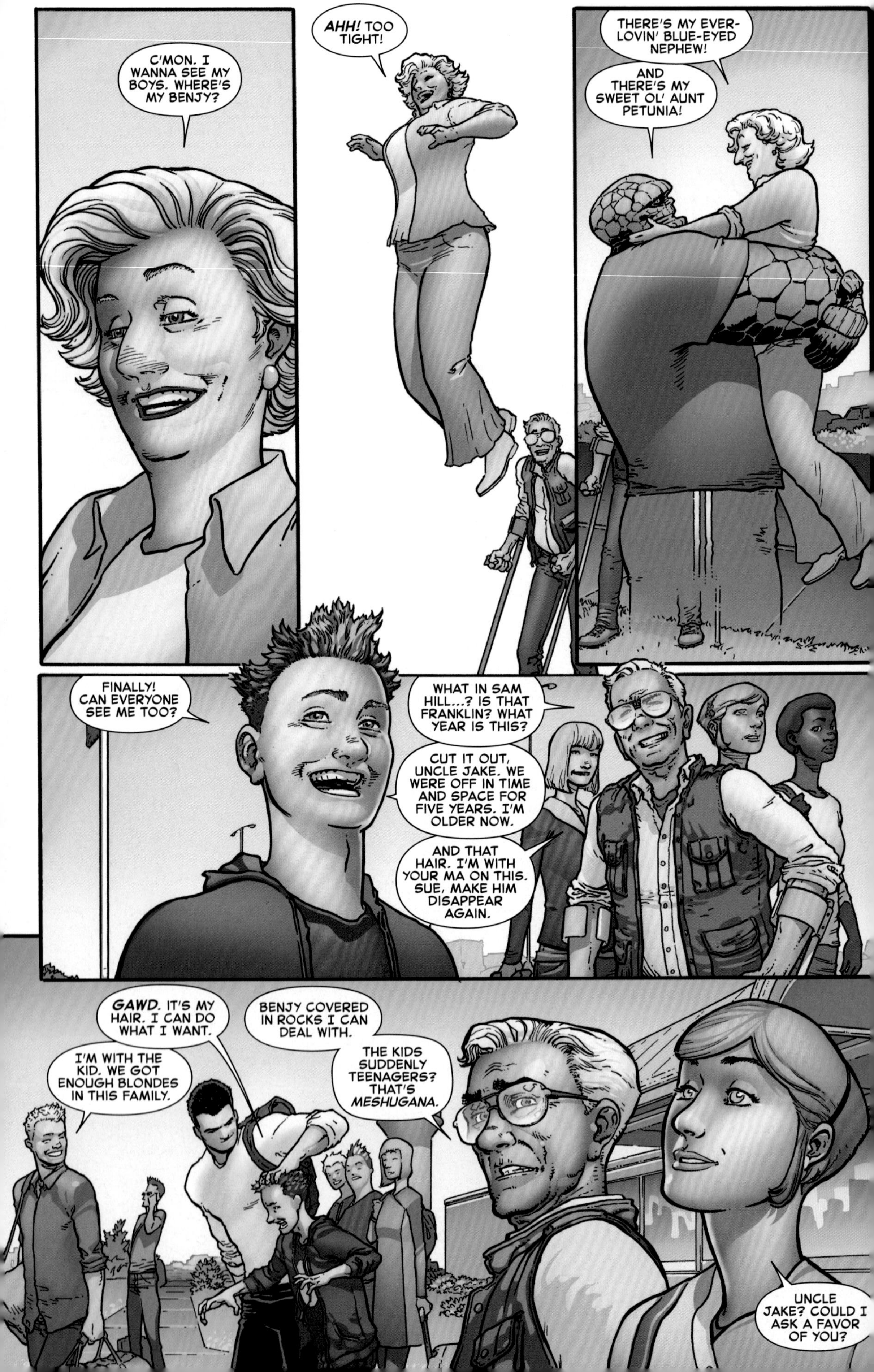
C'MON. I WANNA SEE MY BOYS. WHERE'S MY BENJY?
AHH! TOO TIGHT!
THERE'S MY EVER-LOVIN' BLUE-EYED NEPHEW!
AND THERE'S MY SWEET OL' AUNT PETUNIA!
FINALLY! CAN EVERYONE SEE ME TOO?
WHAT IN SAM HILL...? IS THAT FRANKLIN? WHAT YEAR IS THIS?
CUT IT OUT, UNCLE JAKE. WE WERE OFF IN TIME AND SPACE FOR FIVE YEARS. I'M OLDER NOW.
AND THAT HAIR. I'M WITH YOUR MA ON THIS. SUE, MAKE HIM DISAPPEAR AGAIN.
GAWD. IT'S MY HAIR. I CAN DO WHAT I WANT.
I'M WITH THE KID. WE GOT ENOUGH BLONDES IN THIS FAMILY.
BENJY COVERED IN ROCKS I CAN DEAL WITH.
THE KIDS SUDDENLY TEENAGERS? THAT'S MESHUGANA.
UNCLE JAKE? COULD I ASK A FAVOR OF YOU?

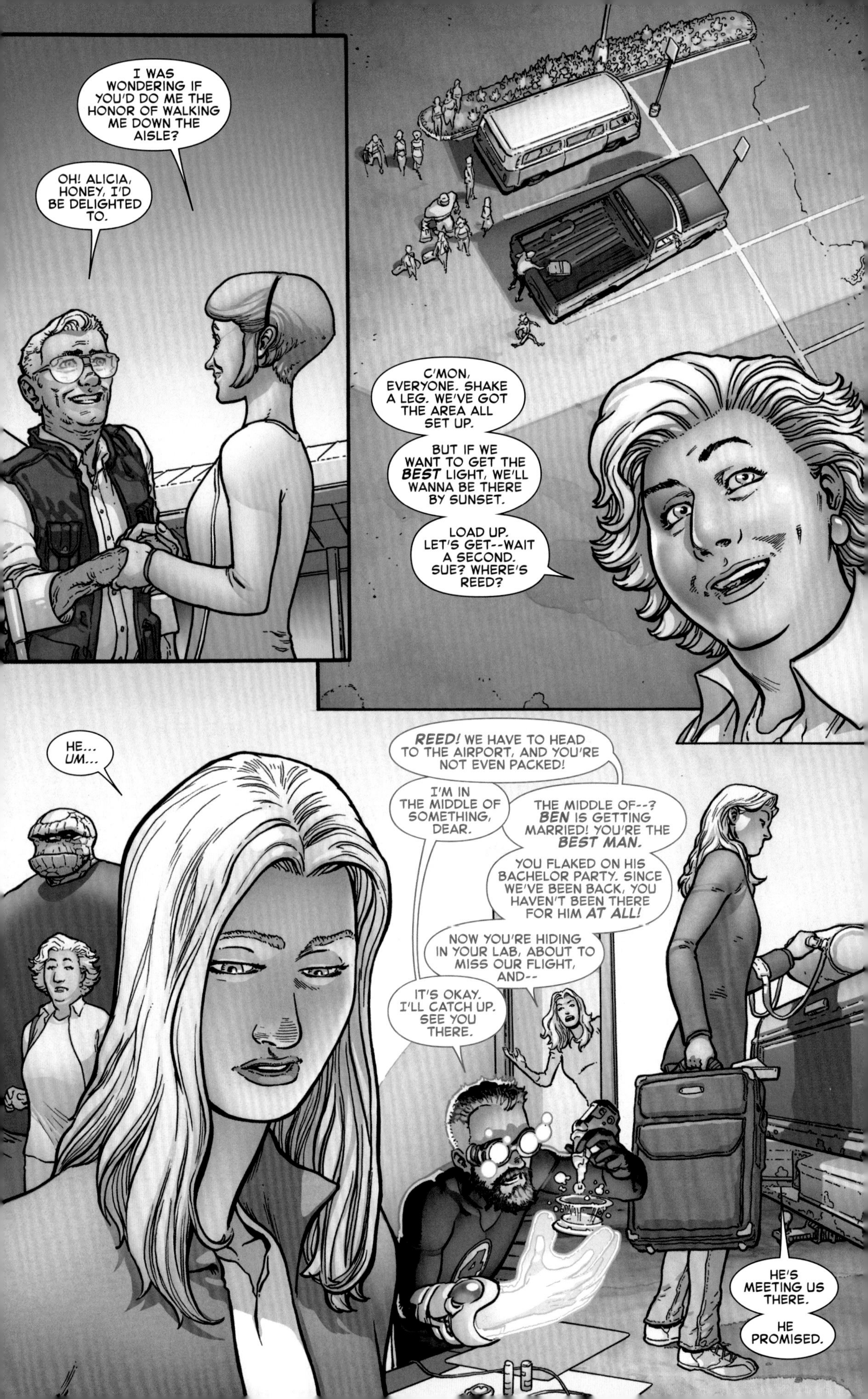
I WAS WONDERING IF YOU'D DO ME THE HONOR OF WALKING ME DOWN THE AISLE?
OH! ALICIA, HONEY, I'D BE DELIGHTED TO.
C'MON, EVERYONE. SHAKE A LEG. WE'VE GOT THE AREA ALL SET UP.
BUT IF WE WANT TO GET THE BEST LIGHT, WE'LL WANNA BE THERE BY SUNSET.
LOAD UP. LET'S GET--WAIT A SECOND. SUE? WHERE'S REED?
HE... UM...
REED! WE HAVE TO HEAD TO THE AIRPORT, AND YOU'RE NOT EVEN PACKED!
I'M IN THE MIDDLE OF SOMETHING, DEAR.
THE MIDDLE OF--? BEN IS GETTING MARRIED! YOU'RE THE BEST MAN.
YOU FLAKED ON HIS BACHELOR PARTY. SINCE WE'VE BEEN BACK, YOU HAVEN'T BEEN THERE FOR HIM AT ALL!
NOW YOU'RE HIDING IN YOUR LAB, ABOUT TO MISS OUR FLIGHT, AND--
IT'S OKAY. I'LL CATCH UP. SEE YOU THERE.
HE'S MEETING US THERE.
HE PROMISED.

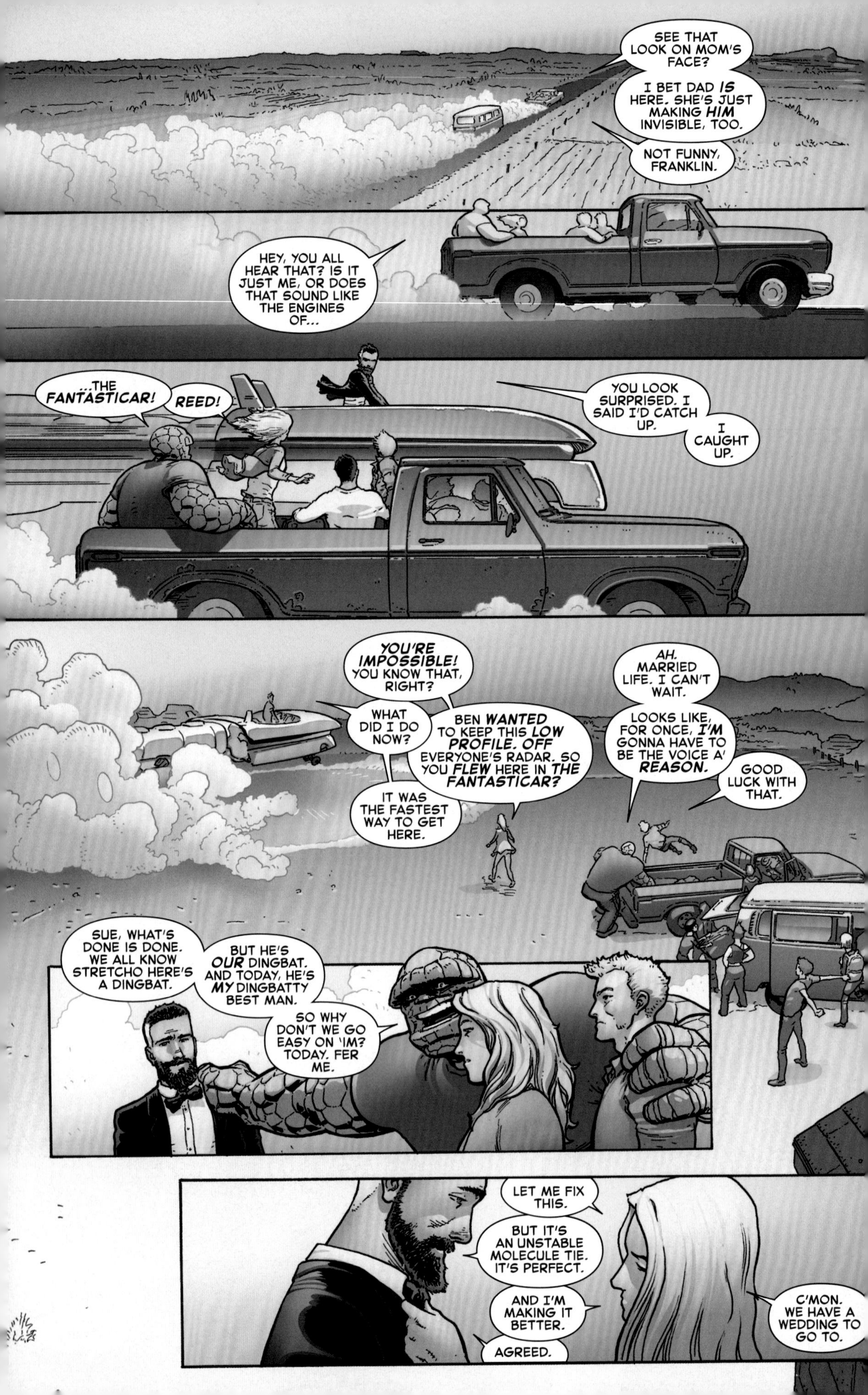

SEE THAT LOOK ON MOM'S FACE?
I BET DAD *IS* HERE. SHE'S JUST MAKING *HIM* INVISIBLE, TOO.
NOT FUNNY, FRANKLIN.
HEY, YOU ALL HEAR THAT? IS IT JUST ME, OR DOES THAT SOUND LIKE THE ENGINES OF...
...THE *FANTASTICAR!*
REED!
YOU LOOK SURPRISED. I SAID I'D CATCH UP.
I CAUGHT UP.
YOU'RE IMPOSSIBLE! YOU KNOW THAT, RIGHT?
WHAT DID I DO NOW?
BEN *WANTED* TO KEEP THIS *LOW PROFILE. OFF* EVERYONE'S RADAR. SO YOU *FLEW* HERE IN *THE FANTASTICAR?*
IT WAS THE FASTEST WAY TO GET HERE.
AH. MARRIED LIFE. I CAN'T WAIT.
LOOKS LIKE, FOR ONCE, *I'M* GONNA HAVE TO BE THE VOICE A' *REASON.*
GOOD LUCK WITH THAT.
SUE, WHAT'S DONE IS DONE. WE ALL KNOW STRETCHO HERE'S A DINGBAT.
BUT HE'S *OUR* DINGBAT. AND TODAY, HE'S *MY* DINGBATTY BEST MAN.
SO WHY DON'T WE GO EASY ON 'IM? TODAY. FER ME.
LET ME FIX THIS.
BUT IT'S AN UNSTABLE MOLECULE TIE. IT'S PERFECT.
AND I'M MAKING IT BETTER.
AGREED.
C'MON. WE HAVE A WEDDING TO GO TO.

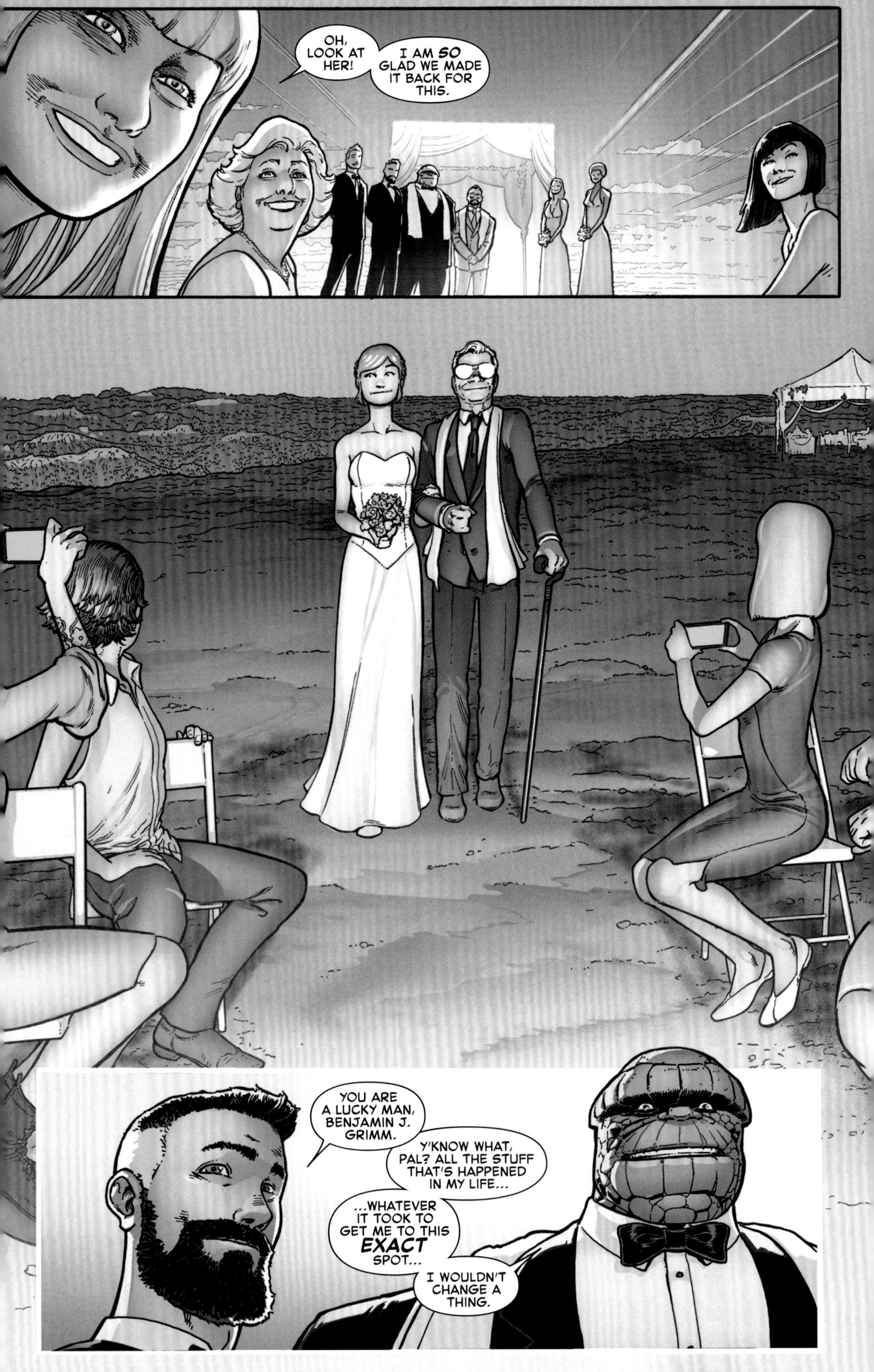
OH, LOOK AT HER!
I AM SO GLAD WE MADE IT BACK FOR THIS.
YOU ARE A LUCKY MAN, BENJAMIN J. GRIMM.
Y'KNOW WHAT, PAL? ALL THE STUFF THAT'S HAPPENED IN MY LIFE...
...WHATEVER IT TOOK TO GET ME TO THIS EXACT SPOT...
I WOULDN'T CHANGE A THING.

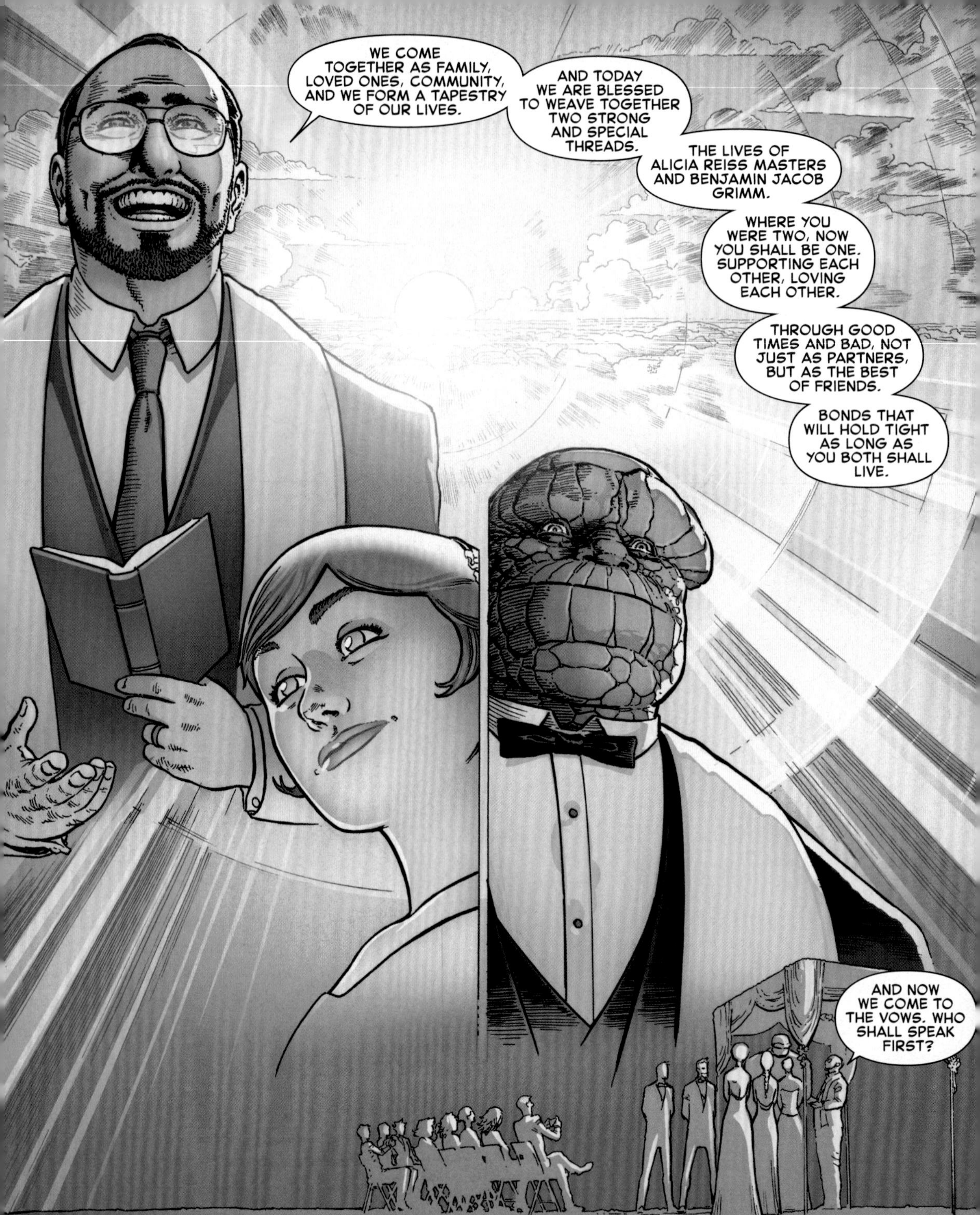
WE COME TOGETHER AS FAMILY, LOVED ONES, COMMUNITY, AND WE FORM A TAPESTRY OF OUR LIVES.
AND TODAY WE ARE BLESSED TO WEAVE TOGETHER TWO STRONG AND SPECIAL THREADS.
THE LIVES OF ALICIA REISS MASTERS AND BENJAMIN JACOB GRIMM.
WHERE YOU WERE TWO, NOW YOU SHALL BE ONE. SUPPORTING EACH OTHER, LOVING EACH OTHER.
THROUGH GOOD TIMES AND BAD, NOT JUST AS PARTNERS, BUT AS THE BEST OF FRIENDS.
BONDS THAT WILL HOLD TIGHT AS LONG AS YOU BOTH SHALL LIVE.
AND NOW WE COME TO THE VOWS. WHO SHALL SPEAK FIRST?

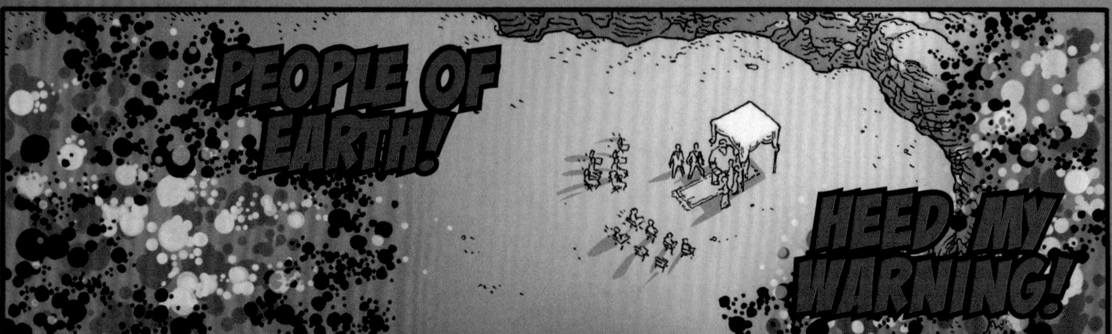
PEOPLE OF EARTH!
HEED MY WARNING!

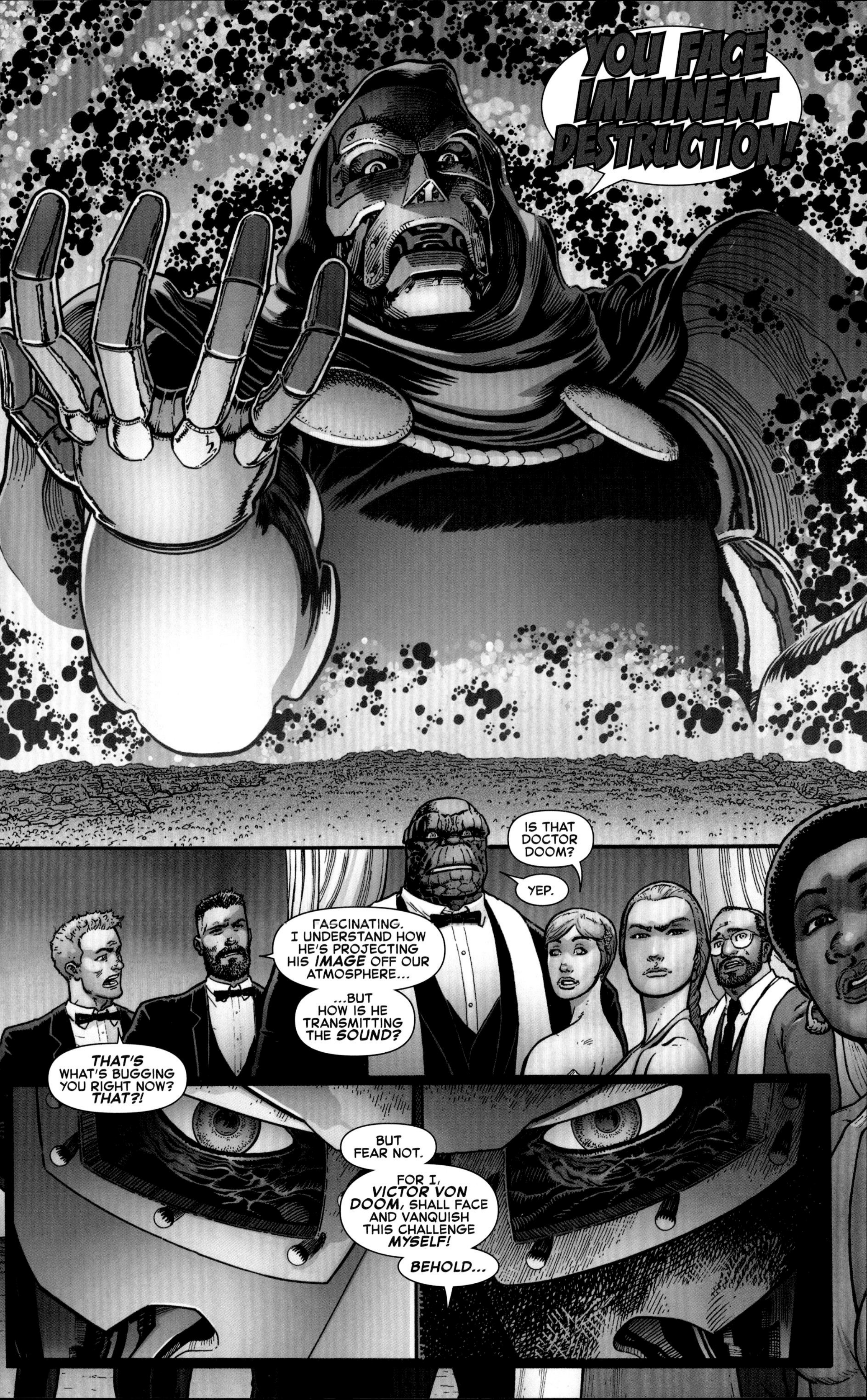
YOU FACE IMMINENT DESTRUCTION!
IS THAT DOCTOR DOOM?
YEP.
FASCINATING. I UNDERSTAND HOW HE'S PROJECTING HIS *IMAGE* OFF OUR ATMOSPHERE...
...BUT HOW IS HE TRANSMITTING THE *SOUND?*
THAT'S WHAT'S BUGGING YOU RIGHT NOW? *THAT?!*
BUT FEAR NOT.
FOR I, *VICTOR VON DOOM,* SHALL FACE AND VANQUISH THIS CHALLENGE *MYSELF!*
BEHOLD...

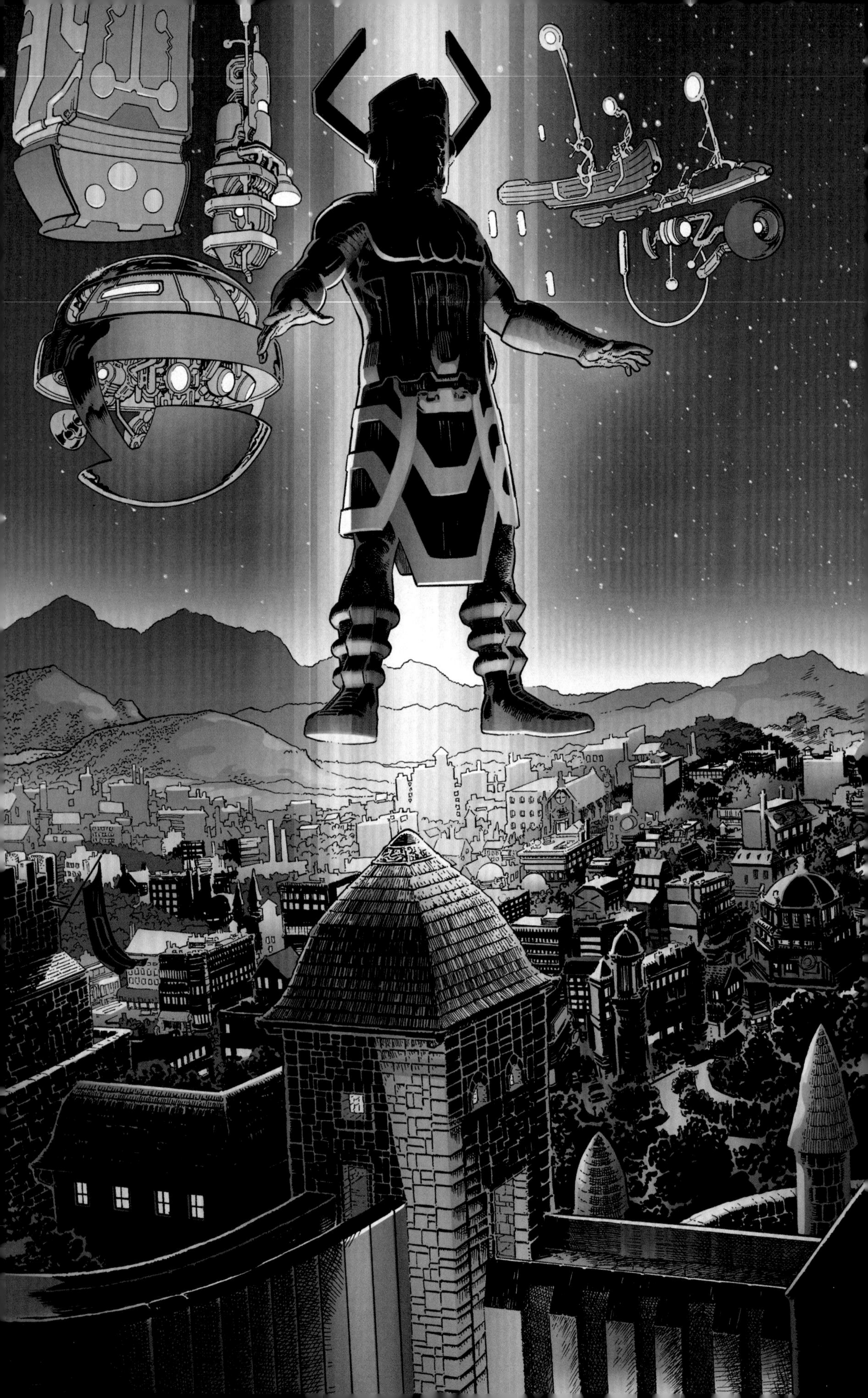

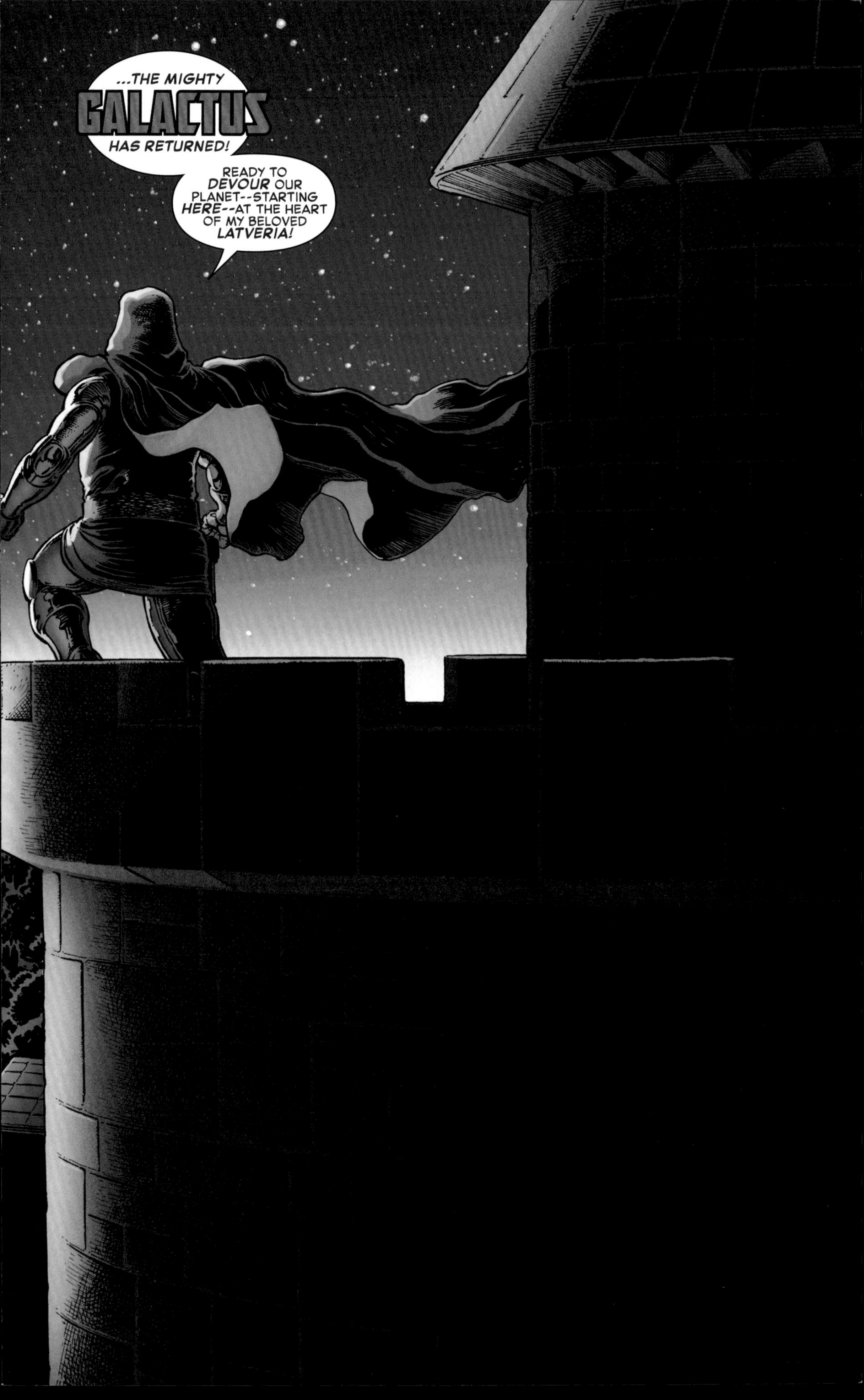
...THE MIGHTY GALACTUS HAS RETURNED!
READY TO DEVOUR OUR PLANET--STARTING HERE--AT THE HEART OF MY BELOVED LATVERIA!

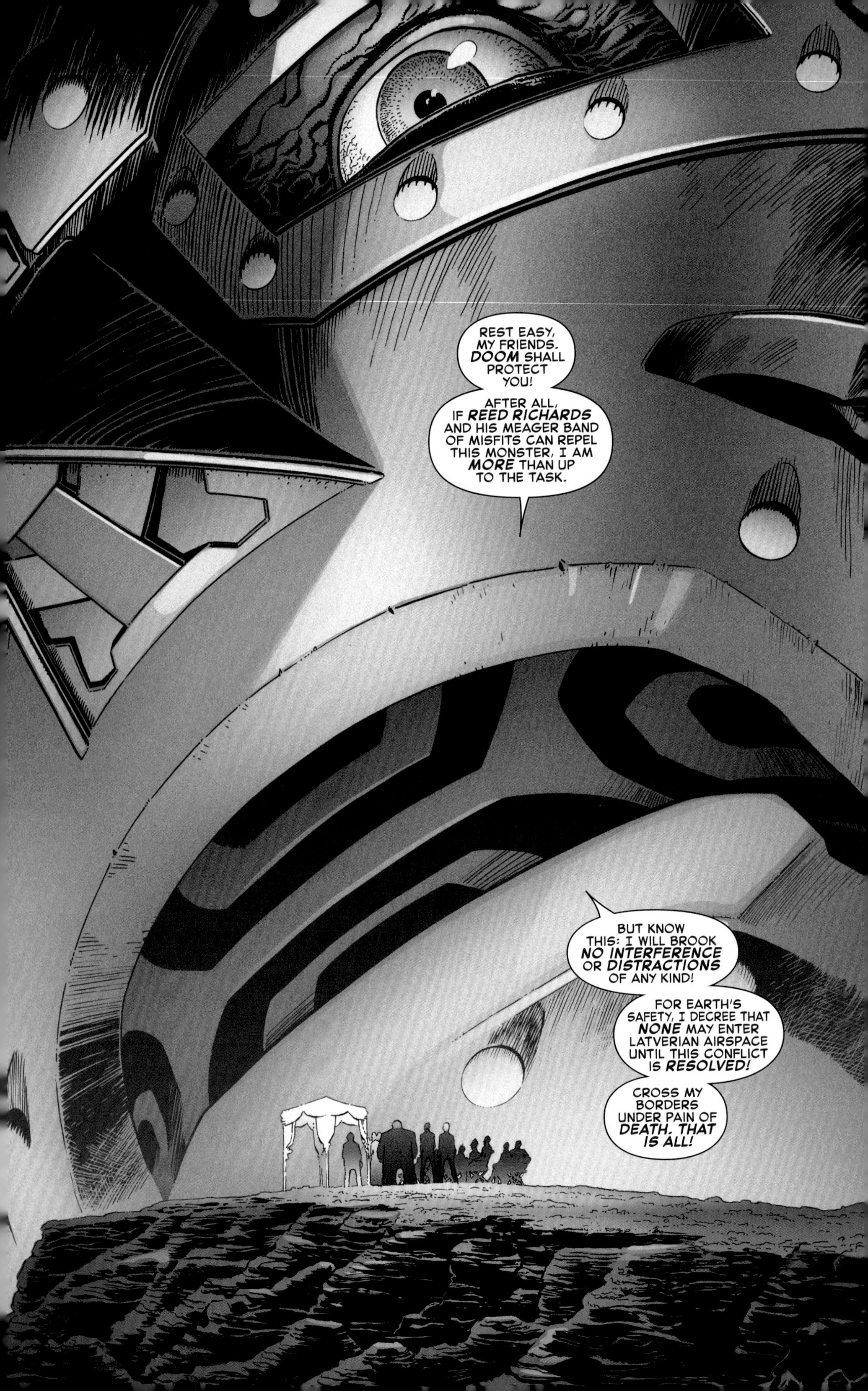

REST EASY, MY FRIENDS. DOOM SHALL PROTECT YOU!
AFTER ALL, IF REED RICHARDS AND HIS MEAGER BAND OF MISFITS CAN REPEL THIS MONSTER, I AM MORE THAN UP TO THE TASK.
BUT KNOW THIS: I WILL BROOK NO INTERFERENCE OR DISTRACTIONS OF ANY KIND!
FOR EARTH'S SAFETY, I DECREE THAT NONE MAY ENTER LATVERIAN AIRSPACE UNTIL THIS CONFLICT IS RESOLVED!
CROSS MY BORDERS UNDER PAIN OF DEATH. THAT IS ALL!

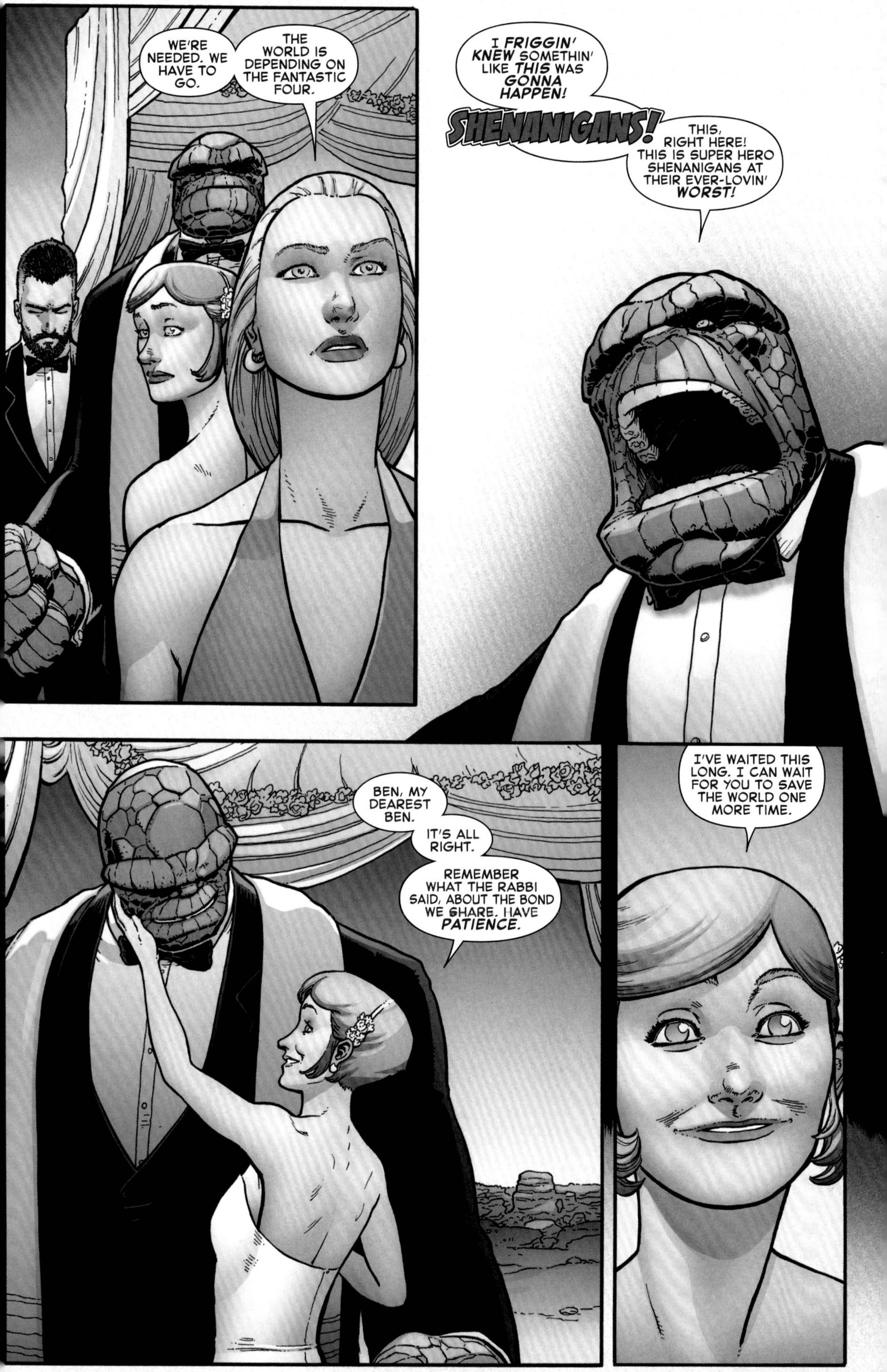
WE'RE NEEDED. WE HAVE TO GO.
THE WORLD IS DEPENDING ON THE FANTASTIC FOUR.
I FRIGGIN' KNEW SOMETHIN' LIKE THIS WAS GONNA HAPPEN!
SHENANIGANS!
THIS, RIGHT HERE! THIS IS SUPER HERO SHENANIGANS AT THEIR EVER-LOVIN' WORST!
BEN, MY DEAREST BEN.
IT'S ALL RIGHT.
REMEMBER WHAT THE RABBI SAID, ABOUT THE BOND WE SHARE. HAVE PATIENCE.
I'VE WAITED THIS LONG. I CAN WAIT FOR YOU TO SAVE THE WORLD ONE MORE TIME.

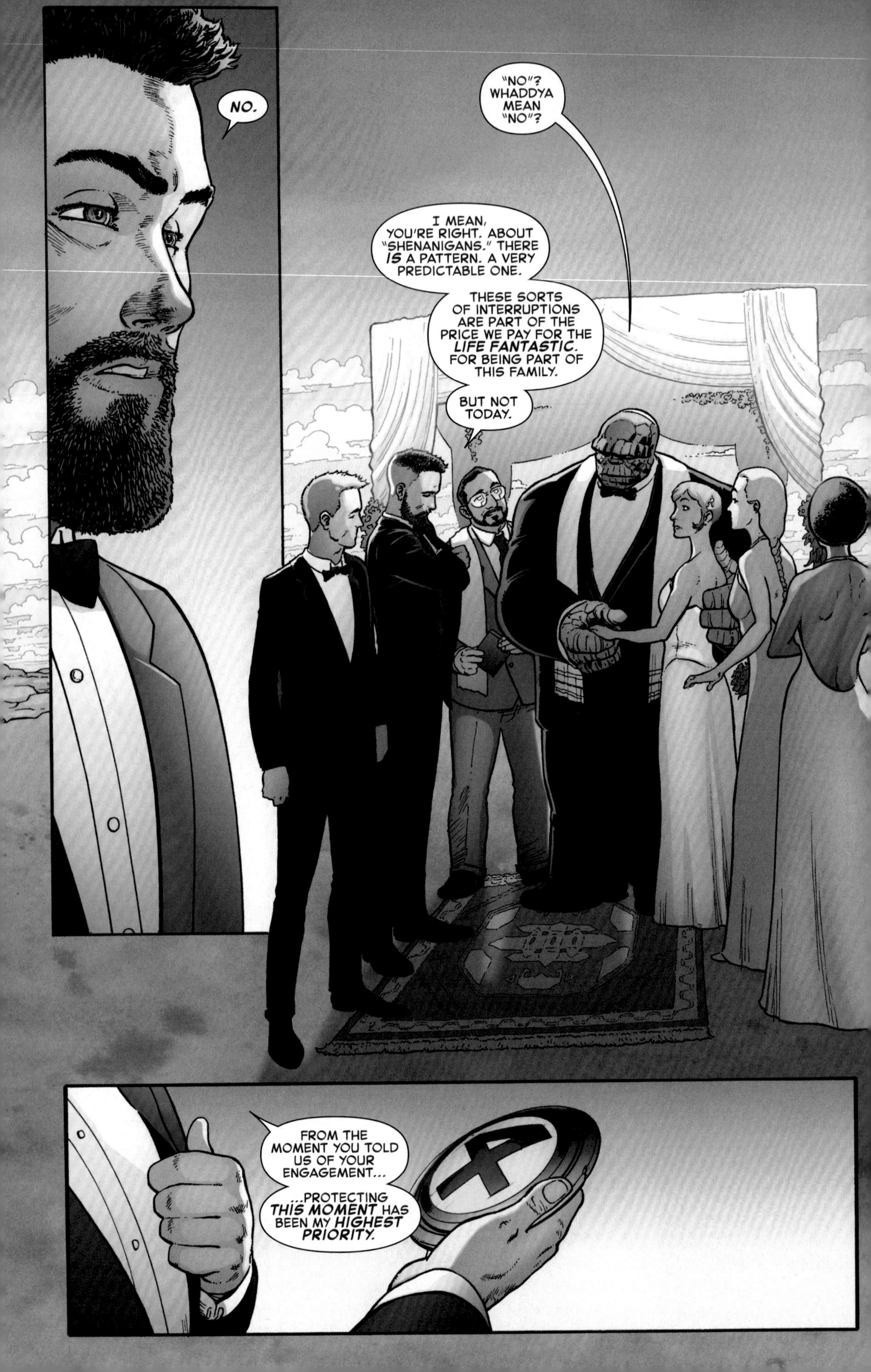
NO.
"NO"? WHADDYA MEAN "NO"?
I MEAN, YOU'RE RIGHT. ABOUT "SHENANIGANS." THERE ***IS*** A PATTERN. A VERY PREDICTABLE ONE.
THESE SORTS OF INTERRUPTIONS ARE PART OF THE PRICE WE PAY FOR THE ***LIFE FANTASTIC.*** FOR BEING PART OF THIS FAMILY.
BUT NOT TODAY.
FROM THE MOMENT YOU TOLD US OF YOUR ENGAGEMENT...
...PROTECTING ***THIS MOMENT*** HAS BEEN MY ***HIGHEST PRIORITY.***

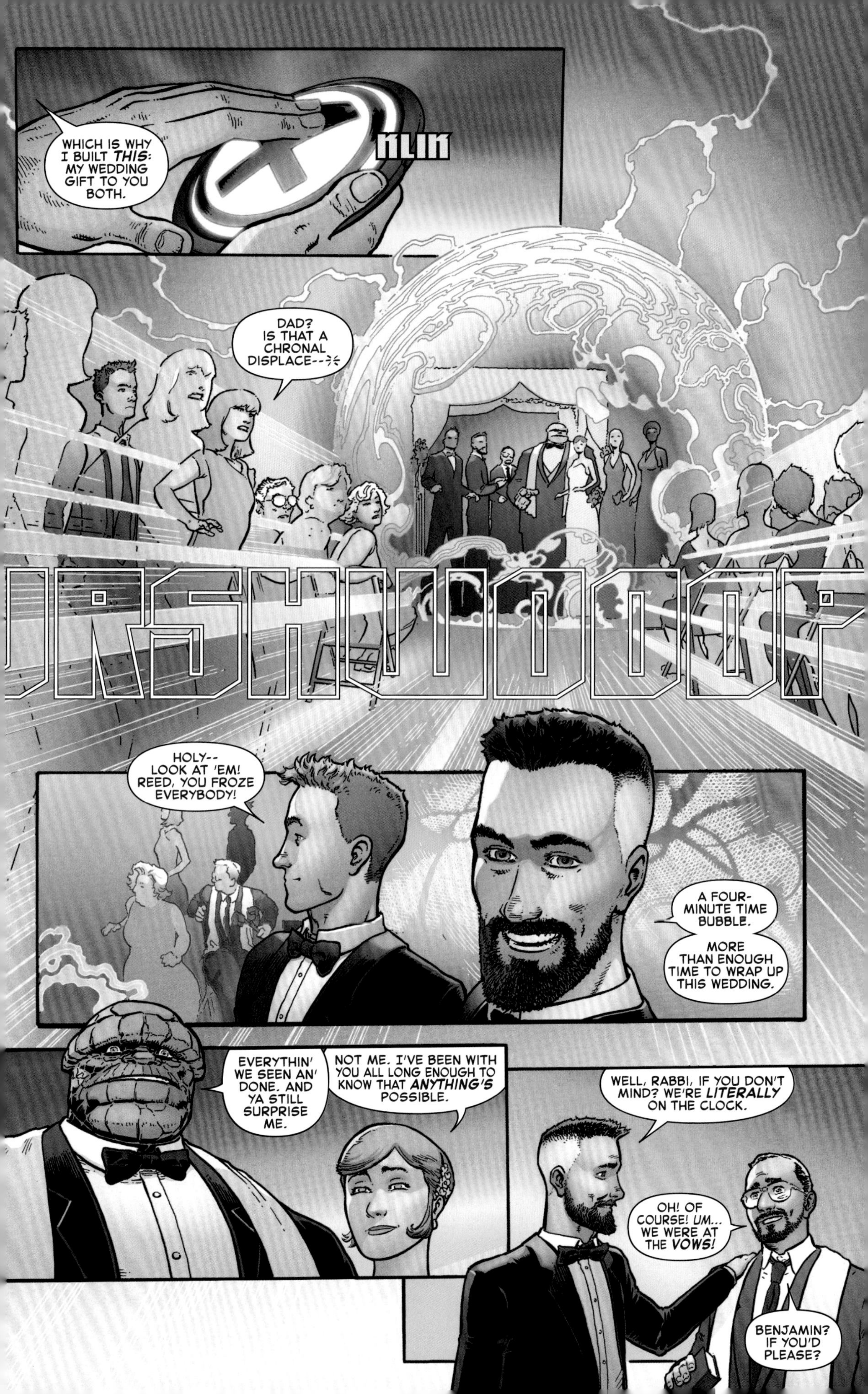

WHICH IS WHY I BUILT THIS: MY WEDDING GIFT TO YOU BOTH.
KLIK
DAD? IS THAT A CHRONAL DISPLACE--
VRSHWOOOOP
HOLY-- LOOK AT 'EM! REED, YOU FROZE EVERYBODY!
A FOUR-MINUTE TIME BUBBLE.
MORE THAN ENOUGH TIME TO WRAP UP THIS WEDDING.
EVERYTHIN' WE SEEN AN' DONE. AND YA STILL SURPRISE ME.
NOT ME. I'VE BEEN WITH YOU ALL LONG ENOUGH TO KNOW THAT ANYTHING'S POSSIBLE.
WELL, RABBI, IF YOU DON'T MIND? WE'RE LITERALLY ON THE CLOCK.
OH! OF COURSE! UM... WE WERE AT THE VOWS!
BENJAMIN? IF YOU'D PLEASE?

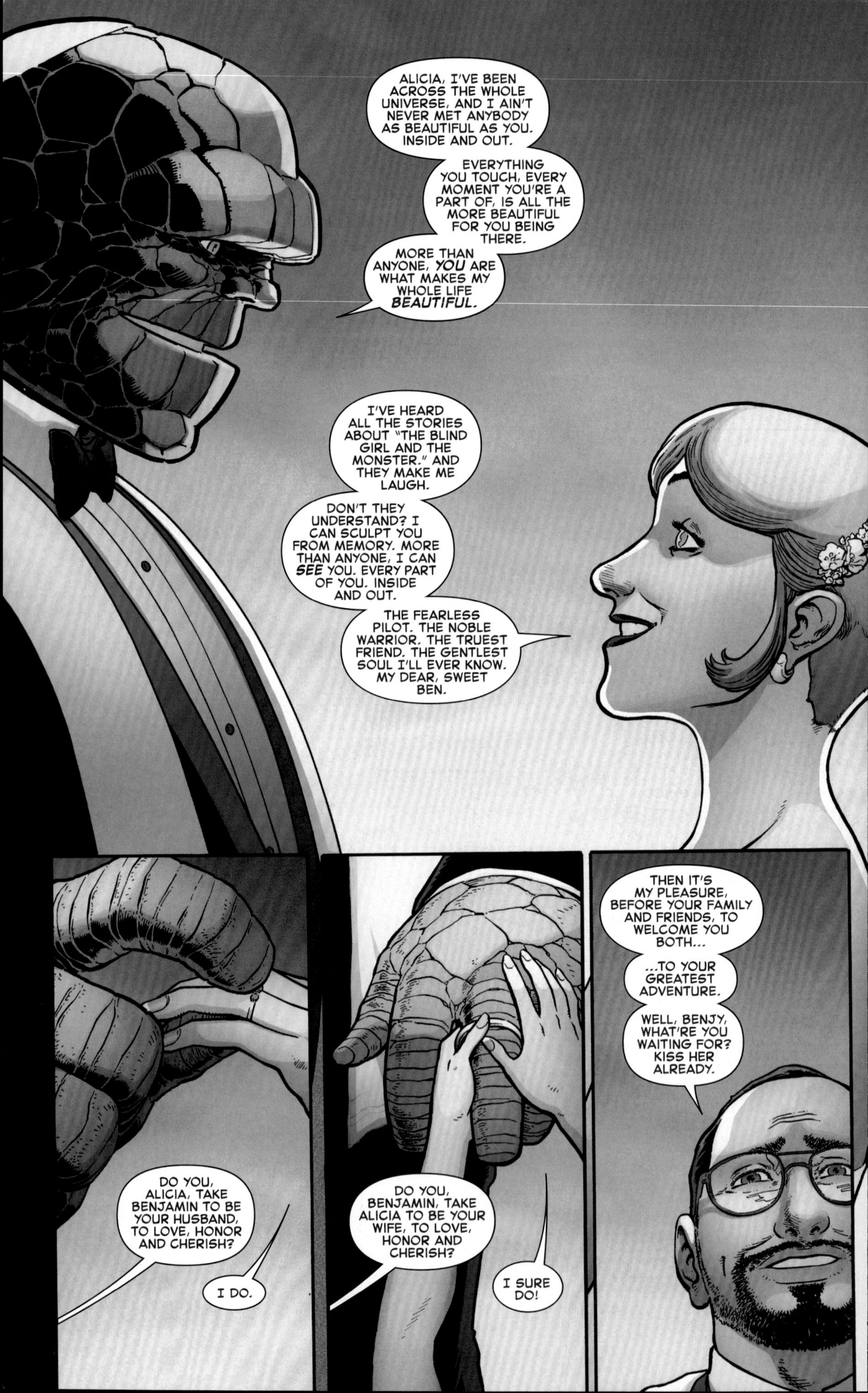
ALICIA, I'VE BEEN ACROSS THE WHOLE UNIVERSE, AND I AIN'T NEVER MET ANYBODY AS BEAUTIFUL AS YOU. INSIDE AND OUT.
EVERYTHING YOU TOUCH, EVERY MOMENT YOU'RE A PART OF, IS ALL THE MORE BEAUTIFUL FOR YOU BEING THERE.
MORE THAN ANYONE, YOU ARE WHAT MAKES MY WHOLE LIFE BEAUTIFUL.
I'VE HEARD ALL THE STORIES ABOUT "THE BLIND GIRL AND THE MONSTER." AND THEY MAKE ME LAUGH.
DON'T THEY UNDERSTAND? I CAN SCULPT YOU FROM MEMORY. MORE THAN ANYONE, I CAN SEE YOU. EVERY PART OF YOU. INSIDE AND OUT.
THE FEARLESS PILOT. THE NOBLE WARRIOR. THE TRUEST FRIEND. THE GENTLEST SOUL I'LL EVER KNOW. MY DEAR, SWEET BEN.
DO YOU, ALICIA, TAKE BENJAMIN TO BE YOUR HUSBAND, TO LOVE, HONOR AND CHERISH?
I DO.
DO YOU, BENJAMIN, TAKE ALICIA TO BE YOUR WIFE, TO LOVE, HONOR AND CHERISH?
I SURE DO!
THEN IT'S MY PLEASURE, BEFORE YOUR FAMILY AND FRIENDS, TO WELCOME YOU BOTH...
...TO YOUR GREATEST ADVENTURE.
WELL, BENJY, WHAT'RE YOU WAITING FOR? KISS HER ALREADY.

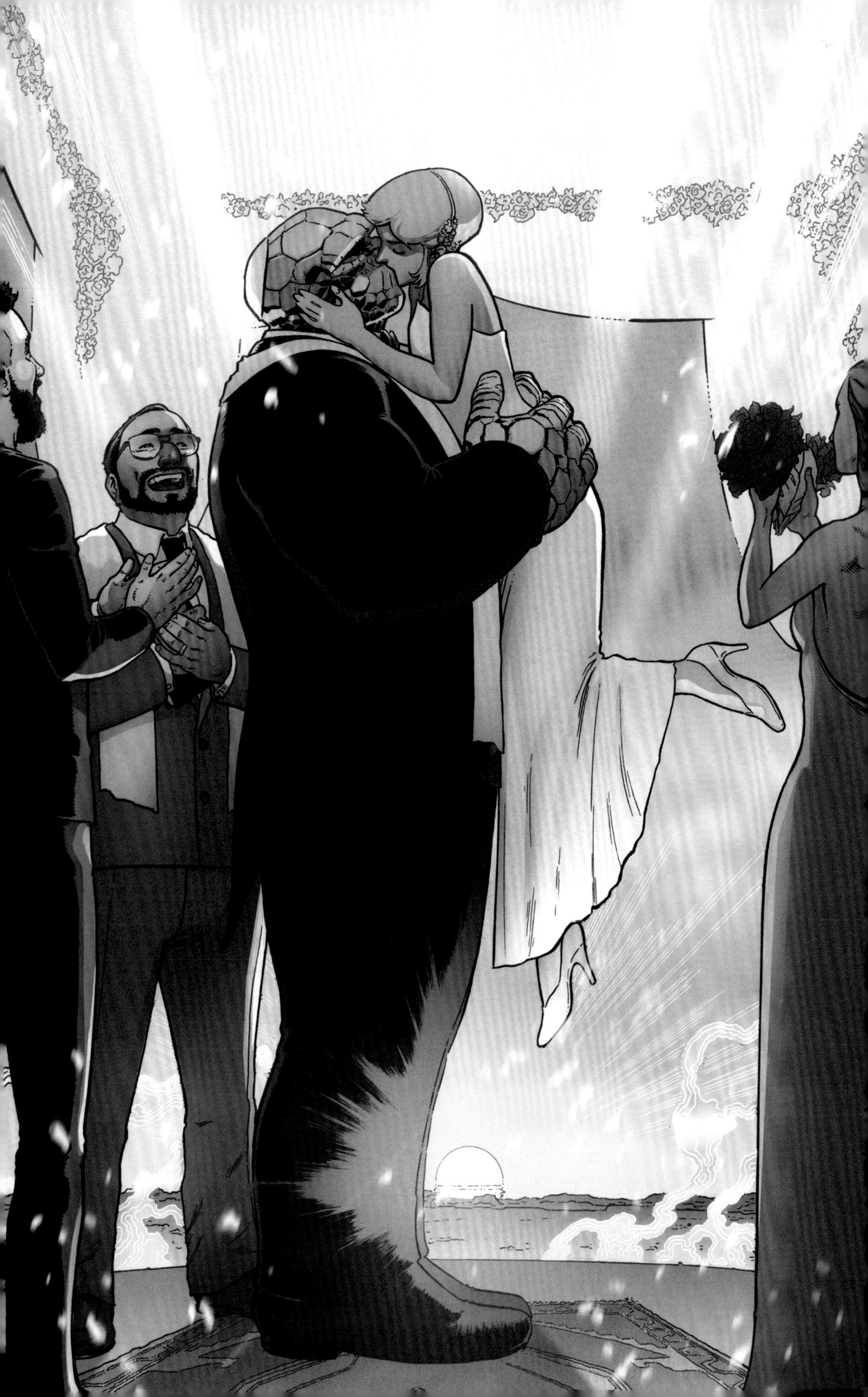

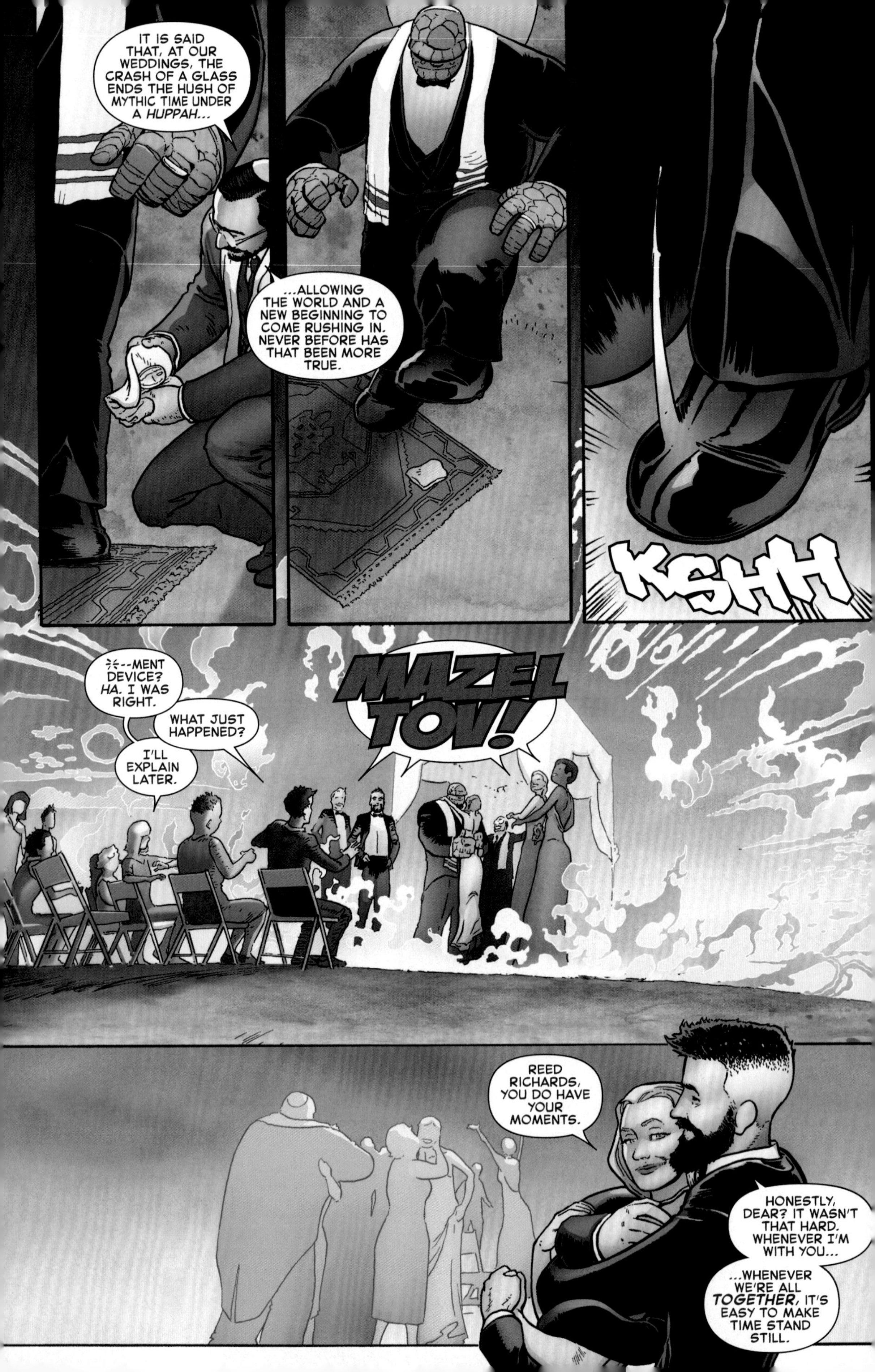
IT IS SAID THAT, AT OUR WEDDINGS, THE CRASH OF A GLASS ENDS THE HUSH OF MYTHIC TIME UNDER A *HUPPAH*...
...ALLOWING THE WORLD AND A NEW BEGINNING TO COME RUSHING IN. NEVER BEFORE HAS THAT BEEN MORE TRUE.
KSHH
--MENT DEVICE? *HA*. I WAS RIGHT.
WHAT JUST HAPPENED?
I'LL EXPLAIN LATER.
MAZEL TOV!
REED RICHARDS, YOU DO HAVE YOUR MOMENTS.
HONESTLY, DEAR? IT WASN'T THAT HARD. WHENEVER I'M WITH YOU...
...WHENEVER WE'RE ALL *TOGETHER*, IT'S EASY TO MAKE TIME STAND STILL.

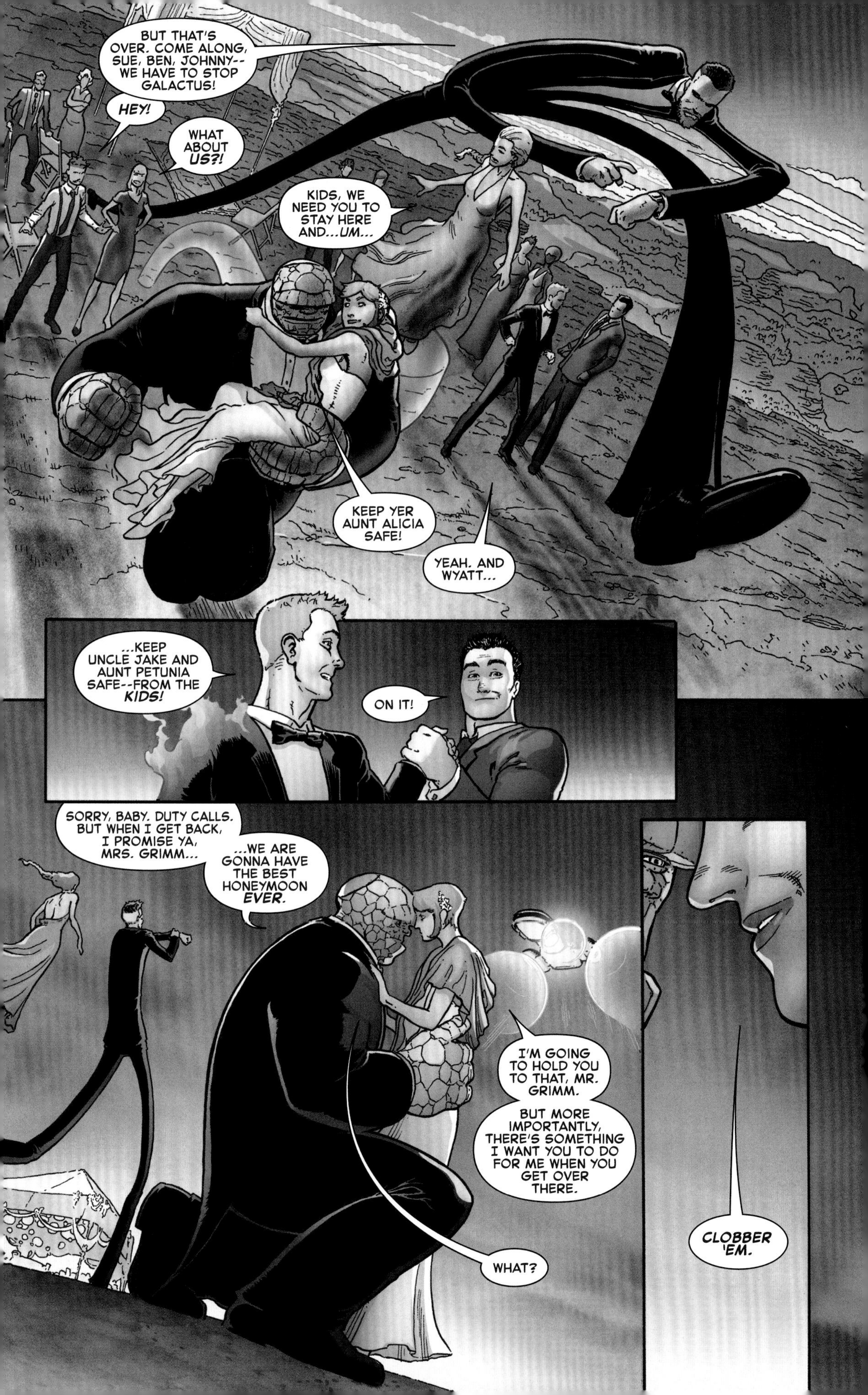
BUT THAT'S OVER. COME ALONG, SUE, BEN, JOHNNY-- WE HAVE TO STOP GALACTUS!
HEY!
WHAT ABOUT US?!
KIDS, WE NEED YOU TO STAY HERE AND...UM...
KEEP YER AUNT ALICIA SAFE!
YEAH. AND WYATT...
...KEEP UNCLE JAKE AND AUNT PETUNIA SAFE--FROM THE KIDS!
ON IT!
SORRY, BABY. DUTY CALLS. BUT WHEN I GET BACK, I PROMISE YA, MRS. GRIMM...
...WE ARE GONNA HAVE THE BEST HONEYMOON EVER.
I'M GOING TO HOLD YOU TO THAT, MR. GRIMM.
BUT MORE IMPORTANTLY, THERE'S SOMETHING I WANT YOU TO DO FOR ME WHEN YOU GET OVER THERE.
WHAT?
CLOBBER 'EM.

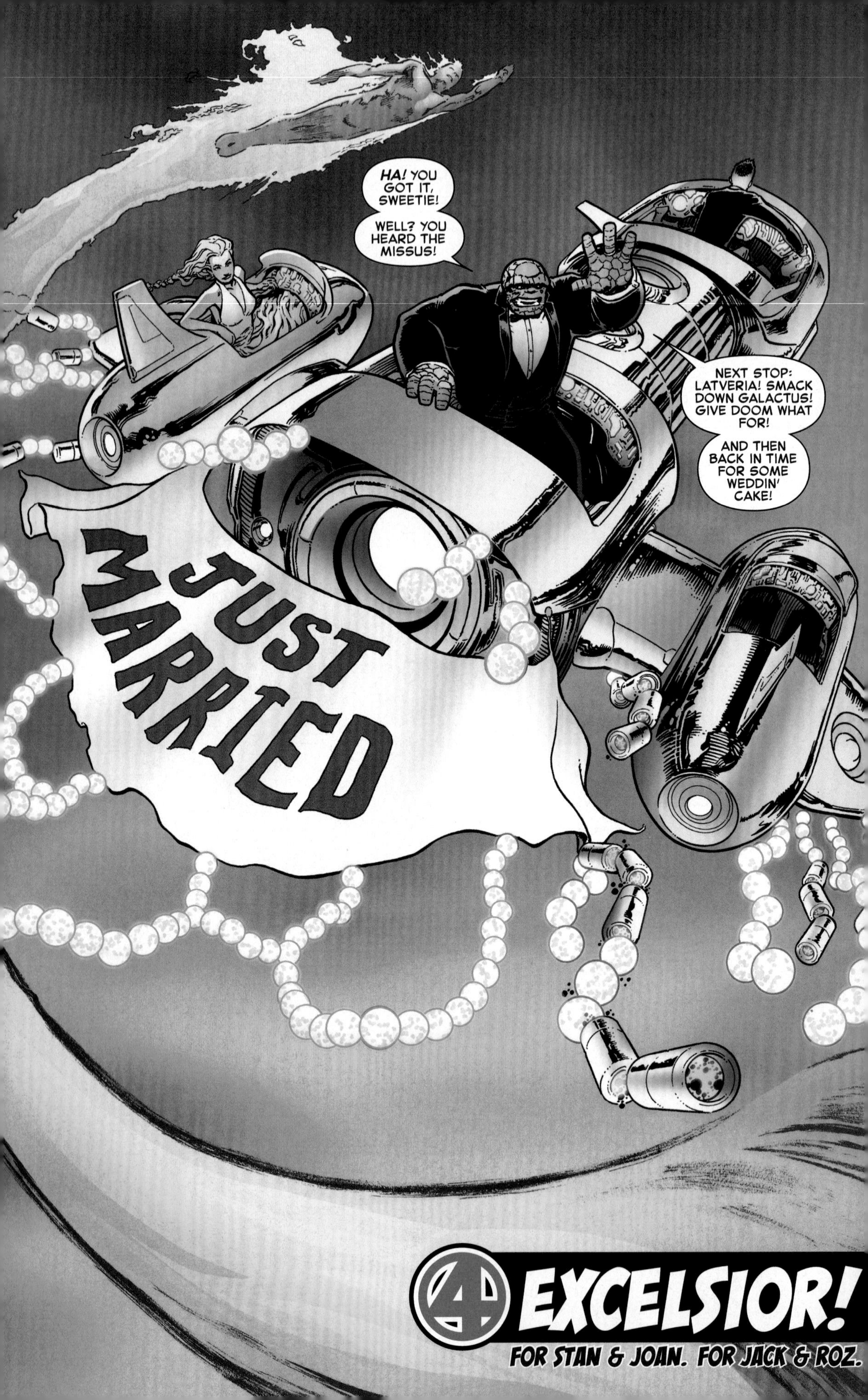

HA! YOU GOT IT, SWEETIE!
WELL? YOU HEARD THE MISSUS!
NEXT STOP: LATVERIA! SMACK DOWN GALACTUS! GIVE DOOM WHAT FOR!
AND THEN BACK IN TIME FOR SOME WEDDIN' CAKE!
JUST MARRIED
EXCELSIOR!
FOR STAN & JOAN. FOR JACK & ROZ.

It's the fateful first encounter of Ben Grimm and Alicia Masters as the Fantastic Four find themselves facing the magical influence of the Puppet Master!

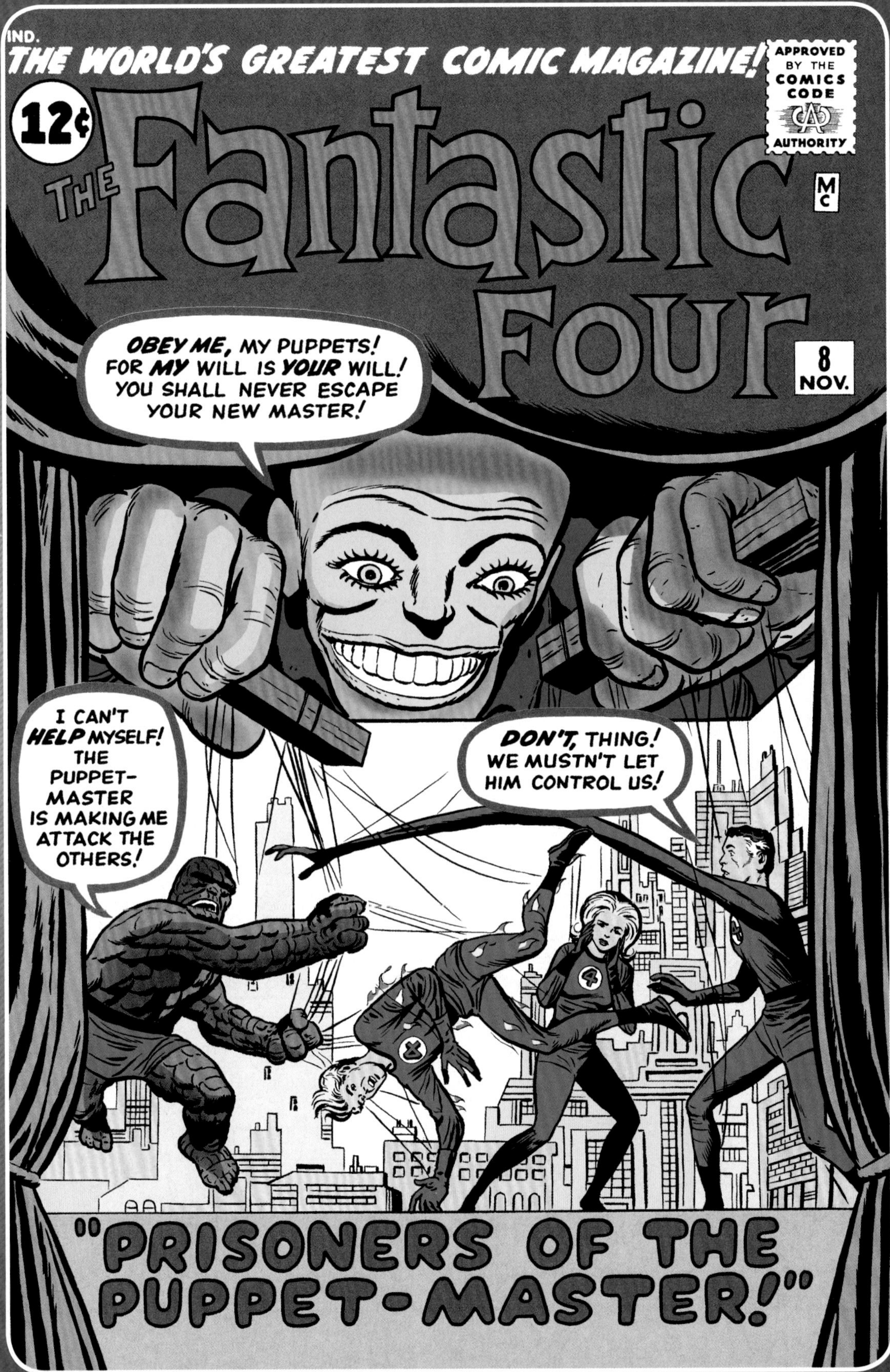

IND.
THE WORLD'S GREATEST COMIC MAGAZINE!
APPROVED BY THE COMICS CODE AUTHORITY
12¢
THE Fantastic Four
MC
8 NOV.
OBEY ME, MY PUPPETS! FOR MY WILL IS YOUR WILL! YOU SHALL NEVER ESCAPE YOUR NEW MASTER!
I CAN'T HELP MYSELF! THE PUPPET-MASTER IS MAKING ME ATTACK THE OTHERS!
DON'T, THING! WE MUSTN'T LET HIM CONTROL US!
"PRISONERS OF THE PUPPET-MASTER!"

THE FANTASTIC FOUR in: PRISONERS OF THE PUPPET MASTER!

Stan Lee + J. KIRBY

THE *THING!* I DIDN'T EXPECT HIM BACK SO SOON!

KEEP HIM OUT, TORCH! DON'T LET HIM IN HERE!

SORRY, THING! REED IS WORKIN' ON SOMETHING *SECRET!*

SO WHAT? *I'M* ONE OF THE FANTASTIC FOUR, AIN'T I?

WE CAN'T EXPLAIN NOW, BUT YOU MUSTN'T ENTER!

V-950

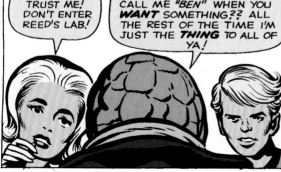

PLEASE, BEN, TRUST ME! DON'T ENTER REED'S LAB!

BAH! HOW COME YOU ONLY CALL ME *"BEN"* WHEN YOU *WANT* SOMETHING?? ALL THE REST OF THE TIME I'M JUST THE *THING* TO ALL OF YA!

HEY! PUT SUE DOWN!

RELAX, SONNY! I AIN'T GONNA HURT HER! I'M JUST GETTIN' HER OUTTA THE WAY, BECAUSE I GOT A FEELIN' THINGS ARE GONNA GET *ROUGH* AROUND HERE!

1

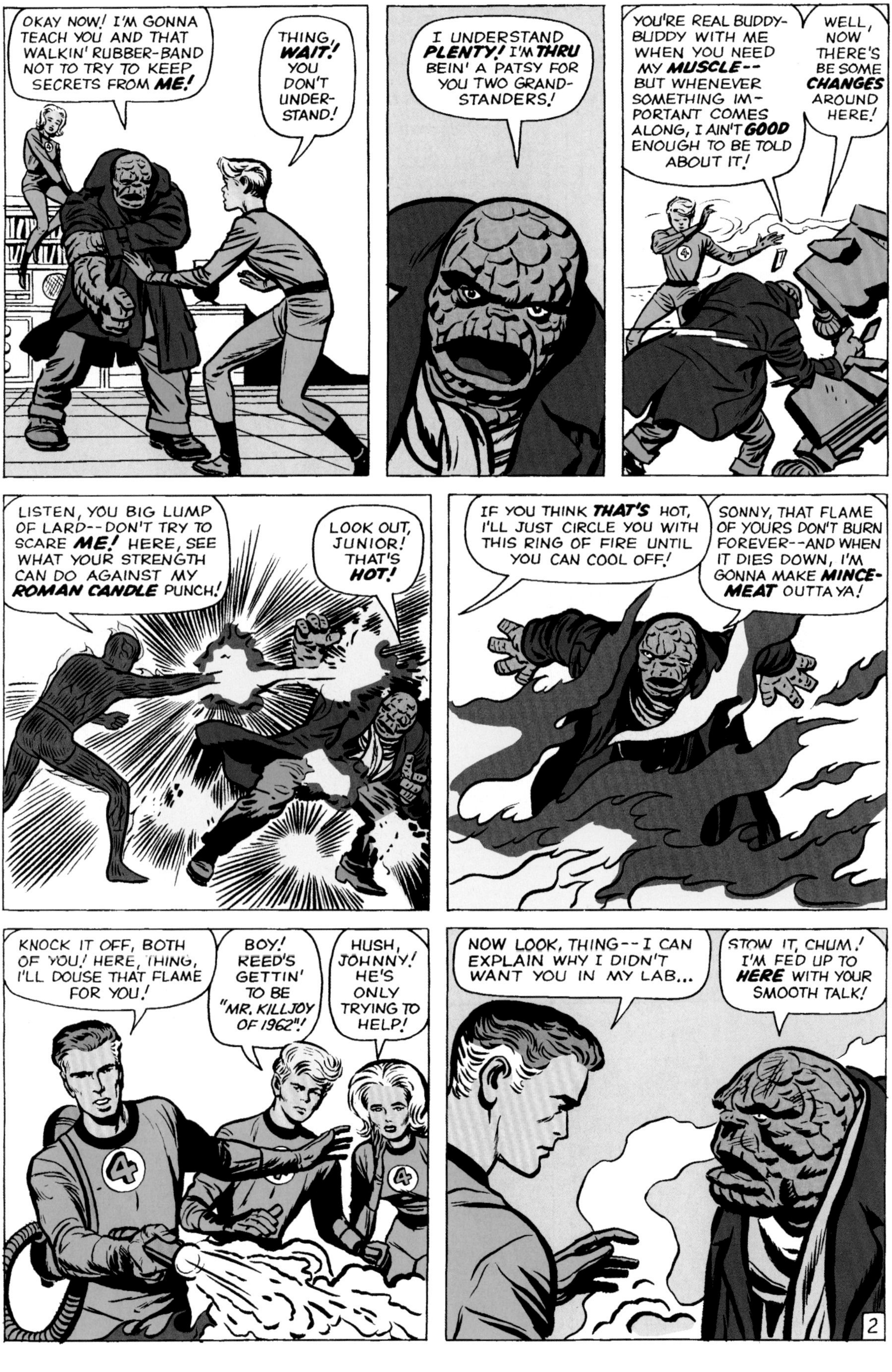
OKAY NOW! I'M GONNA TEACH YOU AND THAT WALKIN' RUBBER-BAND NOT TO TRY TO KEEP SECRETS FROM **ME!**
THING, **WAIT!** YOU DON'T UNDER-STAND!
I UNDERSTAND **PLENTY!** I'M **THRU** BEIN' A PATSY FOR YOU TWO GRAND-STANDERS!
YOU'RE REAL BUDDY-BUDDY WITH ME WHEN YOU NEED MY **MUSCLE--** BUT WHENEVER SOMETHING IM-PORTANT COMES ALONG, I AIN'T **GOOD** ENOUGH TO BE TOLD ABOUT IT!
WELL, NOW THERE'S BE SOME **CHANGES** AROUND HERE!
LISTEN, YOU BIG LUMP OF LARD--DON'T TRY TO SCARE **ME!** HERE, SEE WHAT YOUR STRENGTH CAN DO AGAINST MY **ROMAN CANDLE** PUNCH!
LOOK OUT, JUNIOR! THAT'S **HOT!**
IF YOU THINK **THAT'S** HOT, I'LL JUST CIRCLE YOU WITH THIS RING OF FIRE UNTIL YOU CAN COOL OFF!
SONNY, THAT FLAME OF YOURS DON'T BURN FOREVER--AND WHEN IT DIES DOWN, I'M GONNA MAKE **MINCE-MEAT** OUTTA YA!
KNOCK IT OFF, BOTH OF YOU! HERE, THING, I'LL DOUSE THAT FLAME FOR YOU!
BOY! REED'S GETTIN' TO BE "MR. KILLJOY OF 1962"!
HUSH, JOHNNY! HE'S ONLY TRYING TO HELP!
NOW LOOK, THING--I CAN EXPLAIN WHY I DIDN'T WANT YOU IN MY LAB...
STOW IT, CHUM! I'M FED UP TO **HERE** WITH YOUR SMOOTH TALK!
2

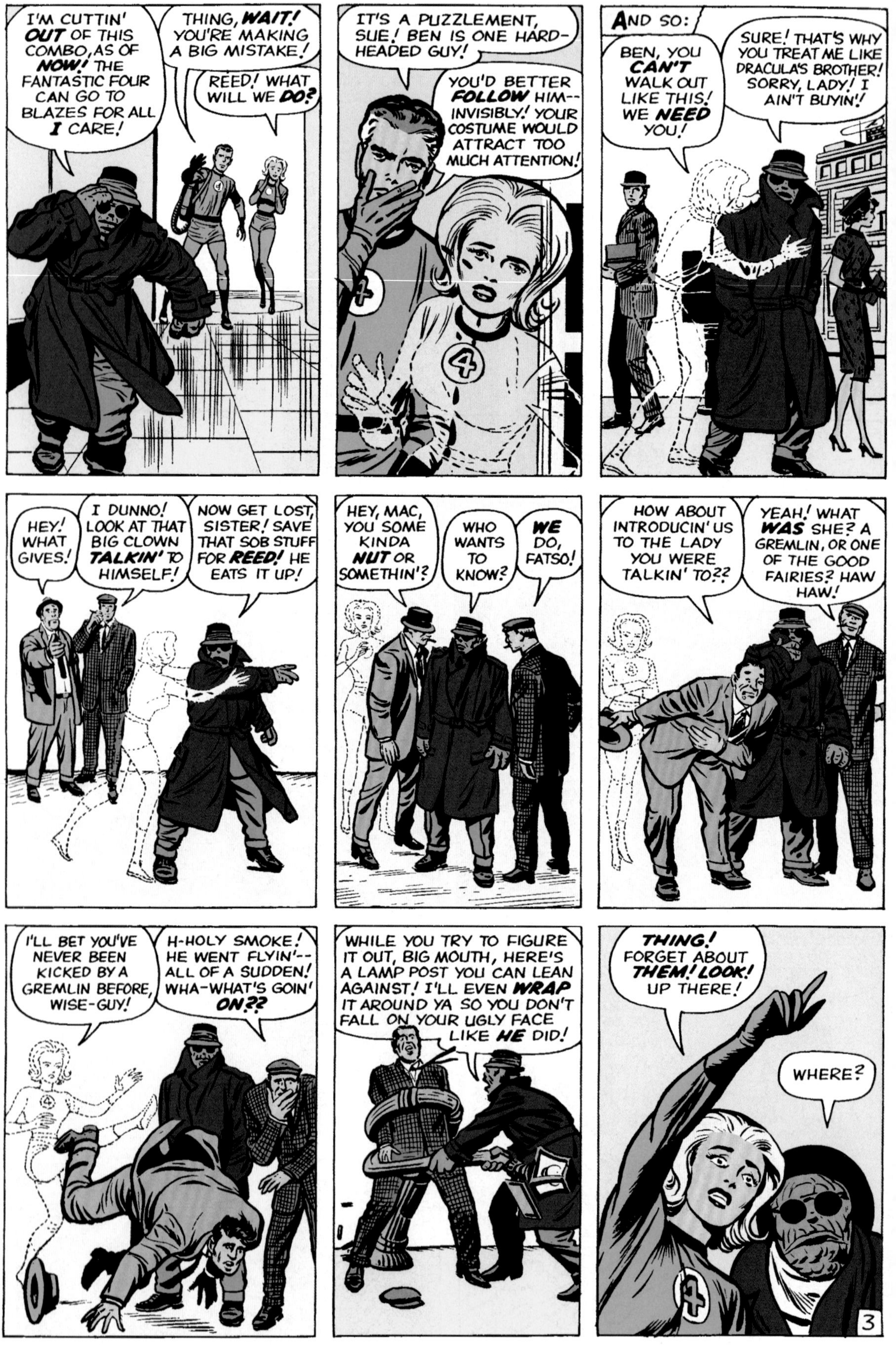
I'M CUTTIN' OUT OF THIS COMBO, AS OF NOW! THE FANTASTIC FOUR CAN GO TO BLAZES FOR ALL I CARE!
THING, WAIT! YOU'RE MAKING A BIG MISTAKE!
REED! WHAT WILL WE DO?
IT'S A PUZZLEMENT, SUE! BEN IS ONE HARD-HEADED GUY!
YOU'D BETTER FOLLOW HIM-- INVISIBLY! YOUR COSTUME WOULD ATTRACT TOO MUCH ATTENTION!
AND SO:
BEN, YOU CAN'T WALK OUT LIKE THIS! WE NEED YOU!
SURE! THAT'S WHY YOU TREAT ME LIKE DRACULA'S BROTHER! SORRY, LADY! I AIN'T BUYIN'!
HEY! WHAT GIVES!
I DUNNO! LOOK AT THAT BIG CLOWN TALKIN' TO HIMSELF!
NOW GET LOST, SISTER! SAVE THAT SOB STUFF FOR REED! HE EATS IT UP!
HEY, MAC, YOU SOME KINDA NUT OR SOMETHIN'?
WHO WANTS TO KNOW?
WE DO, FATSO!
HOW ABOUT INTRODUCIN' US TO THE LADY YOU WERE TALKIN' TO??
YEAH! WHAT WAS SHE? A GREMLIN, OR ONE OF THE GOOD FAIRIES? HAW HAW!
I'LL BET YOU'VE NEVER BEEN KICKED BY A GREMLIN BEFORE, WISE-GUY!
H-HOLY SMOKE! HE WENT FLYIN'-- ALL OF A SUDDEN! WHA-WHAT'S GOIN' ON??
WHILE YOU TRY TO FIGURE IT OUT, BIG MOUTH, HERE'S A LAMP POST YOU CAN LEAN AGAINST! I'LL EVEN WRAP IT AROUND YA SO YOU DON'T FALL ON YOUR UGLY FACE LIKE HE DID!
THING! FORGET ABOUT THEM! LOOK! UP THERE!
WHERE?
3

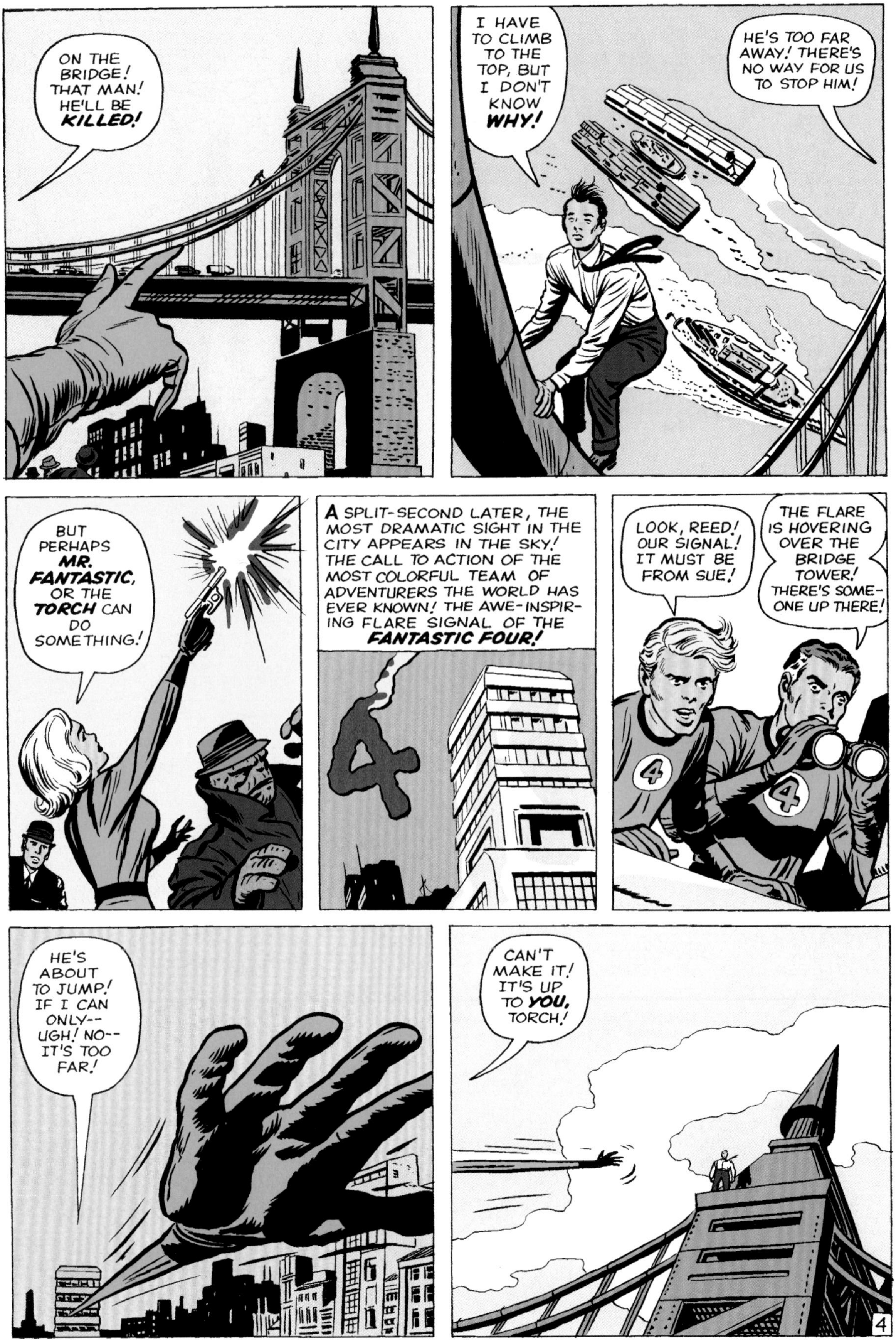
ON THE BRIDGE! THAT MAN! HE'LL BE KILLED!
I HAVE TO CLIMB TO THE TOP, BUT I DON'T KNOW WHY!
HE'S TOO FAR AWAY! THERE'S NO WAY FOR US TO STOP HIM!
BUT PERHAPS MR. FANTASTIC, OR THE TORCH CAN DO SOMETHING!
A SPLIT-SECOND LATER, THE MOST DRAMATIC SIGHT IN THE CITY APPEARS IN THE SKY! THE CALL TO ACTION OF THE MOST COLORFUL TEAM OF ADVENTURERS THE WORLD HAS EVER KNOWN! THE AWE-INSPIRING FLARE SIGNAL OF THE FANTASTIC FOUR!
LOOK, REED! OUR SIGNAL! IT MUST BE FROM SUE!
THE FLARE IS HOVERING OVER THE BRIDGE TOWER! THERE'S SOME-ONE UP THERE!
HE'S ABOUT TO JUMP! IF I CAN ONLY-- UGH! NO-- IT'S TOO FAR!
CAN'T MAKE IT! IT'S UP TO YOU, TORCH!
4

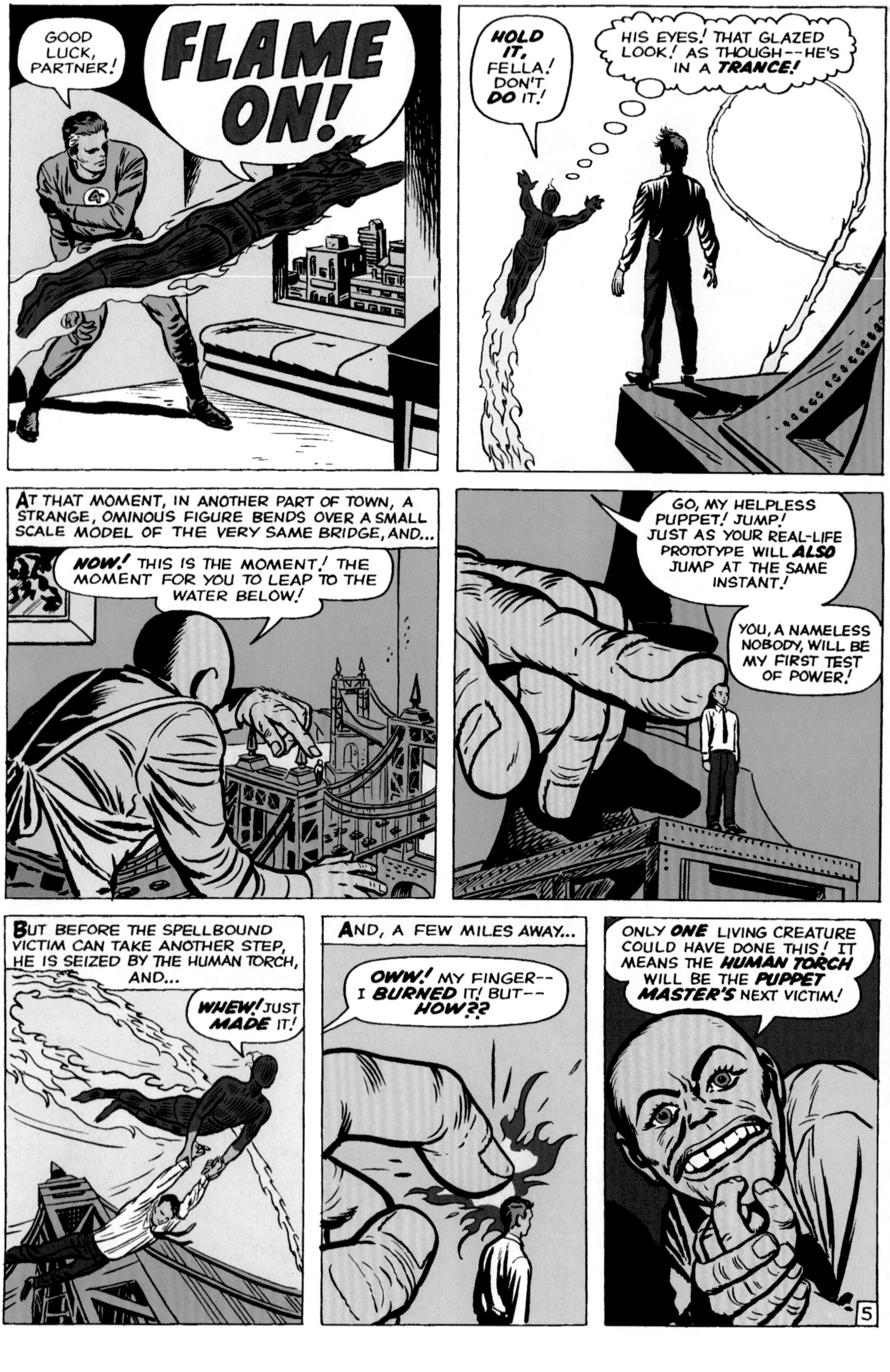
GOOD LUCK, PARTNER!
FLAME ON!
HOLD IT, FELLA! DON'T DO IT!
HIS EYES! THAT GLAZED LOOK! AS THOUGH--HE'S IN A TRANCE!
AT THAT MOMENT, IN ANOTHER PART OF TOWN, A STRANGE, OMINOUS FIGURE BENDS OVER A SMALL SCALE MODEL OF THE VERY SAME BRIDGE, AND...
NOW! THIS IS THE MOMENT! THE MOMENT FOR YOU TO LEAP TO THE WATER BELOW!
GO, MY HELPLESS PUPPET! JUMP! JUST AS YOUR REAL-LIFE PROTOTYPE WILL ALSO JUMP AT THE SAME INSTANT!
YOU, A NAMELESS NOBODY, WILL BE MY FIRST TEST OF POWER!
BUT BEFORE THE SPELLBOUND VICTIM CAN TAKE ANOTHER STEP, HE IS SEIZED BY THE HUMAN TORCH, AND...
WHEW! JUST MADE IT!
AND, A FEW MILES AWAY...
OWW! MY FINGER-- I BURNED IT! BUT-- HOW??
ONLY ONE LIVING CREATURE COULD HAVE DONE THIS! IT MEANS THE HUMAN TORCH WILL BE THE PUPPET MASTER'S NEXT VICTIM!
5

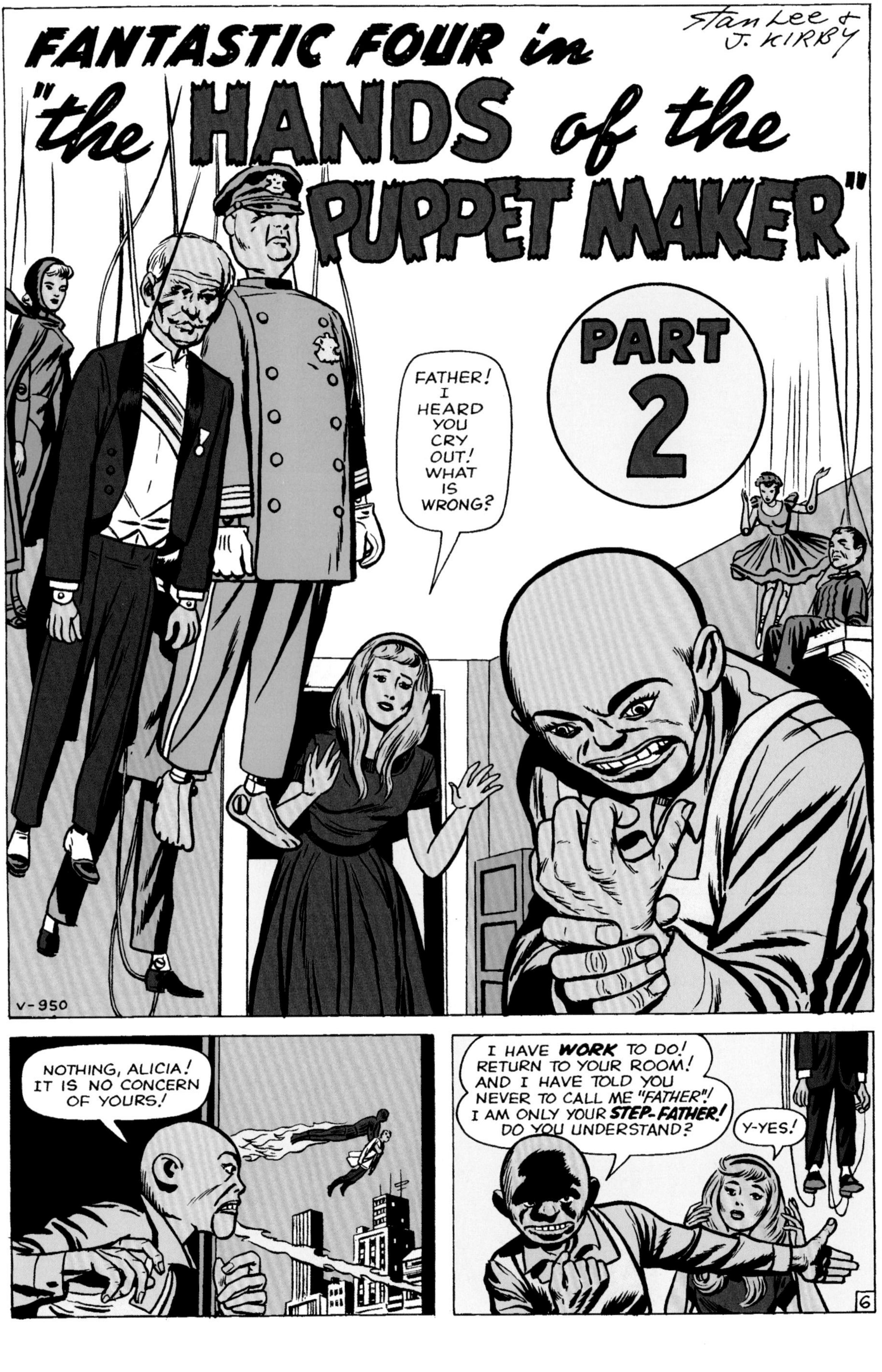
Stan Lee &
J. Kirby
FANTASTIC FOUR in
"the HANDS of the PUPPET MAKER"
PART 2
FATHER! I HEARD YOU CRY OUT! WHAT IS WRONG?
V-950
NOTHING, ALICIA! IT IS NO CONCERN OF YOURS!
I HAVE WORK TO DO! RETURN TO YOUR ROOM! AND I HAVE TOLD YOU NEVER TO CALL ME "FATHER"! I AM ONLY YOUR STEP-FATHER! DO YOU UNDERSTAND?
Y-YES!
6

IT IS LUCKY FOR ME THAT SHE IS BLIND! SHE HAS NO IDEA OF WHAT MY *"WORK"* REALLY IS!

BUT WHAT WOULD SHE SAY IF SHE COULD KNOW THAT EVER SINCE I DISCOVERED THIS QUANTITY OF RADIOACTIVE CLAY, I HAVE BEEN CARVING IT TO GAIN *POWER* FOR MYSELF!

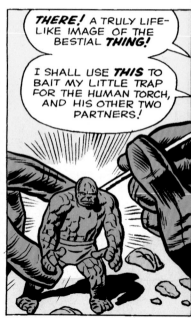

THERE! A TRULY LIFE-LIKE IMAGE OF THE BESTIAL *THING!*

I SHALL USE *THIS* TO BAIT MY LITTLE TRAP FOR THE HUMAN TORCH, AND HIS OTHER TWO PARTNERS!

ALL I NEED DO IS PLACE THIS CLAY PUPPET IN A REPLICA OF MY ROOM! NOW HIS LIVING COUNTERPART HAS NO CHOICE BUT TO COME HERE ALSO!

AND, TRUE TO THE PUPPET MASTER'S PREDICTION...

THING! WAIT! WHERE ARE YOU GOING??

MUST WALK ACROSS TOWN! CAN STOP FOR NOTHING!

HE'S LIKE A MAN IN A TRANCE! WHAT'S *HAPPENED* TO HIM?? IT'S AS THOUGH AN INVISIBLE MAGNET IS *PULLING* HIM CLOSER-- AND CLOSER!

HE ENTERED THAT ROOM AS THOUGH OBEYING A SILENT COMMAND!

I AM HERE!

*P*UZZLED, SUE ENTERS BEHIND THE THING! BUT THE EXTRA-SHARP SENSES OF A BLIND GIRL LEAD TO HER UNDOING!

FATHER! THERE ARE *TWO* STRANGERS HERE! I CAN SENSE *ANOTHER* HEART-BEAT! I CAN HEAR ANOTHER'S BREATHING!

THERE IS ONLY *ONE* OTHER WHOM IT CAN BE! THE INVISIBLE MEMBER OF THE FANTASTIC FOUR!

WELL, SHE SHALL NOT FIND THE PUPPET MASTER UNPREPARED!

7

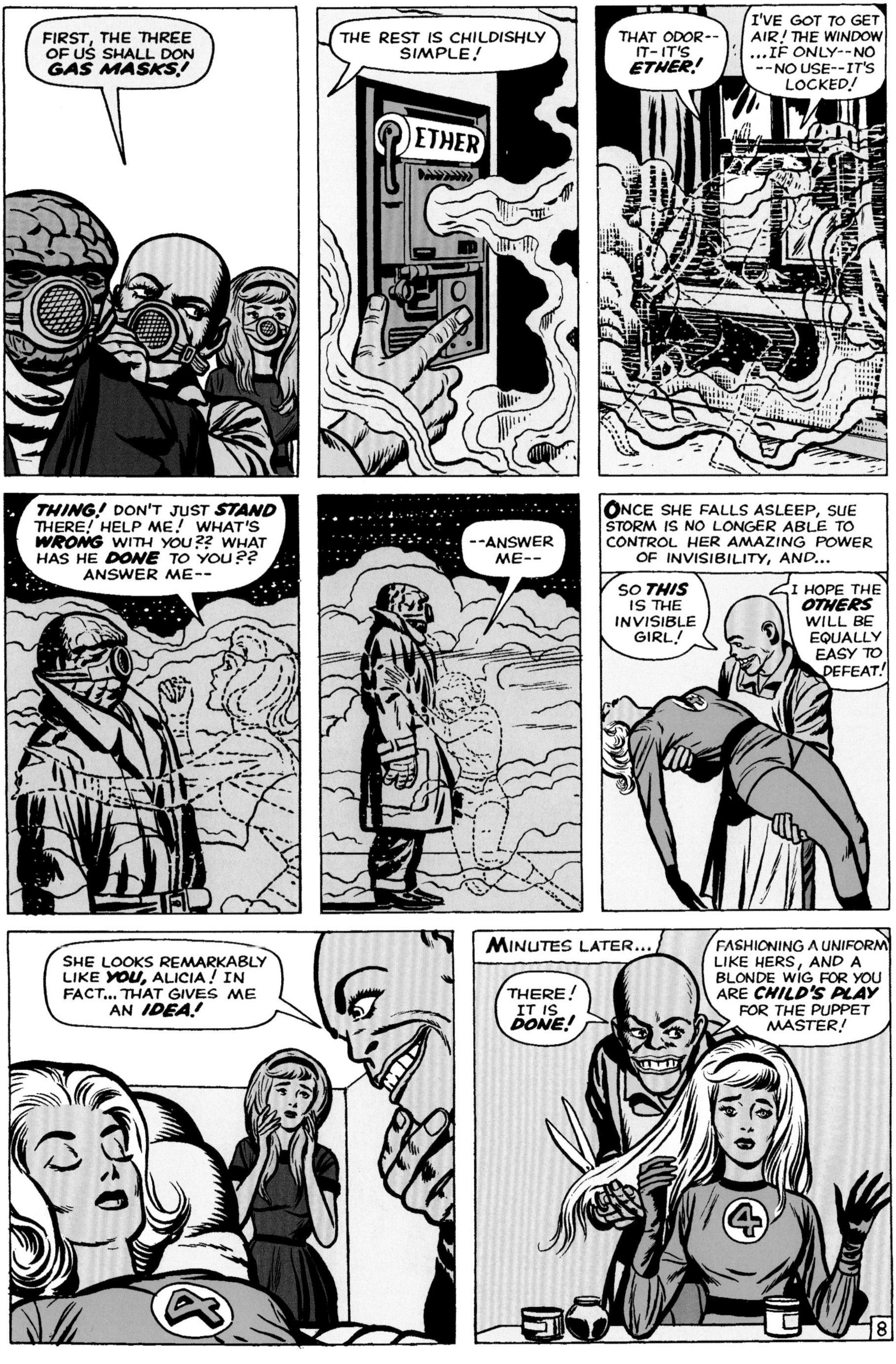

FIRST, THE THREE OF US SHALL DON GAS MASKS!
THE REST IS CHILDISHLY SIMPLE!
ETHER
THAT ODOR-- IT-IT'S ETHER!
I'VE GOT TO GET AIR! THE WINDOW ...IF ONLY--NO --NO USE--IT'S LOCKED!
THING! DON'T JUST STAND THERE! HELP ME! WHAT'S WRONG WITH YOU?? WHAT HAS HE DONE TO YOU?? ANSWER ME--
--ANSWER ME--
ONCE SHE FALLS ASLEEP, SUE STORM IS NO LONGER ABLE TO CONTROL HER AMAZING POWER OF INVISIBILITY, AND...
SO THIS IS THE INVISIBLE GIRL!
I HOPE THE OTHERS WILL BE EQUALLY EASY TO DEFEAT!
SHE LOOKS REMARKABLY LIKE YOU, ALICIA! IN FACT... THAT GIVES ME AN IDEA!
MINUTES LATER...
FASHIONING A UNIFORM LIKE HERS, AND A BLONDE WIG FOR YOU ARE CHILD'S PLAY FOR THE PUPPET MASTER!
THERE! IT IS DONE!
8

AND NOW, ALICIA, WHILE OUR UNINVITED GUEST SLEEPS, **YOU** WILL TAKE HER PLACE! YOU WILL PLAY A HARMLESS LITTLE PRANK FOR ME!

A LITTLE PRANK? BUT WHAT, FATHER?

DO NOT QUESTION ME! JUST OBEY!

THIS MAN--HIS FACE FEELS STRONG AND POWERFUL! AND YET, I CAN SENSE A GENTLENESS TO HIM--THERE IS SOMETHING TRAGIC--SOMETHING SENSITIVE!

ENOUGH OF YOUR PRATTLE! STAND BACK! I WANT TO **TEST** HIS STRENGTH!

I HAVE PUT A STEEL HAMMER IN HIS HAND...

AND NOW, AT MY COMMAND...

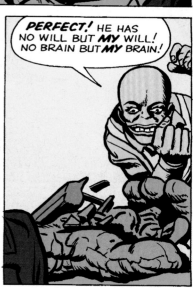

PERFECT! HE HAS NO WILL BUT **MY** WILL! NO BRAIN BUT **MY** BRAIN!

GO WITH HIM, ALICIA! SAY NOTHING, BUT DO NOT LEAVE HIS SIDE!

THIS IS ALL SO STRANGE! I DO NOT UNDERSTAND!

BUT I MUST DO AS I AM TOLD!

AND WHEN THEY PLAY OUT THEIR LITTLE ACT, I SHALL PROVE MY POWER IN **ANOTHER** WAY! I SHALL USE A **NEW** PUPPET ...THE PERSONAL TRUSTEE OF THE WARDEN OF STATE PRISON!

9

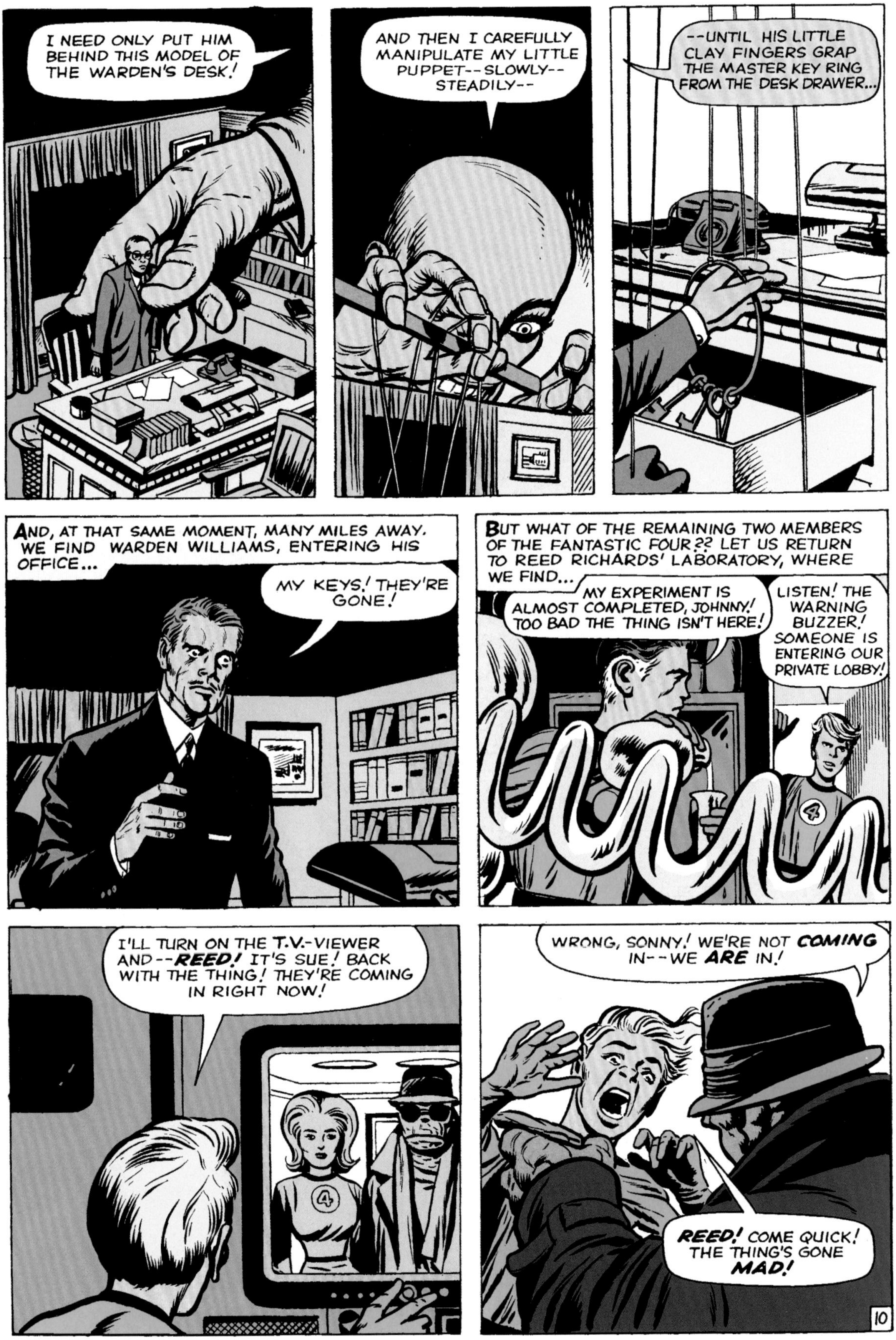
I NEED ONLY PUT HIM BEHIND THIS MODEL OF THE WARDEN'S DESK!
AND THEN I CAREFULLY MANIPULATE MY LITTLE PUPPET--SLOWLY--STEADILY--
--UNTIL HIS LITTLE CLAY FINGERS GRAP THE MASTER KEY RING FROM THE DESK DRAWER...
AND, AT THAT SAME MOMENT, MANY MILES AWAY, WE FIND WARDEN WILLIAMS, ENTERING HIS OFFICE...
MY KEYS! THEY'RE GONE!
BUT WHAT OF THE REMAINING TWO MEMBERS OF THE FANTASTIC FOUR?? LET US RETURN TO REED RICHARDS' LABORATORY, WHERE WE FIND...
MY EXPERIMENT IS ALMOST COMPLETED, JOHNNY! TOO BAD THE THING ISN'T HERE!
LISTEN! THE WARNING BUZZER! SOMEONE IS ENTERING OUR PRIVATE LOBBY!
I'LL TURN ON THE T.V.-VIEWER AND--REED! IT'S SUE! BACK WITH THE THING! THEY'RE COMING IN RIGHT NOW!
WRONG, SONNY! WE'RE NOT COMING IN--WE ARE IN!
REED! COME QUICK! THE THING'S GONE MAD!
10

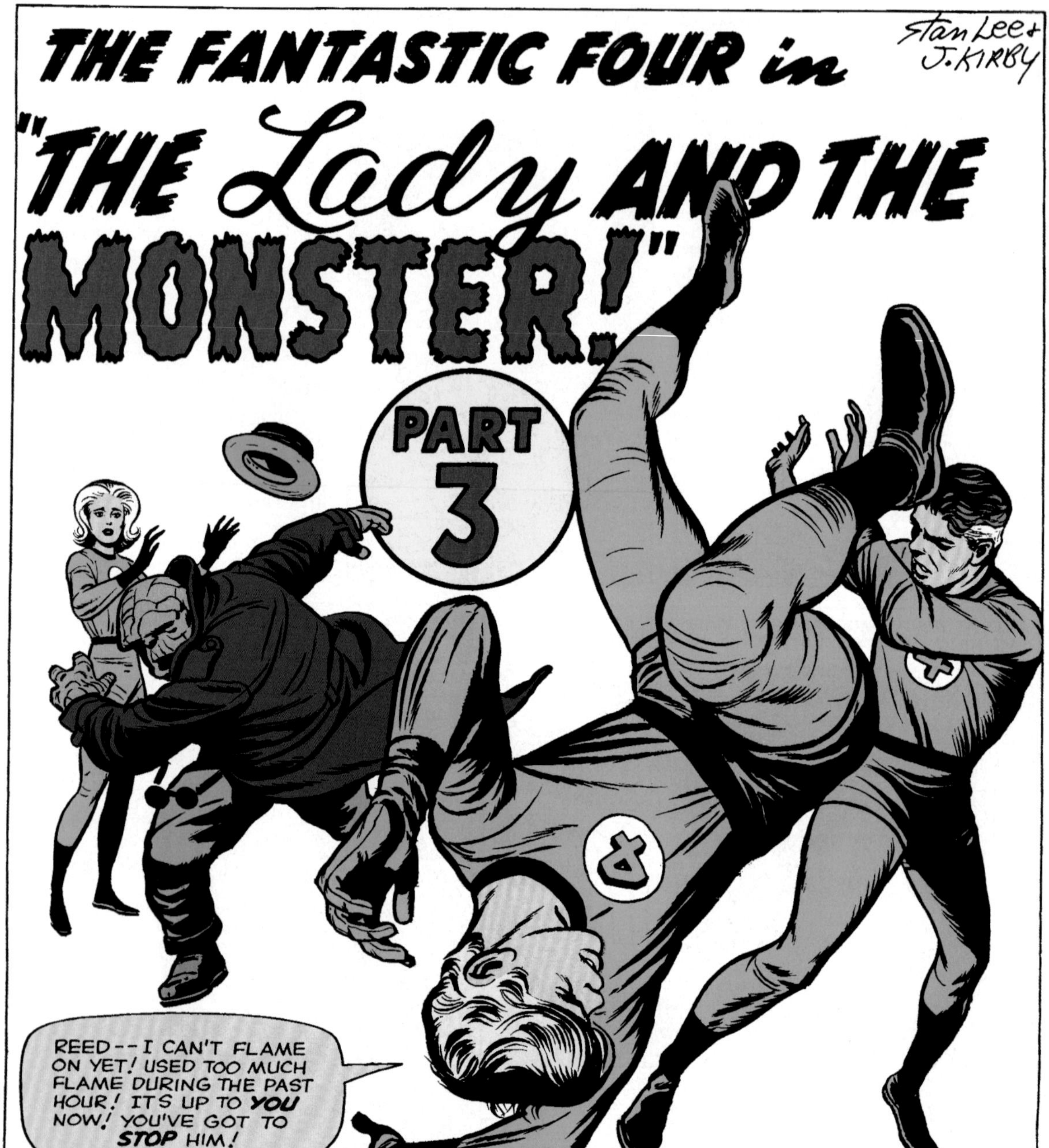
THE FANTASTIC FOUR in
"THE Lady AND THE MONSTER!"
Stan Lee & J. KIRBY
PART 3
REED--I CAN'T FLAME ON YET! USED TOO MUCH FLAME DURING THE PAST HOUR! IT'S UP TO **YOU** NOW! YOU'VE GOT TO **STOP** HIM!

V-950

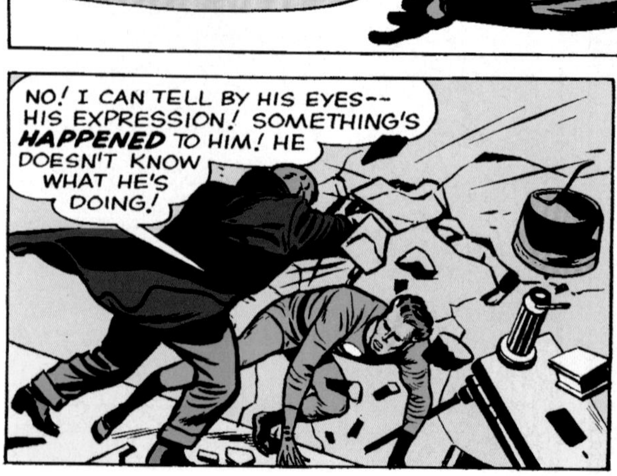
NO! I CAN TELL BY HIS EYES--HIS EXPRESSION! SOMETHING'S **HAPPENED** TO HIM! HE DOESN'T KNOW WHAT HE'S DOING!

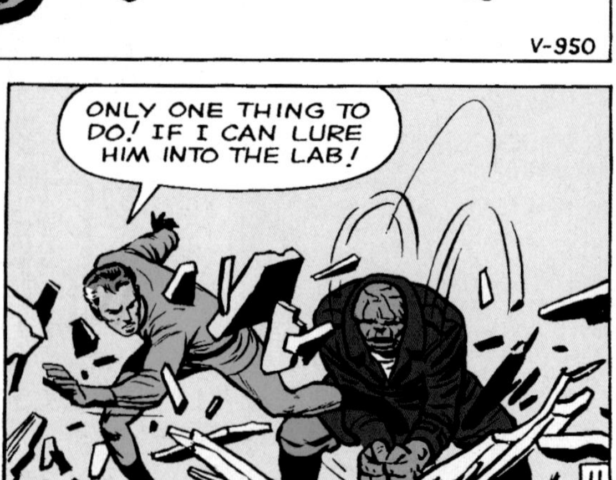
ONLY ONE THING TO DO! IF I CAN LURE HIM INTO THE LAB!

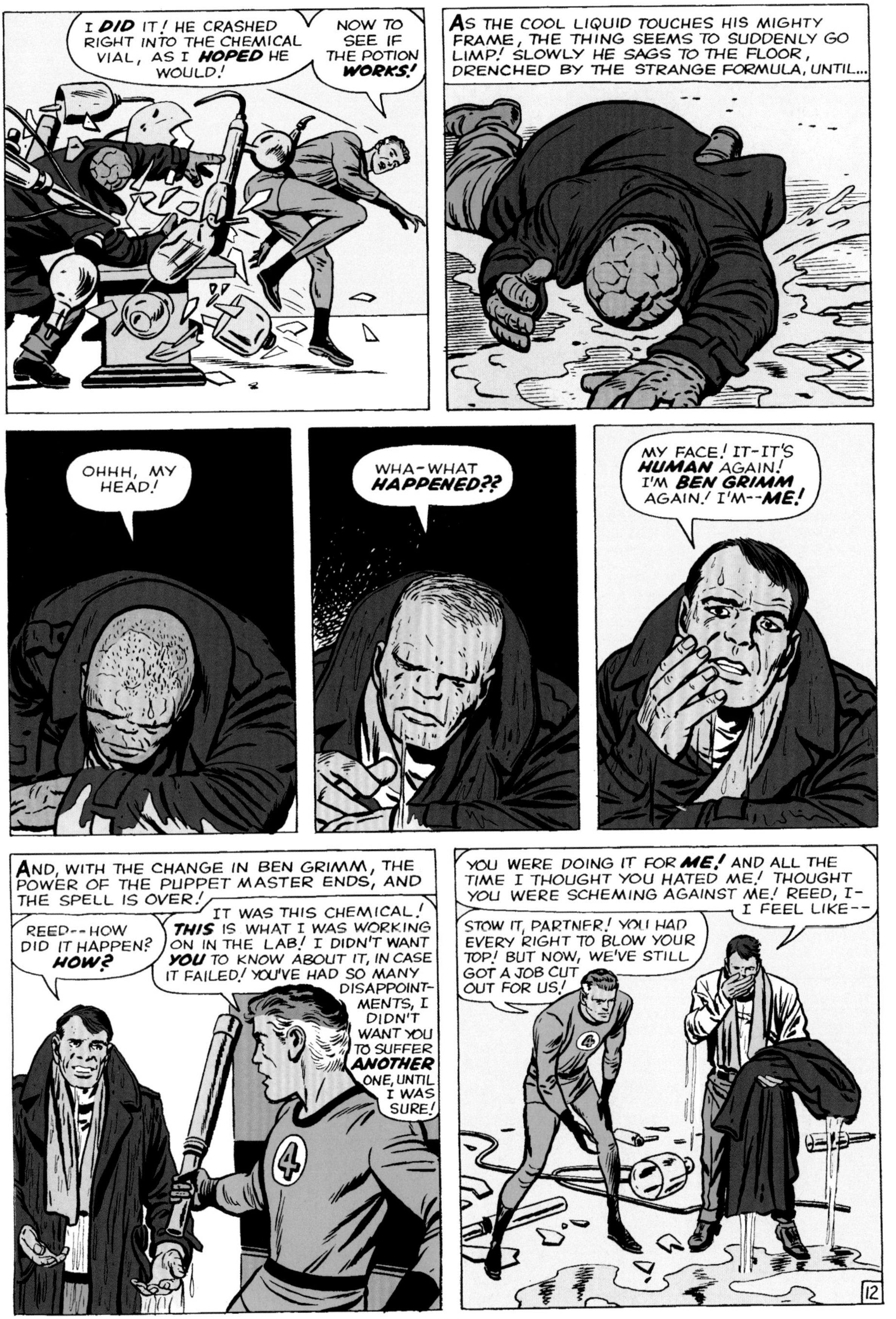
I DID IT! HE CRASHED RIGHT INTO THE CHEMICAL VIAL, AS I HOPED HE WOULD!
NOW TO SEE IF THE POTION WORKS!
AS THE COOL LIQUID TOUCHES HIS MIGHTY FRAME, THE THING SEEMS TO SUDDENLY GO LIMP! SLOWLY HE SAGS TO THE FLOOR, DRENCHED BY THE STRANGE FORMULA, UNTIL...
OHHH, MY HEAD!
WHA-WHAT HAPPENED??
MY FACE! IT-IT'S HUMAN AGAIN! I'M BEN GRIMM AGAIN! I'M--ME!
AND, WITH THE CHANGE IN BEN GRIMM, THE POWER OF THE PUPPET MASTER ENDS, AND THE SPELL IS OVER!
REED--HOW DID IT HAPPEN? HOW?
IT WAS THIS CHEMICAL! THIS IS WHAT I WAS WORKING ON IN THE LAB! I DIDN'T WANT YOU TO KNOW ABOUT IT, IN CASE IT FAILED! YOU'VE HAD SO MANY DISAPPOINTMENTS, I DIDN'T WANT YOU TO SUFFER ANOTHER ONE, UNTIL I WAS SURE!
YOU WERE DOING IT FOR ME! AND ALL THE TIME I THOUGHT YOU HATED ME! THOUGHT YOU WERE SCHEMING AGAINST ME! REED, I-I FEEL LIKE--
STOW IT, PARTNER! YOU HAD EVERY RIGHT TO BLOW YOUR TOP! BUT NOW, WE'VE STILL GOT A JOB CUT OUT FOR US!
12

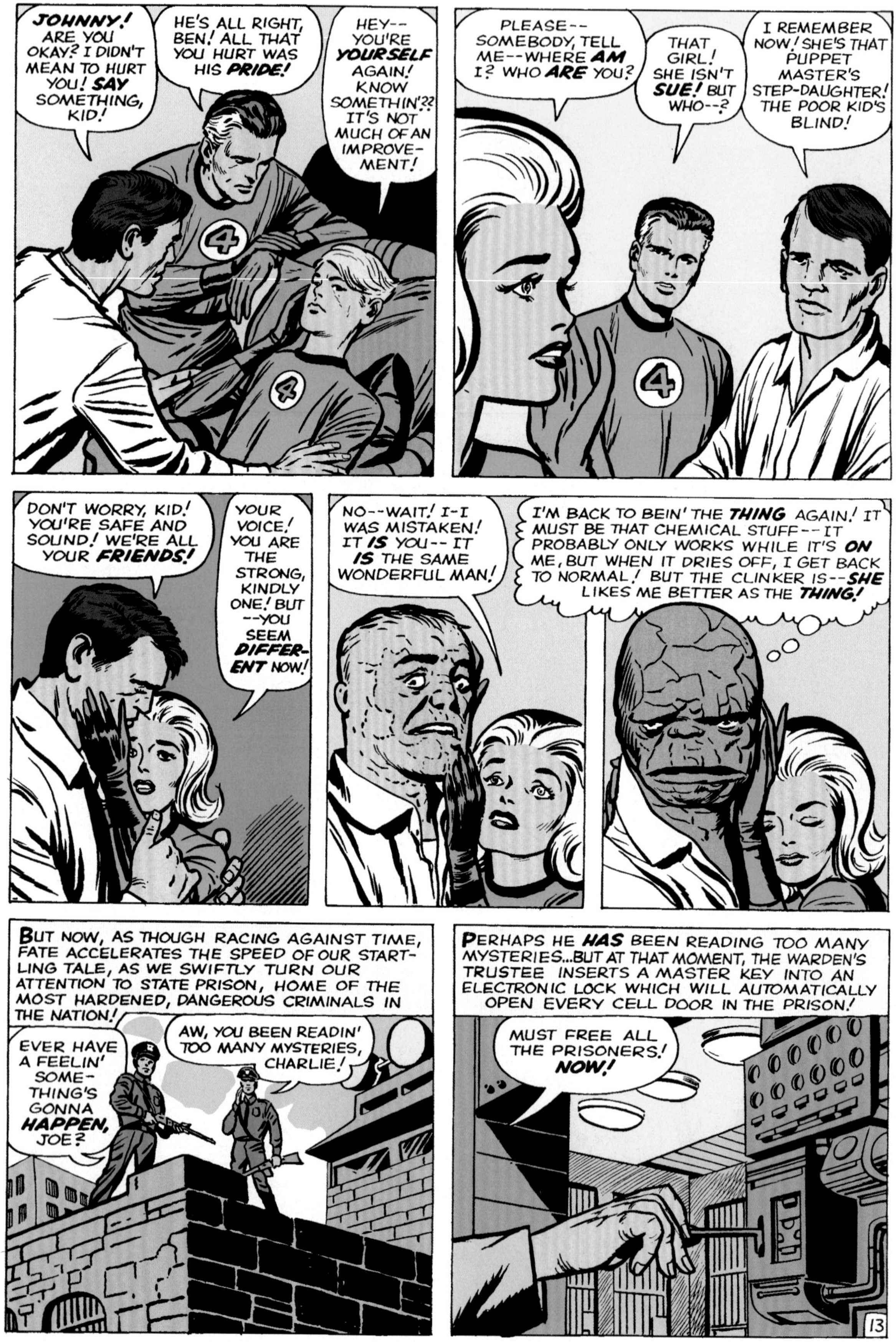

JOHNNY! ARE YOU OKAY? I DIDN'T MEAN TO HURT YOU! SAY SOMETHING, KID!
HE'S ALL RIGHT, BEN! ALL THAT YOU HURT WAS HIS PRIDE!
HEY-- YOU'RE YOURSELF AGAIN! KNOW SOMETHIN'?? IT'S NOT MUCH OF AN IMPROVEMENT!
PLEASE-- SOMEBODY, TELL ME--WHERE AM I? WHO ARE YOU?
THAT GIRL! SHE ISN'T SUE! BUT WHO--?
I REMEMBER NOW! SHE'S THAT PUPPET MASTER'S STEP-DAUGHTER! THE POOR KID'S BLIND!
DON'T WORRY, KID! YOU'RE SAFE AND SOUND! WE'RE ALL YOUR FRIENDS!
YOUR VOICE! YOU ARE THE STRONG, KINDLY ONE! BUT --YOU SEEM DIFFERENT NOW!
NO--WAIT! I-I WAS MISTAKEN! IT IS YOU-- IT IS THE SAME WONDERFUL MAN!
I'M BACK TO BEIN' THE THING AGAIN! IT MUST BE THAT CHEMICAL STUFF--IT PROBABLY ONLY WORKS WHILE IT'S ON ME, BUT WHEN IT DRIES OFF, I GET BACK TO NORMAL! BUT THE CLINKER IS--SHE LIKES ME BETTER AS THE THING!
BUT NOW, AS THOUGH RACING AGAINST TIME, FATE ACCELERATES THE SPEED OF OUR STARTLING TALE, AS WE SWIFTLY TURN OUR ATTENTION TO STATE PRISON, HOME OF THE MOST HARDENED, DANGEROUS CRIMINALS IN THE NATION!
EVER HAVE A FEELIN' SOMETHING'S GONNA HAPPEN, JOE?
AW, YOU BEEN READIN' TOO MANY MYSTERIES, CHARLIE!
PERHAPS HE HAS BEEN READING TOO MANY MYSTERIES...BUT AT THAT MOMENT, THE WARDEN'S TRUSTEE INSERTS A MASTER KEY INTO AN ELECTRONIC LOCK WHICH WILL AUTOMATICALLY OPEN EVERY CELL DOOR IN THE PRISON!
MUST FREE ALL THE PRISONERS! NOW!
13

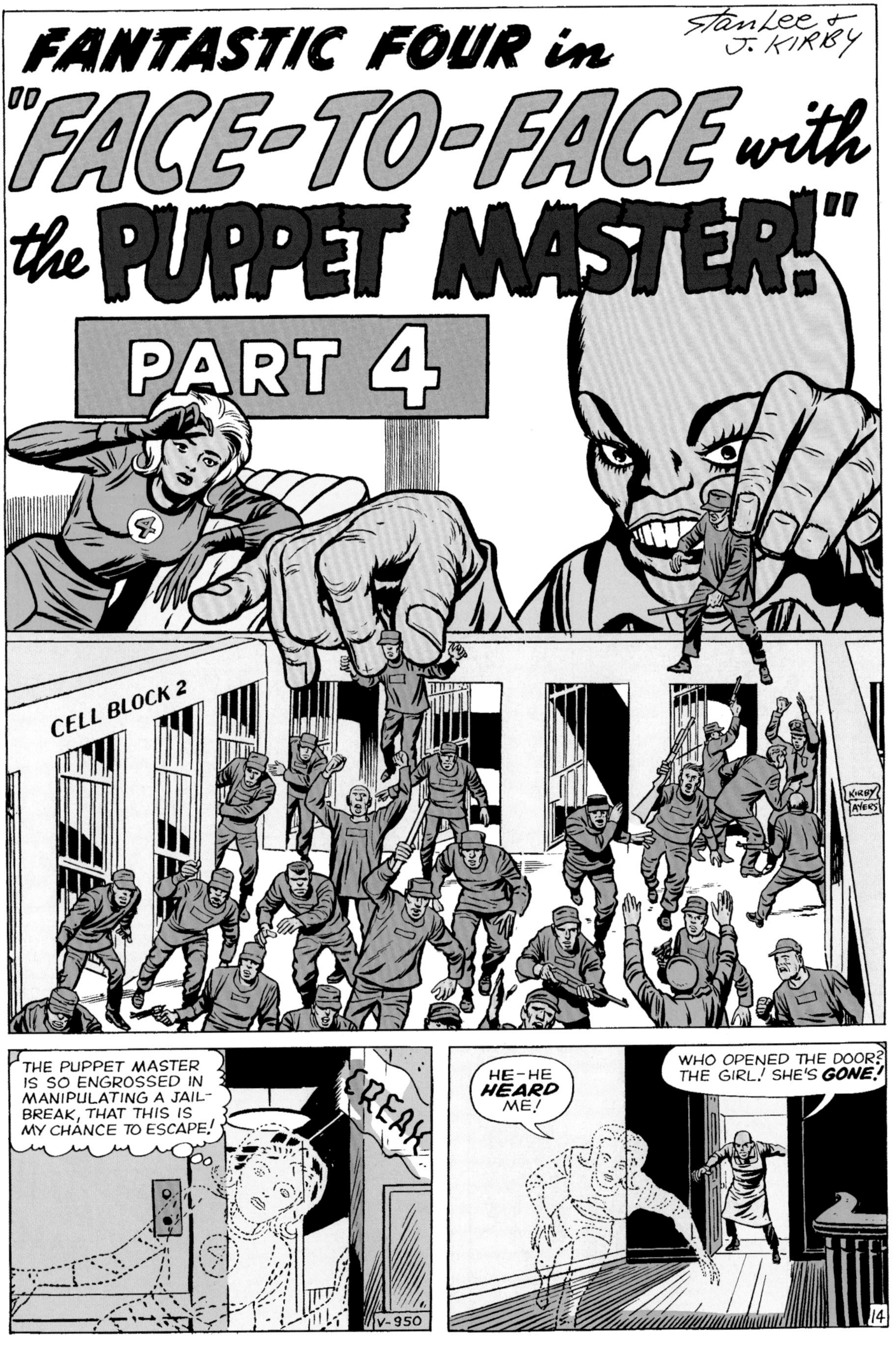
Stan Lee + J. Kirby
FANTASTIC FOUR in
"FACE-TO-FACE with the PUPPET MASTER!"
PART 4
CELL BLOCK 2
KIRBY AYERS
THE PUPPET MASTER IS SO ENGROSSED IN MANIPULATING A JAIL-BREAK, THAT THIS IS MY CHANCE TO ESCAPE!
CREAK
V-950
HE-HE HEARD ME!
WHO OPENED THE DOOR? THE GIRL! SHE'S GONE!
14

EVEN THE INVISIBLE GIRL CANNOT ESCAPE *ME!* LUCKILY, I HAD THE FORSIGHT TO MAKE A PUPPET OF HER...

...ALL I NEED DO IS GRASP THE PUPPET'S ANKLES, AND...

OH! I-I'M *FALLING!* AS THOUGH SOMETHING IS HOLDING MY ANKLES!

THE SUDDEN SHOCK CAUSES HER TO FORGET HERSELF AND BECOME VISIBLE AGAIN!

THERE SHE *IS!*

I'VE ONLY ONE CHANCE! MY *FLARE GUN!*

LUCKILY, THE FANTASTICAR IS SWEEPING THE SKIES IN A FRANTIC SEARCH FOR THE INVISIBLE GIRL, AND SO...

THERE'S SUE'S SIGNAL!

IT'S COMIN' FROM THE STOOP OF THAT BUILDING! *LET'S GO!*

SHE MUST BE IN HERE!

BUT, INSIDE THE BUILDING WHICH SERVES AS HIS LABORATORY, THE PUPPET MASTER HAS ONE *OTHER* CREATION, WAITING FOR HIS ATTACKERS! HIS LARGEST, MOST POWERFUL PUPPET!

MY GIANT, MENTALLY-CONTROLLED PUPPET WILL HOLD THEM OFF LONG ENOUGH FOR ME TO MAKE MY GETAWAY-- WITH *YOU* AS MY HOSTAGE!

CAREFUL, THING! LOOK AT *THAT!*

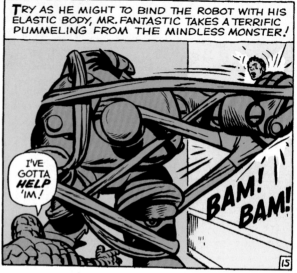

TRY AS HE MIGHT TO BIND THE ROBOT WITH HIS ELASTIC BODY, MR. FANTASTIC TAKES A TERRIFIC PUMMELING FROM THE MINDLESS MONSTER!

I'VE GOTTA *HELP* 'IM!

BAM! BAM!

15

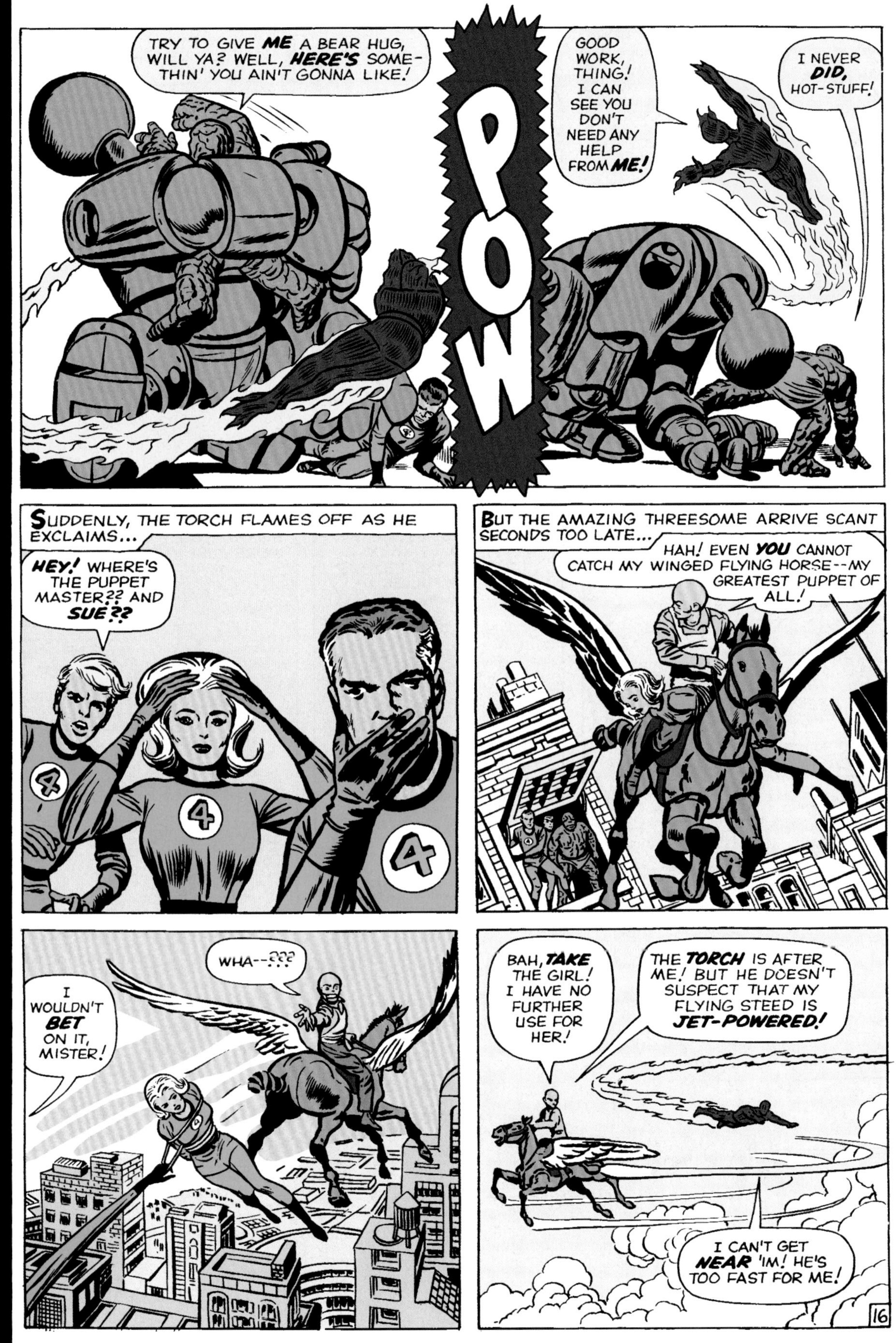
TRY TO GIVE ME A BEAR HUG, WILL YA? WELL, HERE'S SOME-THIN' YOU AIN'T GONNA LIKE!
POW
GOOD WORK, THING! I CAN SEE YOU DON'T NEED ANY HELP FROM ME!
I NEVER DID, HOT-STUFF!
SUDDENLY, THE TORCH FLAMES OFF AS HE EXCLAIMS...
HEY! WHERE'S THE PUPPET MASTER?? AND SUE??
BUT THE AMAZING THREESOME ARRIVE SCANT SECONDS TOO LATE...
HAH! EVEN YOU CANNOT CATCH MY WINGED FLYING HORSE--MY GREATEST PUPPET OF ALL!
I WOULDN'T BET ON IT, MISTER!
WHA--???
BAH, TAKE THE GIRL! I HAVE NO FURTHER USE FOR HER!
THE TORCH IS AFTER ME! BUT HE DOESN'T SUSPECT THAT MY FLYING STEED IS JET-POWERED!
I CAN'T GET NEAR 'IM! HE'S TOO FAST FOR ME!
16

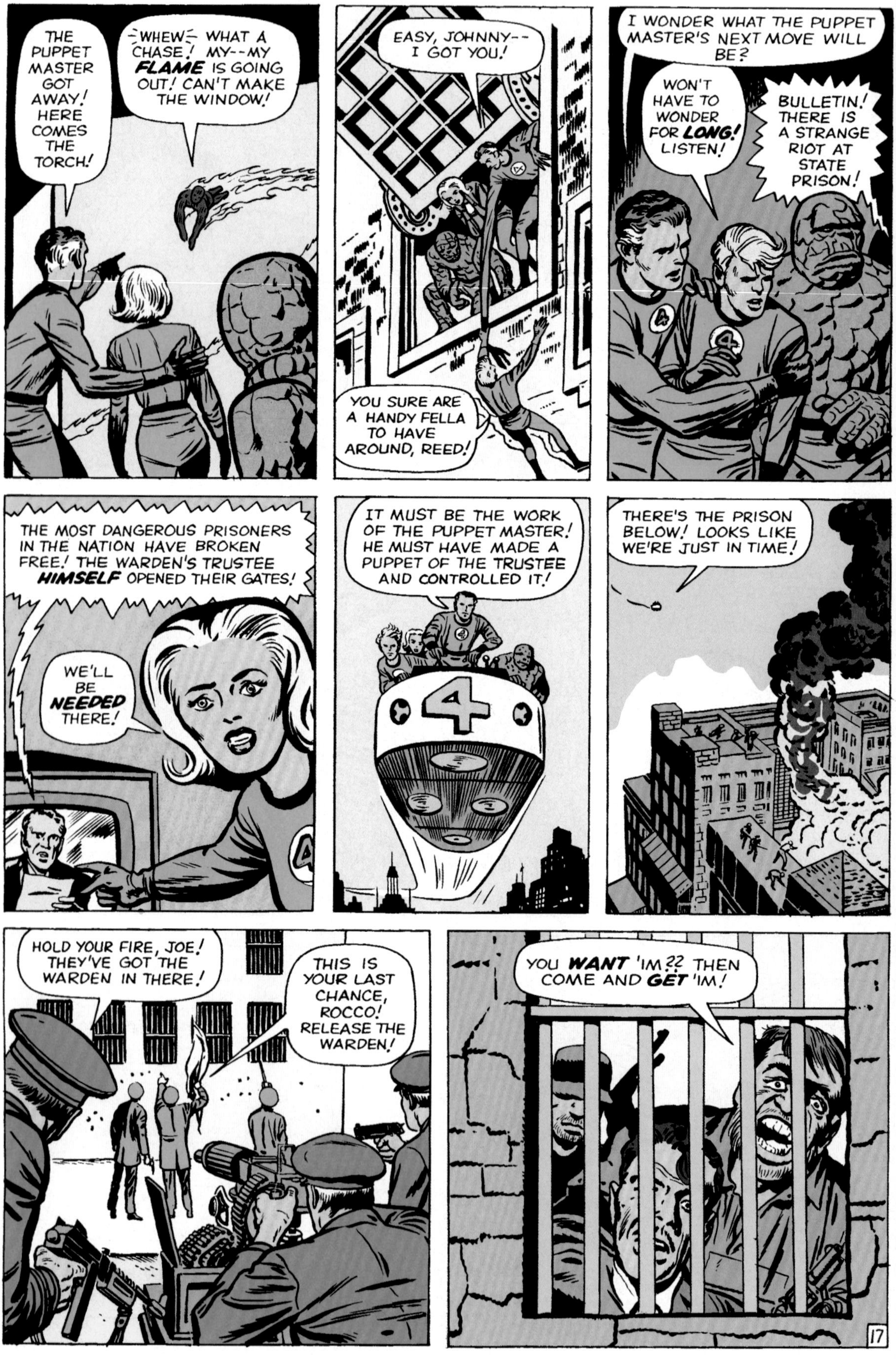
THE PUPPET MASTER GOT AWAY! HERE COMES THE TORCH!
-WHEW!- WHAT A CHASE! MY--MY FLAME IS GOING OUT! CAN'T MAKE THE WINDOW!
EASY, JOHNNY-- I GOT YOU!
YOU SURE ARE A HANDY FELLA TO HAVE AROUND, REED!
I WONDER WHAT THE PUPPET MASTER'S NEXT MOVE WILL BE?
WON'T HAVE TO WONDER FOR LONG! LISTEN!
BULLETIN! THERE IS A STRANGE RIOT AT STATE PRISON!
THE MOST DANGEROUS PRISONERS IN THE NATION HAVE BROKEN FREE! THE WARDEN'S TRUSTEE HIMSELF OPENED THEIR GATES!
WE'LL BE NEEDED THERE!
IT MUST BE THE WORK OF THE PUPPET MASTER! HE MUST HAVE MADE A PUPPET OF THE TRUSTEE AND CONTROLLED IT!
THERE'S THE PRISON BELOW! LOOKS LIKE WE'RE JUST IN TIME!
HOLD YOUR FIRE, JOE! THEY'VE GOT THE WARDEN IN THERE!
THIS IS YOUR LAST CHANCE, ROCCO! RELEASE THE WARDEN!
YOU WANT 'IM?? THEN COME AND GET 'IM!

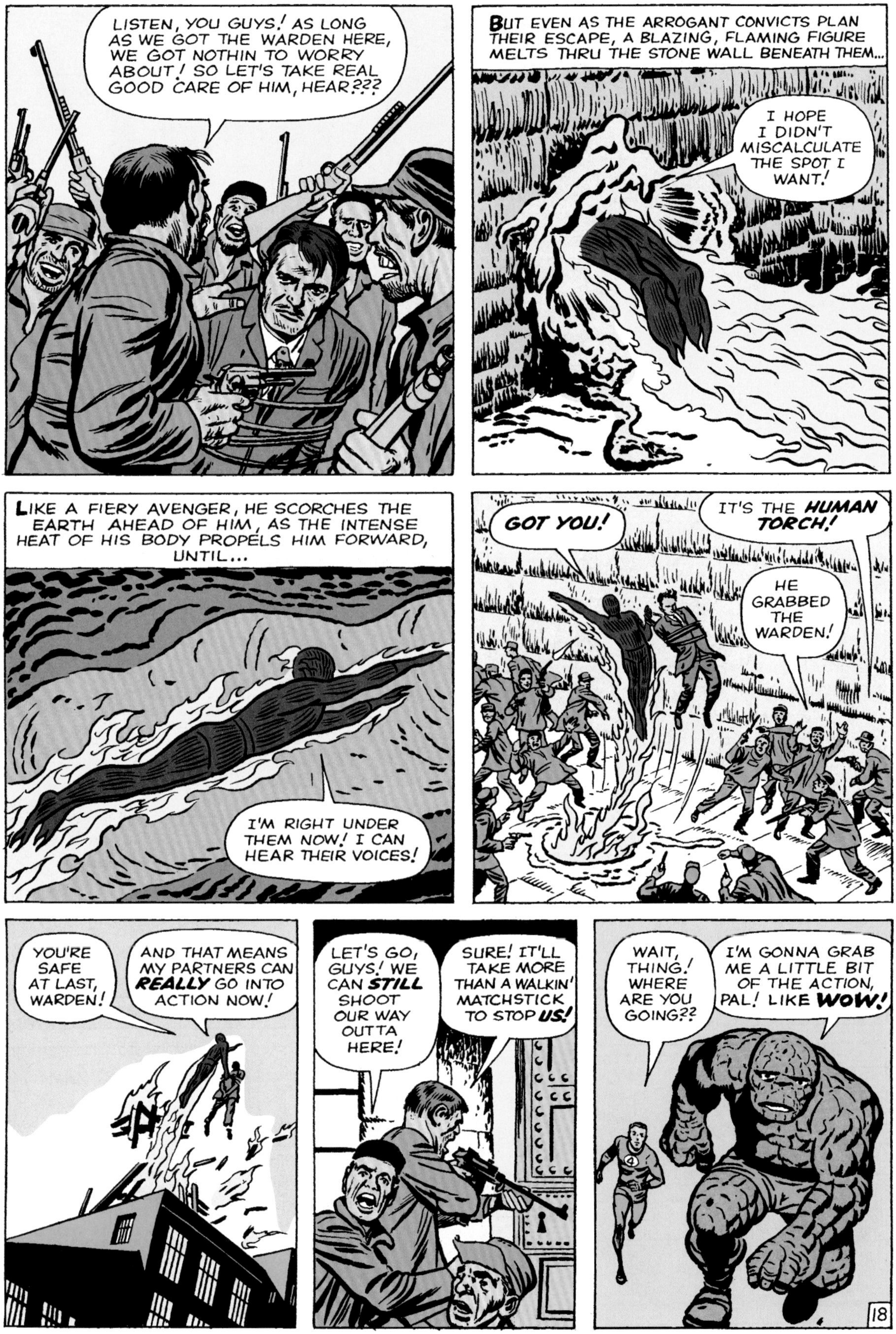

LISTEN, YOU GUYS! AS LONG AS WE GOT THE WARDEN HERE, WE GOT NOTHIN TO WORRY ABOUT! SO LET'S TAKE REAL GOOD CARE OF HIM, HEAR???
BUT EVEN AS THE ARROGANT CONVICTS PLAN THEIR ESCAPE, A BLAZING, FLAMING FIGURE MELTS THRU THE STONE WALL BENEATH THEM...
I HOPE I DIDN'T MISCALCULATE THE SPOT I WANT!
LIKE A FIERY AVENGER, HE SCORCHES THE EARTH AHEAD OF HIM, AS THE INTENSE HEAT OF HIS BODY PROPELS HIM FORWARD, UNTIL...
I'M RIGHT UNDER THEM NOW! I CAN HEAR THEIR VOICES!
GOT YOU!
IT'S THE HUMAN TORCH!
HE GRABBED THE WARDEN!
YOU'RE SAFE AT LAST, WARDEN!
AND THAT MEANS MY PARTNERS CAN REALLY GO INTO ACTION NOW!
LET'S GO, GUYS! WE CAN STILL SHOOT OUR WAY OUTTA HERE!
SURE! IT'LL TAKE MORE THAN A WALKIN' MATCHSTICK TO STOP US!
WAIT, THING! WHERE ARE YOU GOING??
I'M GONNA GRAB ME A LITTLE BIT OF THE ACTION, PAL! LIKE WOW!
18

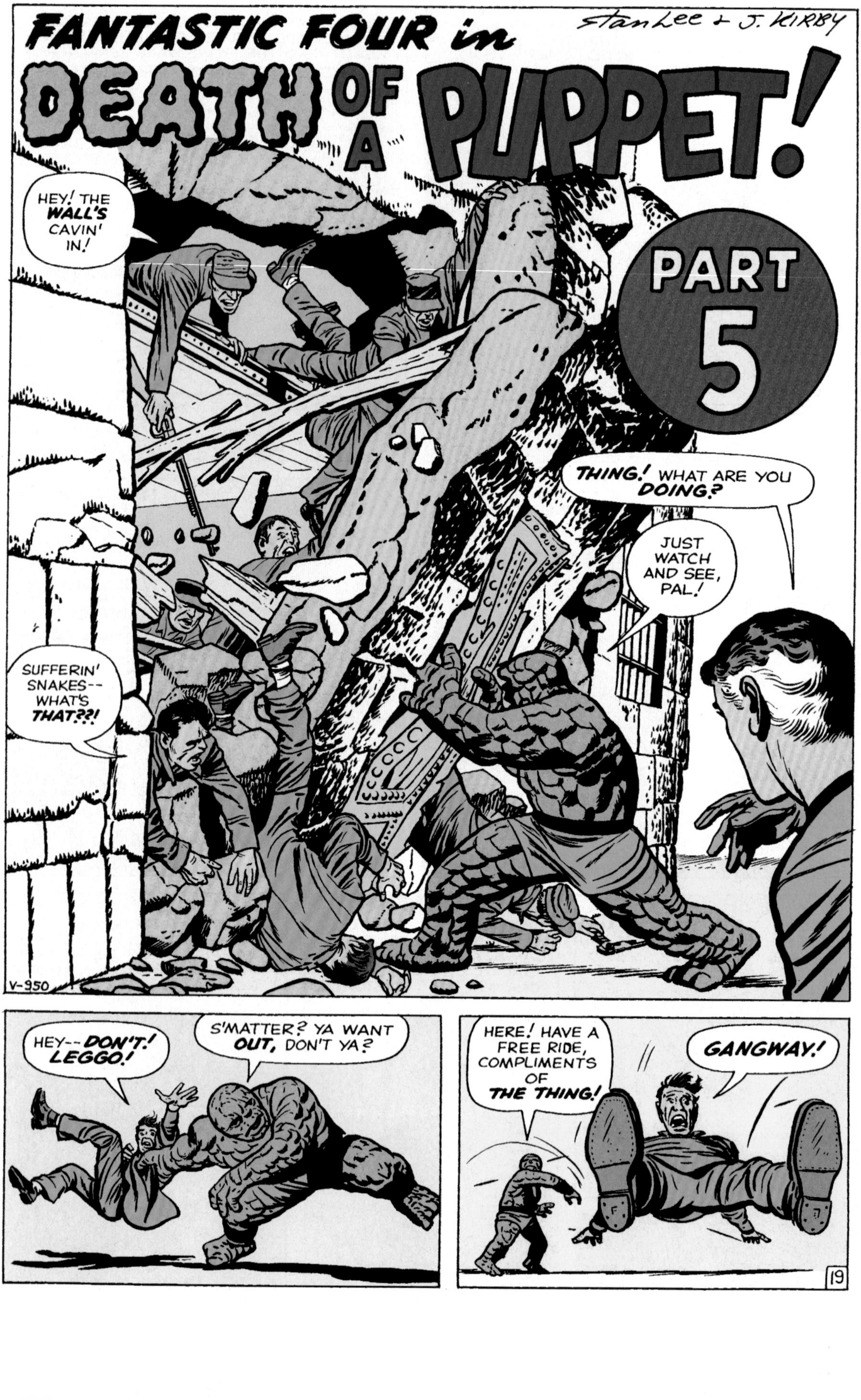

FANTASTIC FOUR in
DEATH OF A PUPPET!
Stan Lee + J. Kirby
PART 5
HEY! THE WALL'S CAVIN' IN!
SUFFERIN' SNAKES--WHAT'S THAT??!
THING! WHAT ARE YOU DOING?
JUST WATCH AND SEE, PAL!
V-950
HEY--DON'T! LEGGO!
S'MATTER? YA WANT OUT, DON'T YA?
HERE! HAVE A FREE RIDE, COMPLIMENTS OF THE THING!
GANGWAY!
19

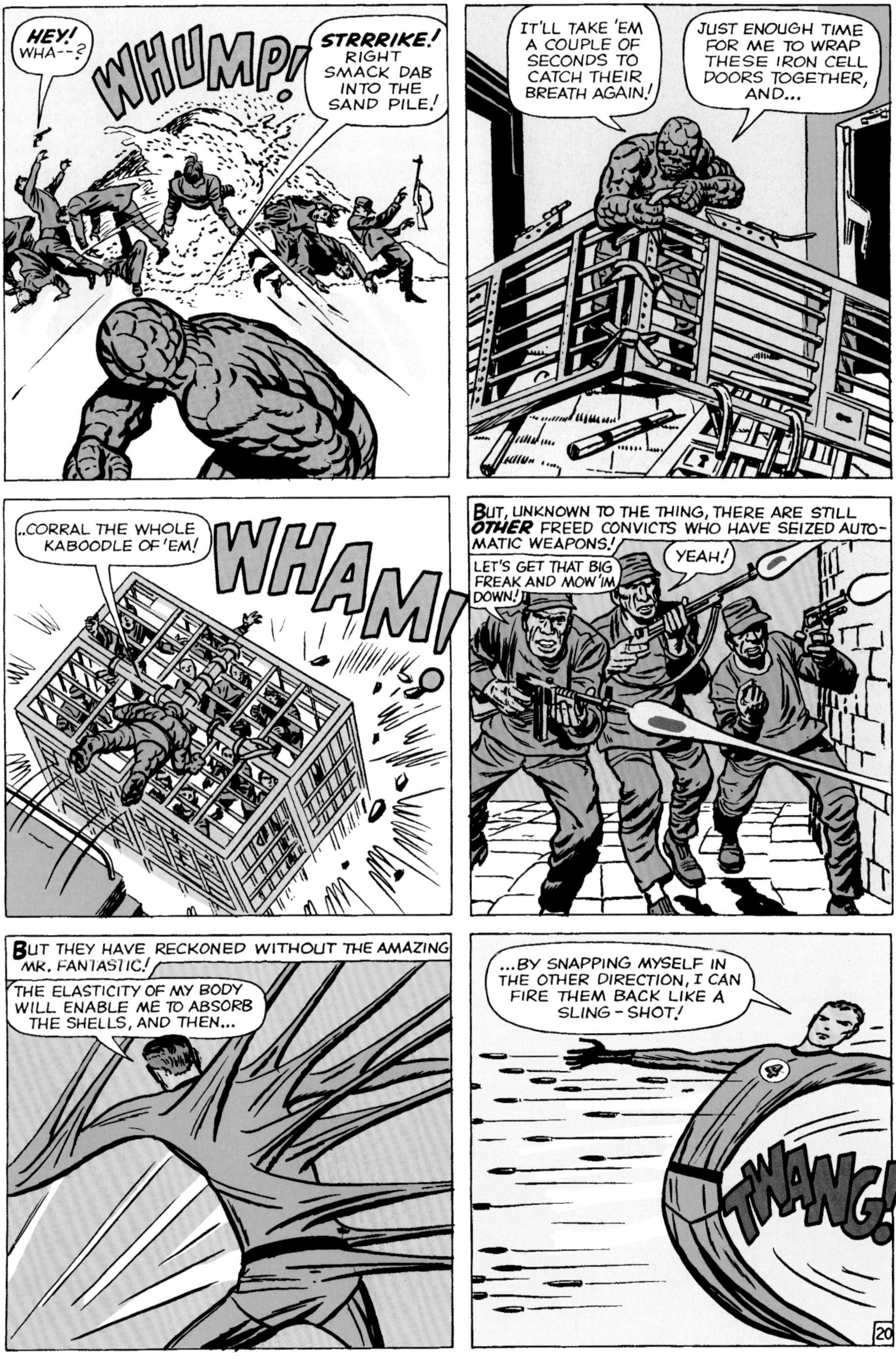
HEY! WHA--?
WHUMP!
STRRRIKE! RIGHT SMACK DAB INTO THE SAND PILE!
IT'LL TAKE 'EM A COUPLE OF SECONDS TO CATCH THEIR BREATH AGAIN!
JUST ENOUGH TIME FOR ME TO WRAP THESE IRON CELL DOORS TOGETHER, AND...
..CORRAL THE WHOLE KABOODLE OF 'EM!
WHAM!
BUT, UNKNOWN TO THE THING, THERE ARE STILL OTHER FREED CONVICTS WHO HAVE SEIZED AUTOMATIC WEAPONS!
LET'S GET THAT BIG FREAK AND MOW 'IM DOWN!
YEAH!
BUT THEY HAVE RECKONED WITHOUT THE AMAZING MR. FANTASTIC!
THE ELASTICITY OF MY BODY WILL ENABLE ME TO ABSORB THE SHELLS, AND THEN...
...BY SNAPPING MYSELF IN THE OTHER DIRECTION, I CAN FIRE THEM BACK LIKE A SLING-SHOT!
THWANG!

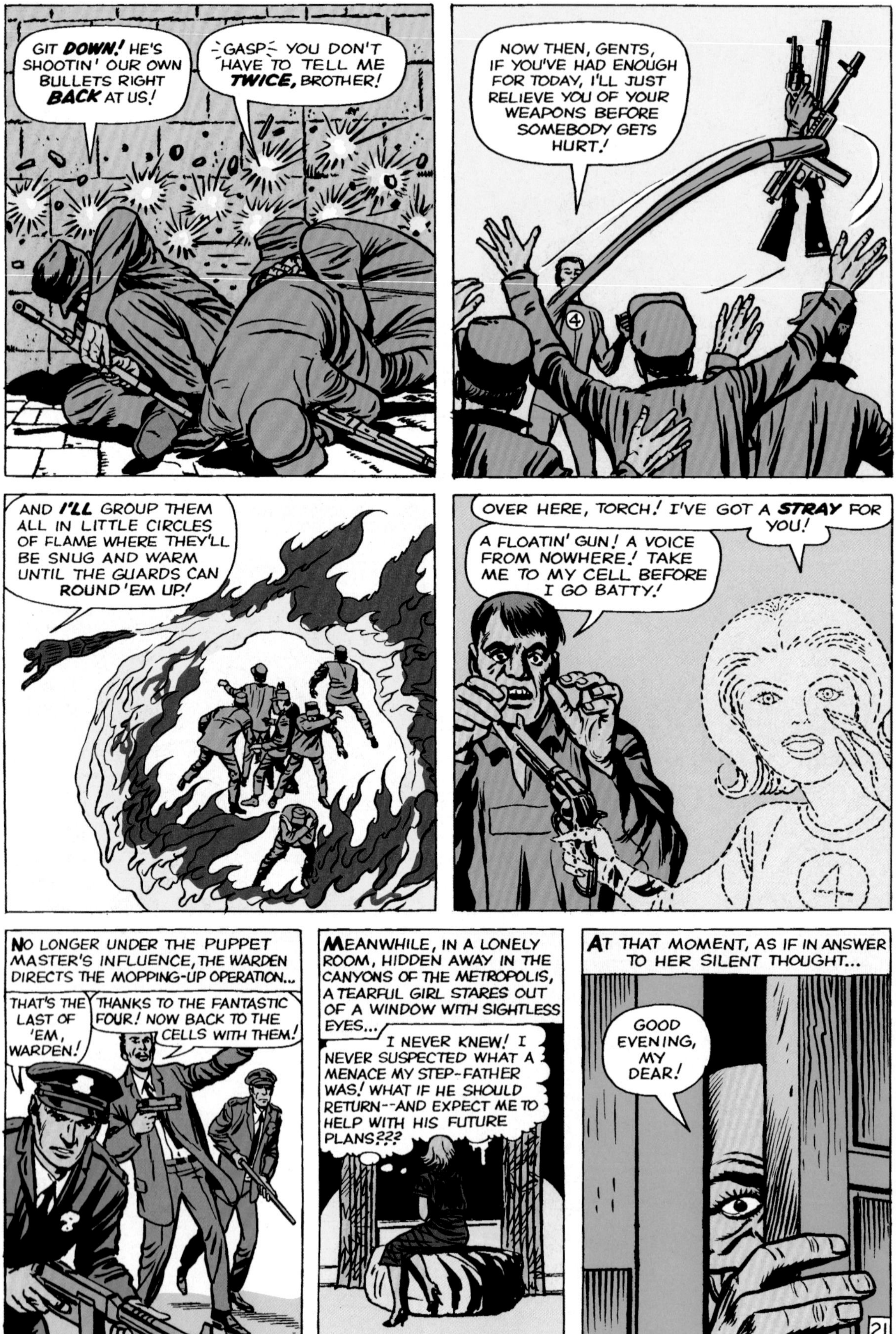
GIT DOWN! HE'S SHOOTIN' OUR OWN BULLETS RIGHT BACK AT US!
-GASP- YOU DON'T HAVE TO TELL ME TWICE, BROTHER!
NOW THEN, GENTS, IF YOU'VE HAD ENOUGH FOR TODAY, I'LL JUST RELIEVE YOU OF YOUR WEAPONS BEFORE SOMEBODY GETS HURT!
AND I'LL GROUP THEM ALL IN LITTLE CIRCLES OF FLAME WHERE THEY'LL BE SNUG AND WARM UNTIL THE GUARDS CAN ROUND 'EM UP!
OVER HERE, TORCH! I'VE GOT A STRAY FOR YOU!
A FLOATIN' GUN! A VOICE FROM NOWHERE! TAKE ME TO MY CELL BEFORE I GO BATTY!
NO LONGER UNDER THE PUPPET MASTER'S INFLUENCE, THE WARDEN DIRECTS THE MOPPING-UP OPERATION...
THAT'S THE LAST OF 'EM, WARDEN!
THANKS TO THE FANTASTIC FOUR! NOW BACK TO THE CELLS WITH THEM!
MEANWHILE, IN A LONELY ROOM, HIDDEN AWAY IN THE CANYONS OF THE METROPOLIS, A TEARFUL GIRL STARES OUT OF A WINDOW WITH SIGHTLESS EYES...
I NEVER KNEW! I NEVER SUSPECTED WHAT A MENACE MY STEP-FATHER WAS! WHAT IF HE SHOULD RETURN--AND EXPECT ME TO HELP WITH HIS FUTURE PLANS???
AT THAT MOMENT, AS IF IN ANSWER TO HER SILENT THOUGHT...
GOOD EVENING, MY DEAR!
21

I HAVE RETURNED IN ORDER TO MANIPULATE MY GREATEST PUPPET OF ALL!

I WISH YOU COULD **SEE** IT, ALICIA! IT IS A SMALL FIGURE OF **ME**-- BUT NOT AS I AM NOW! NO, IT IS THE PUPPET MASTER-- RULER OF ALL THE WORLD!

NOW THAT I HAVE TESTED MY POWER AND KNOW THAT IT WORKS, I CAN DO **ANYTHING!** I CAN CONTROL ARMIES, NATIONS, **ANYTHING!** KINGS AND DICTATORS WILL DO MY BIDDING! DO YOU HEAR ME, ALICIA?

I-I HEAR YOU!

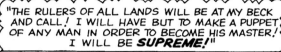

"MY FIRST OFFICIAL ACT WILL BE TO TEAR DOWN THE U.N., FOR IT WILL NO LONGER BE NEEDED! THE **PUPPET MASTER** WILL CONTROL THE DESTINY OF NATIONS!"

"THE RULERS OF ALL LANDS WILL BE AT MY BECK AND CALL! I WILL HAVE BUT TO MAKE A PUPPET OF ANY MAN IN ORDER TO BECOME HIS MASTER! I WILL BE **SUPREME!**"

"**NONE** WILL BE MIGHTY ENOUGH TO DEFY ME! EVEN THE FANTASTIC FOUR WILL BE SLAVES OF THE PUPPET MASTER! AND FOR **THEM,** I SHALL HAVE A **SPECIAL** FATE RESERVED! FOR THEIR DEFEAT WILL BE MY GREATEST VICTORY!"

PUPPET MASTER REX

22

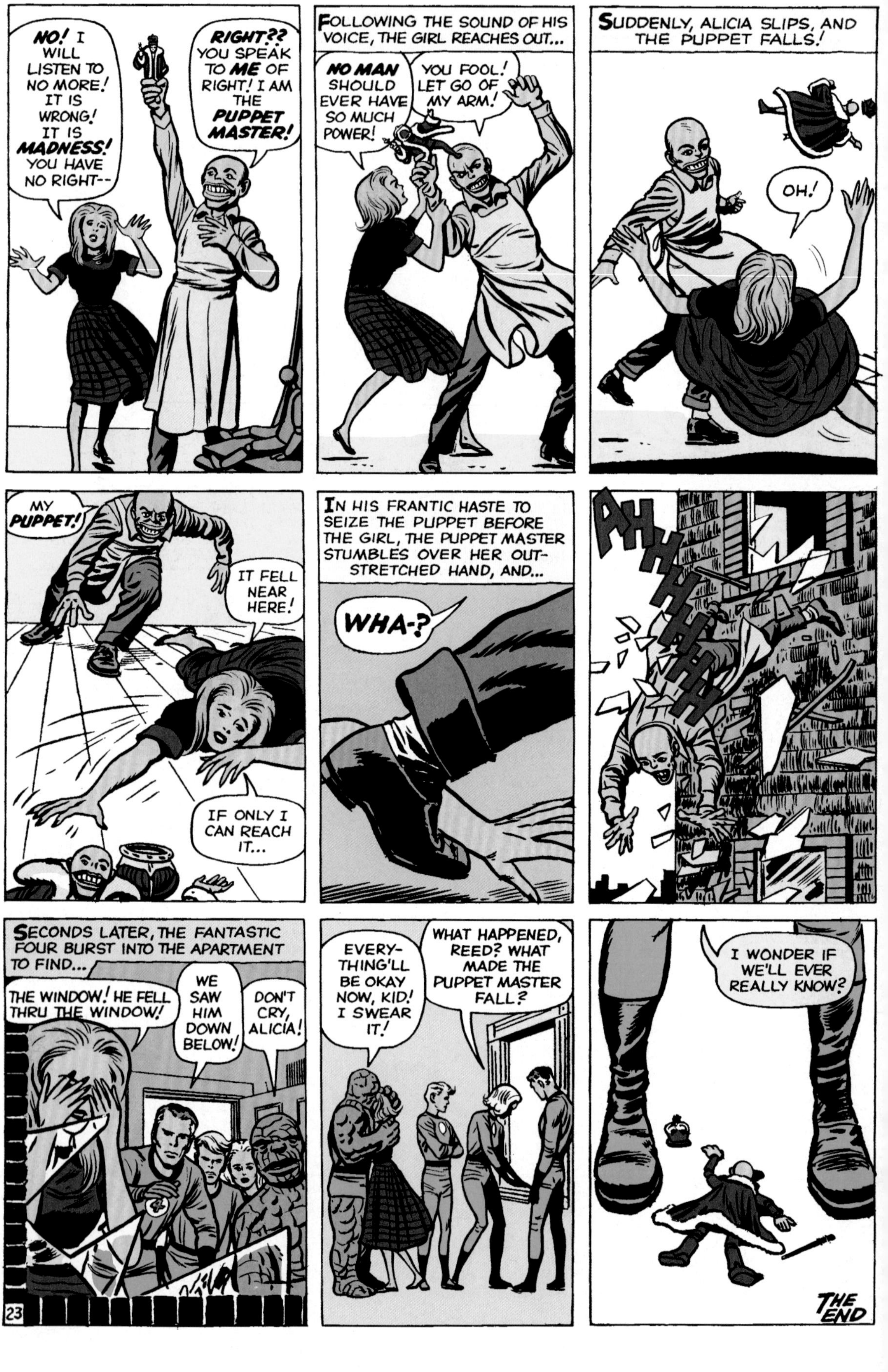
NO! I WILL LISTEN TO NO MORE! IT IS WRONG! IT IS MADNESS! YOU HAVE NO RIGHT--
RIGHT?? YOU SPEAK TO ME OF RIGHT! I AM THE PUPPET MASTER!
FOLLOWING THE SOUND OF HIS VOICE, THE GIRL REACHES OUT...
NO MAN SHOULD EVER HAVE SO MUCH POWER!
YOU FOOL! LET GO OF MY ARM!
SUDDENLY, ALICIA SLIPS, AND THE PUPPET FALLS!
OH!
MY PUPPET!
IT FELL NEAR HERE!
IF ONLY I CAN REACH IT...
IN HIS FRANTIC HASTE TO SEIZE THE PUPPET BEFORE THE GIRL, THE PUPPET MASTER STUMBLES OVER HER OUT-STRETCHED HAND, AND...
WHA-?
AHHHHHHH
SECONDS LATER, THE FANTASTIC FOUR BURST INTO THE APARTMENT TO FIND...
THE WINDOW! HE FELL THRU THE WINDOW!
WE SAW HIM DOWN BELOW!
DON'T CRY, ALICIA!
23
EVERY-THING'LL BE OKAY NOW, KID! I SWEAR IT!
WHAT HAPPENED, REED? WHAT MADE THE PUPPET MASTER FALL?
I WONDER IF WE'LL EVER REALLY KNOW?
THE END

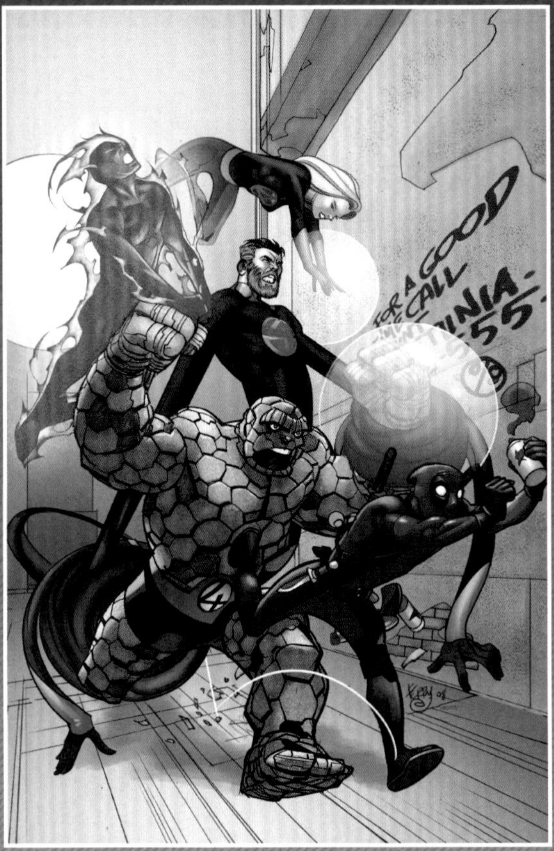
FOR A GOOD
CALL

Wedding Special #1 variant by
Pasqual Ferry & **Chris Sotomayor**

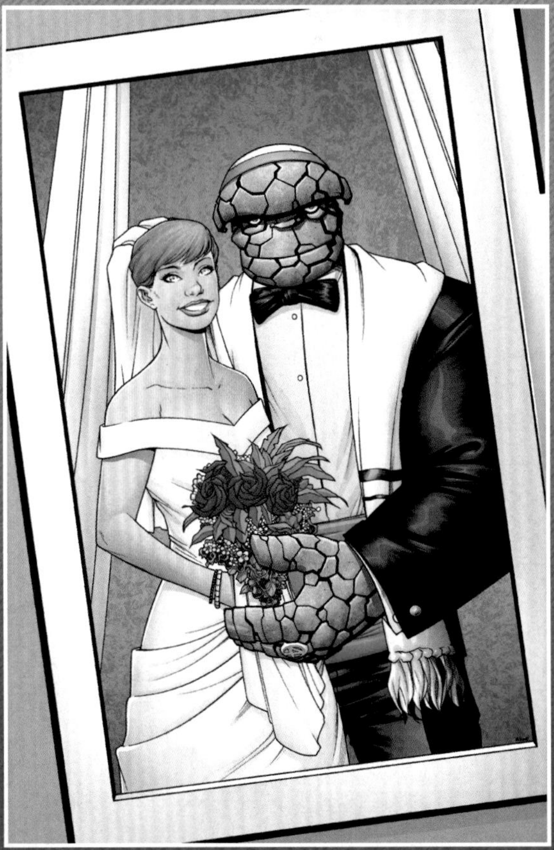

Wedding Special #1 variant by
Mike McKone & **Matt Yackey**

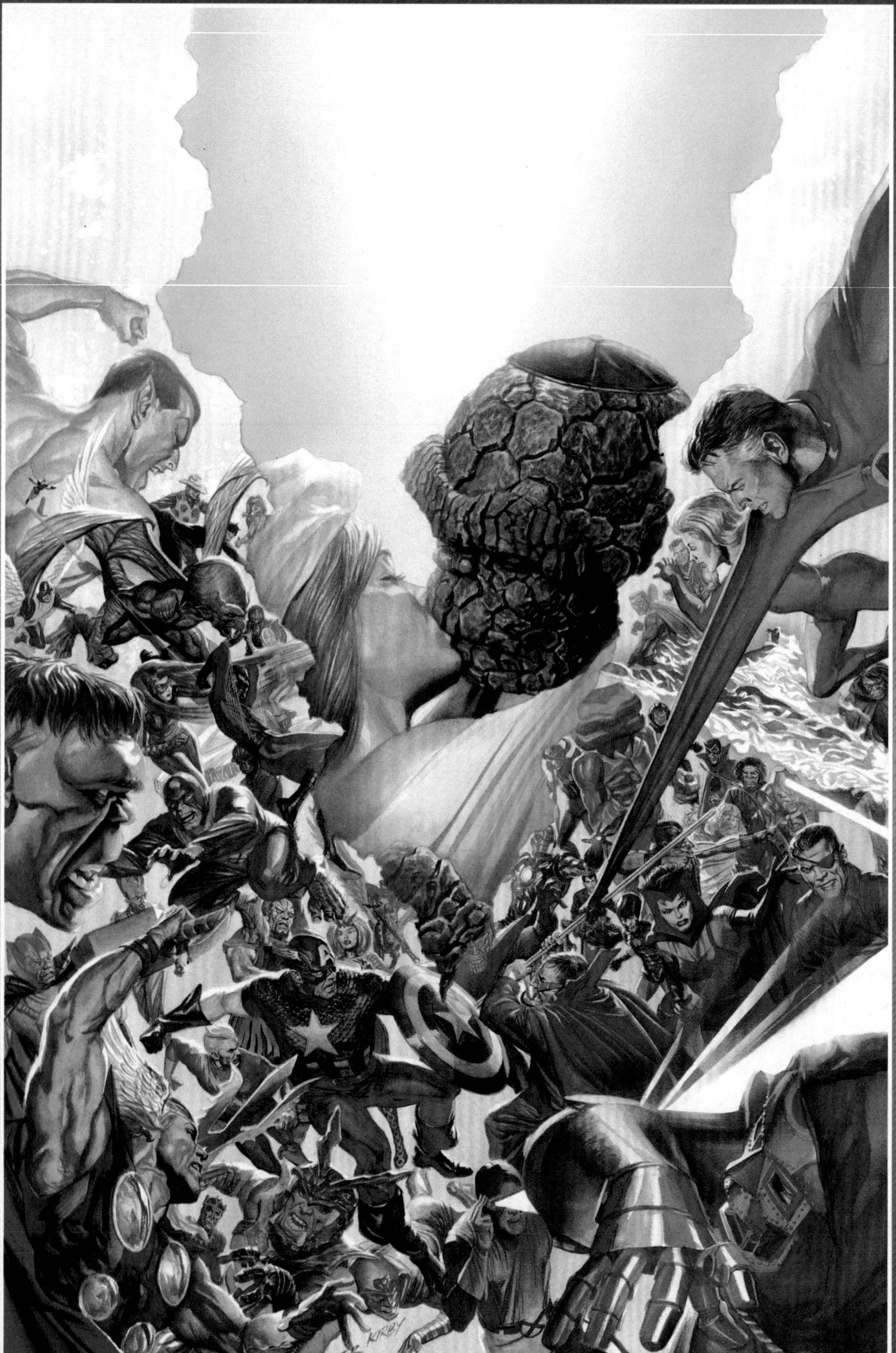
AFTER KIRBY

#5 variant by **Alex Ross**

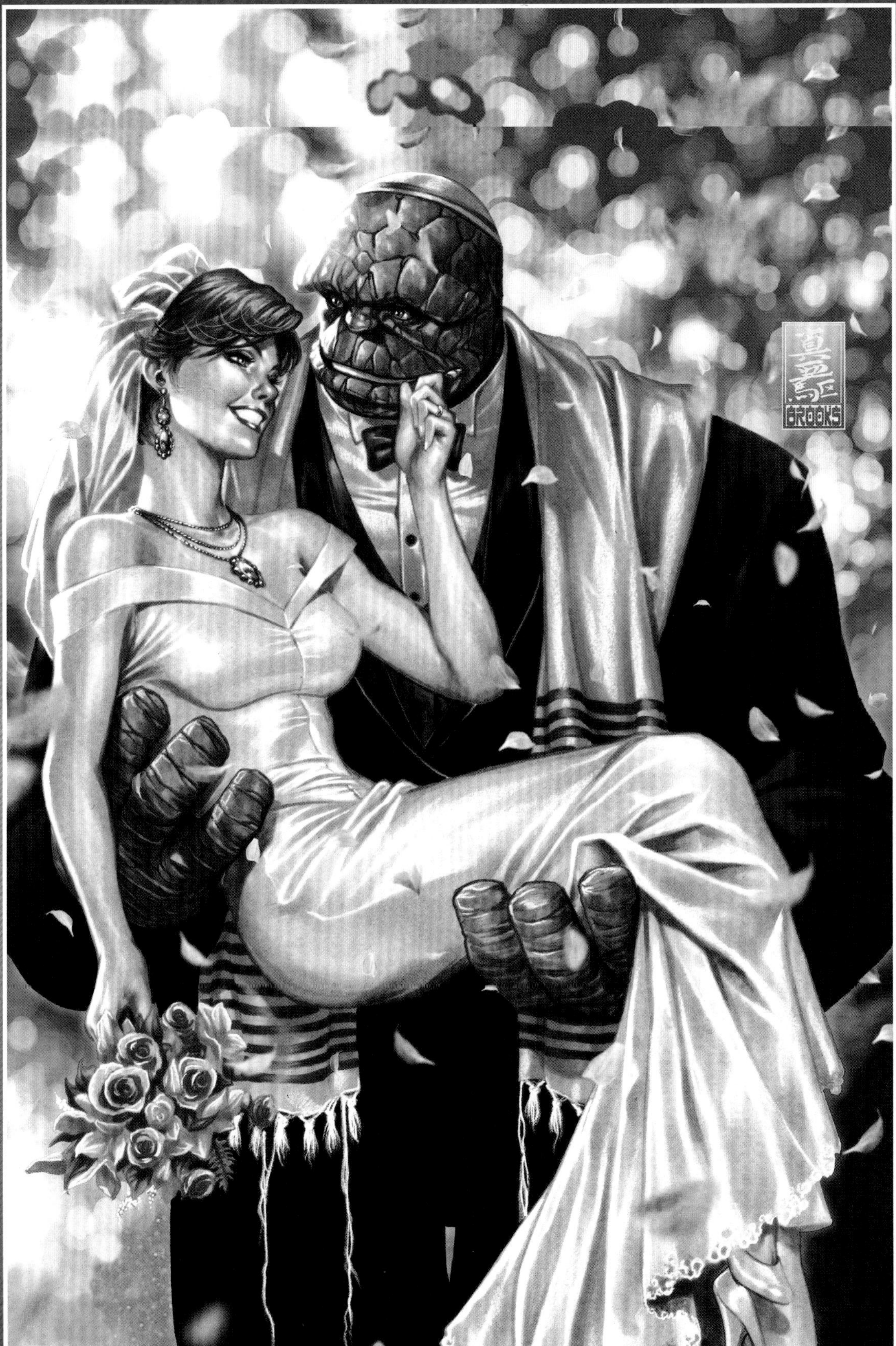
BROOKS

#5 variant by **Mark Brooks**

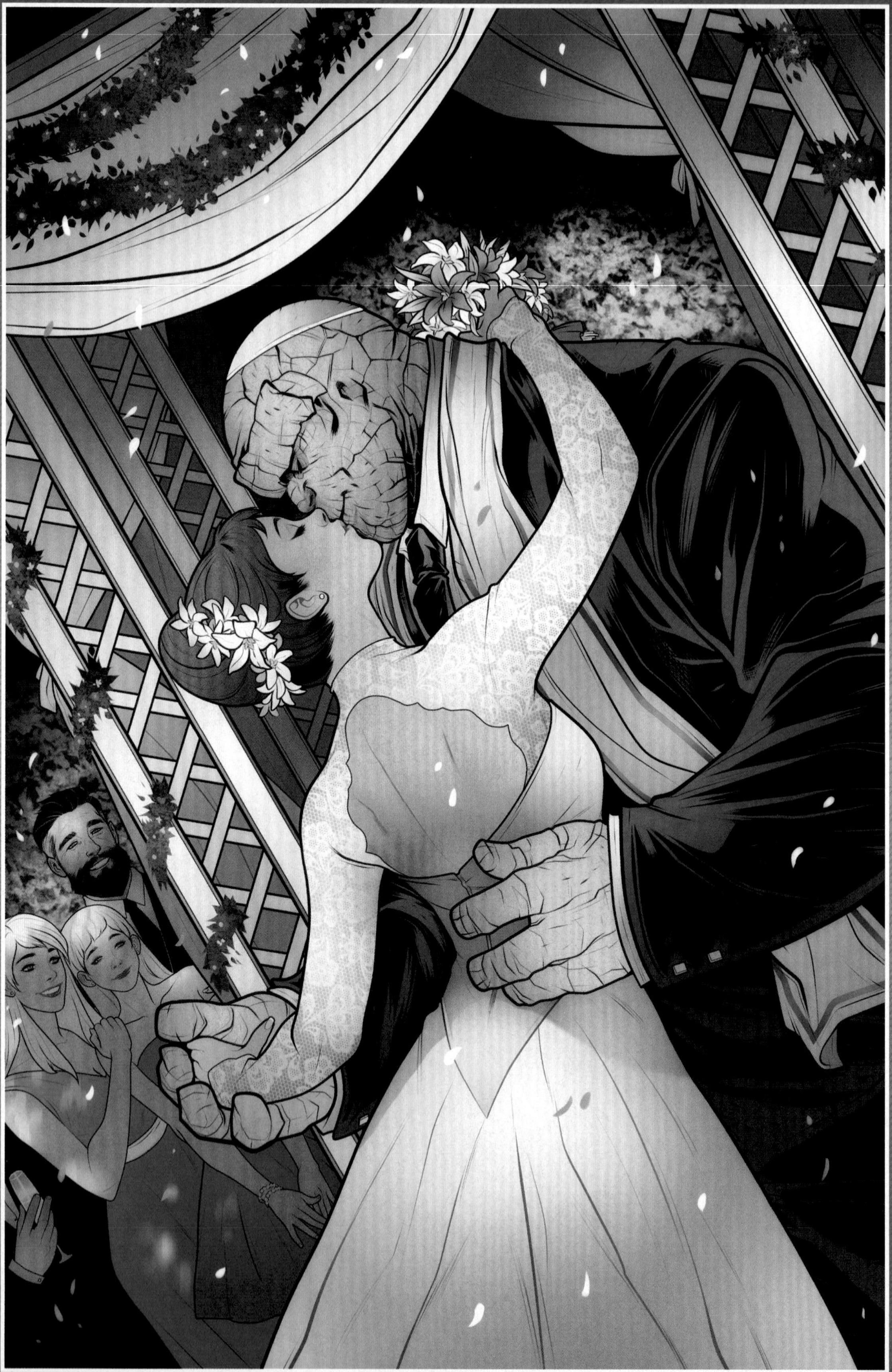

#5 variant by **Elizabeth Torque**

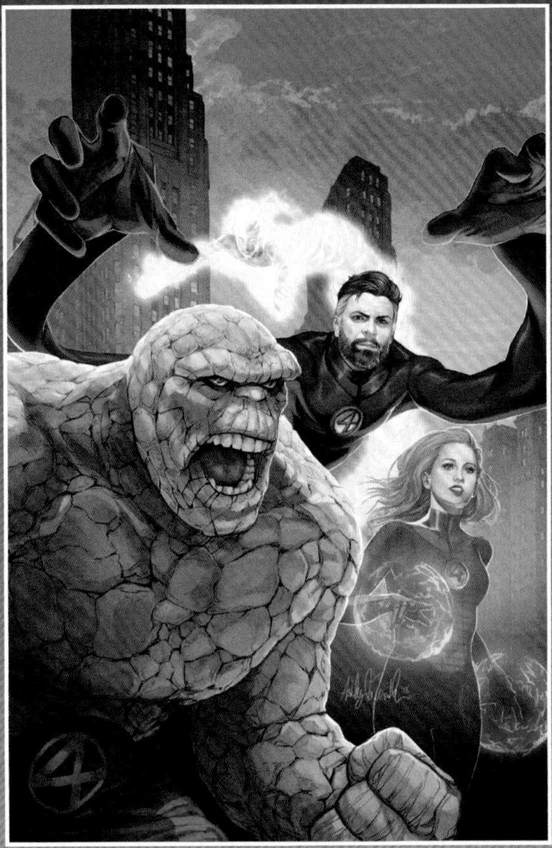

#5 variant by
Ashley Witter

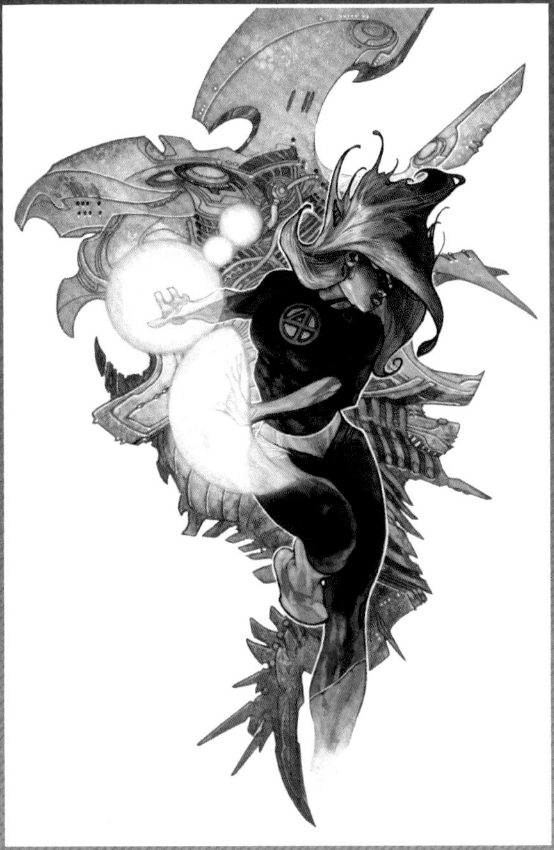

#5 variant by
Simone Bianchi

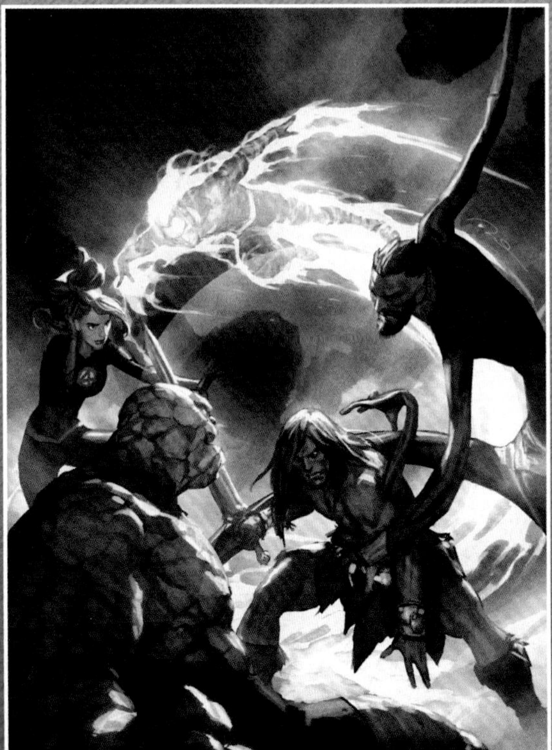

#5 Conan Vs. variant by
Gerald Parel

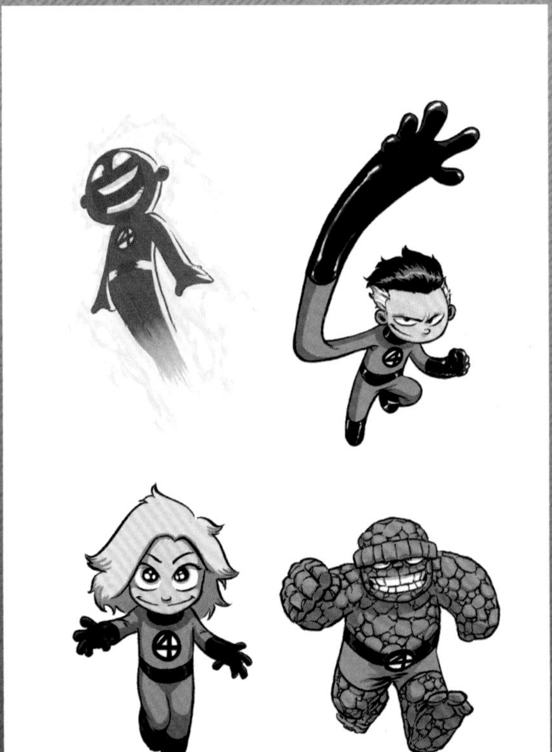

#5 variant by
Skottie Young

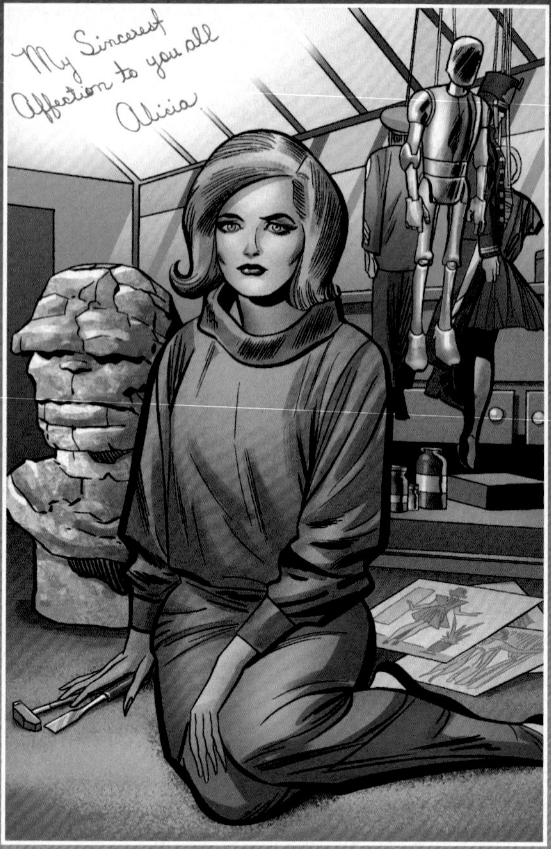
My Sincerest
Affection to you all
Alicia

#5 Alicia remastered variant by
Jack Kirby, Chic Stone & **Paul Mounts**

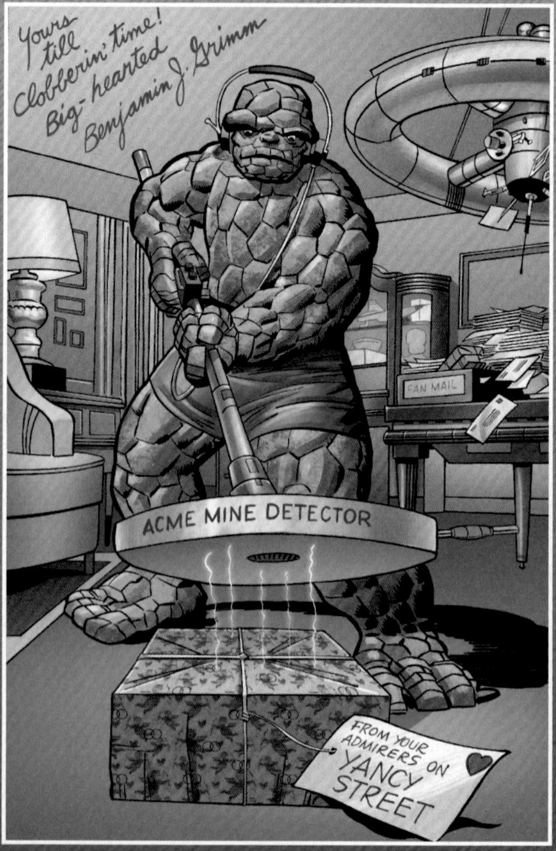
Yours till Clobberin' time!
Big-hearted
Benjamin J. Grimm
FAN MAIL
ACME MINE DETECTOR
FROM YOUR ADMIRERS ON
YANCY STREET

#5 Thing remastered variant by
Jack Kirby, Chic Stone & **Paul Mounts**